Praise for
Finding Resilience

"*Finding Resilience: A Teen's Journey Through Lyme Disease* is a powerful firsthand account of the devastating impact that Lyme can have on an entire family. Rachel and Dorothy bring the reader along for their raw and emotional journey through loss, suffering, and eventually triumph. Anyone whose life has been touched by chronic illness will connect with this heartfelt memoir and find strength in Rachel's seemingly impossible, yet ultimately successful, battle to regain her health. A must-read for those needing a boost of resilience."

—**NICOLE BELL,** patient advocate, author of the award-winning
and best-selling memoir *What Lurks in the Woods: Struggle
and Hope in the Midst of Chronic Illness*

"*Finding Resilience* is a guiding light for young people and parents navigating chronic illness, as Rachel and Dorothy have so beautifully captured a journey that is difficult to put into words. As Lyme disease cases continue to skyrocket, someone in your life will benefit from knowing their story. *Finding Resilience* is a reminder of the healing power of sharing stories—especially the challenging ones. Bravo to Rachel and Dorothy for bravely leading the way."

—**LINDSAY KEYS,** writer, filmmaker, co-director of
The Quiet Epidemic

"When I first met Rachel, she was a teenager in a reclining wheelchair in the midst of very dark times. Watching her recover her health and make a positive difference in the world has been beyond inspiring. In her new book, *Finding Resilience: A Teen's Journey Through Lyme Disease*, Rachel and her mother, Dorothy, take the reader on a journey from the depths of despair to a life regained. Her recovery gives hope to those currently struggling with their own health challenges. It will warm your heart. There's no question that she has found resilience; in fact, she's gone far beyond."

—SCOTT FORSGREN, The Better Health Guy

"*Finding Resilience: A Teen's Journey Through Lyme Disease* is a story of overwhelming obstacles with a successful ending as a result of persistence, family support, and eventually finding knowledgeable health-care providers. The beginning of the book is basically a story I have unfortunately heard, with many variations, thousands of times. It describes how our youth are becoming disabled by a disabled health-care system. How did we end up with a health-care system in which so many fail to adequately listen to their patients, fail to perform an adequate assessment, fail to use sound medical judgment, and defend against their failures by blaming the patient when dealing with a complex chronic disease? The book progresses with diary entries from both Rachel and her mother, Dorothy. In the beginning of the book the reader is expecting Rachel to be sentenced to a life of pain and disability in a wheelchair for a condition that some may attribute to being 'psychogenic.' However, it doesn't end that way. I look forward to seeing the release of this inspirational book!"

—ROBERT C. BRANSFIELD, MD; Distinguished Life Fellow, American Psychiatric Association, who has treated thousands of Lyme disease patients over the past thirty-plus years; Former president, International Lyme and Associated Diseases Society

"No family should have to go through what the Lelands went through when Rachel got Lyme disease and other tick-borne co-infections. The treatment they received from many doctors, school officials, and others was deplorable but, unfortunately, not uncommon with how many families are treated. Hopefully, the book will shift much of the thinking from those type of establishments."

—FRED DIAMOND, author of *Love, Hope, Lyme:*
What Family Members, Partners, and Friends Who Love
a Chronic Lyme Survivor Need to Know

"In this beautifully written book based on the journal she kept throughout her illness, Rachel shares the actual experiences of her adolescent self. What Dorothy has added is her perspective as a mother, reflecting on the often terrifying events recounted by her daughter. With its openness and honesty, this book will certainly help many Lyme patients suffering from similar traumas to feel less isolated."

—SANDY BERENBAUM, LCSW, BCD, psychotherapist,
co-author of *When Your Child Has Lyme Disease:*
A Parent's Survival Guide

Finding Resilience

A Teen's Journey Through Lyme Disease

Rachel Leland

Dorothy Kupcha Leland

RIVER GROVE
BOOKS

Some names and identifying characteristics of persons referenced in this book have been changed to protect their privacy.

Published by River Grove Books
Austin, TX
www.rivergrovebooks.com

Distributed by River Grove Books

Design and composition by Greenleaf Book Group and Kim Lance
Cover design by Greenleaf Book Group and Kim Lance
Cover photo by Bryan Lindsay Photography

Publisher's Cataloging-in-Publication data is available.

Print ISBN: 978-1-63299-752-4

eBook ISBN: 978-1-63299-753-1

First Edition

Contents

Authors' Note

This book is based on the journals, videos, correspondence, writings, and recollections of the authors. Although we are telling our story as we experienced it, some names and other identifying details have been fictionalized.

Our goal is to describe our own experiences in Rachel's struggle to overcome the challenges of Lyme disease and to regain her good health. We describe many of the tests, treatments, medications, and other medical care that Rachel received. However, we are not doctors, and we are writing from one patient's and one parent's perspectives. We discuss many difficult topics, including depression and suicidal thoughts. We are not offering medical advice, and we strongly caution each of our readers not to rely on our book in dealing with any medical problems that they may encounter. The reader should seek the advice and care of qualified medical professionals.

Prologue

I was thirteen years old when I wrote my very first journal entry on May 1, 2005. I was in the seventh grade, and my world had begun crumbling down around me at a terrifying pace. One day I was an accomplished athlete playing her heart out in a competitive soccer league, and the next I was using a wheelchair to get from one junior high class to another. Seemingly out of the blue, my body had decided I was the enemy, sending bolts of pain shooting through my neck, back, and legs every minute of the day until I couldn't even manage walking anymore. The worst part was that no one seemed to have any idea what was going on.

What came next was a long, frightening, and often frustrating search for answers. As my parents and I went to doctor after doctor without any clear explanation for my rapidly deteriorating health, my fear and anxiety skyrocketed. Wanting to help me cope, my mom suggested I write down all my experiences in a journal. I found an old notebook we had around the house, and hoping to make sense of my overwhelming new feelings, I began to write. When I composed those first few entries, I had no idea how important that journal would turn out to be, as a place to record my confusion and the dark emotions that sometimes engulfed me. Writing allowed me to bear witness to myself—a self I felt no one else in the world could even see, let alone understand.

This feeling of isolation only grew during the years that I grappled with chronic illness. Furthermore, I struggled greatly with the concept of hope. Looking back through adult eyes, I can see that my mounting despair was due, in large part, to the fact that I had no role models for my new way of living. I needed someone to show me that I could survive this experience and go on to lead a joyful, meaningful life. Unable to imagine any light at the end of this tunnel, I found myself stuck in a deep, dark hole with seemingly no way out. But, while I did not have anybody like me to guide my way, I did have the love and support of family and friends, and this kept me going. They held my hands in that place of darkness, encouraging me to keep traveling the long and winding path that finally brought me out of the abyss—and to better health.

Once I found my way out of that bleak situation, and for many years after, my journal collected dust. It had served its purpose, and now I couldn't bear to revisit the traumatic events I had detailed so painstakingly all those years before. When I dared to divulge anything about that part of my life to the outside world, it was only through carefully crafted inspirational messages on social media. These posts were always truthful, but deep inside I knew that their relentlessly upbeat tone didn't accurately reflect my lived experience. But then, something unexpected shifted my perspective.

One day, I came across an old photo of me taken when my health had first begun declining. Being confronted with evidence of the difficulty I'd overcome at such a young age brought back a flood of emotions I had been denying for so many years. Suddenly, I felt compelled to share the reality of how disheartened and despondent I'd been as a young teen.

I knew that if this picture could stir up such deep feelings in me, it might do the same for others. For the first time, I felt ready to reveal something authentic about what I'd gone through with chronic illness. I opened Instagram, selected the picture of me in the wheelchair, and in the caption beneath it, I wrote my truth—just as I had in my journal years before. My experience had been scary, frustrating, and hard. It still *was* hard. And it pained me to see this photo of a girl who I knew was about to endure so much anguish. It broke my heart to see her smiling for the camera, unaware of how upside down her life was about to become. But as I weighed whether to share this more in-depth post, I knew that if even one person who saw this picture could feel the sense of connection I had so desperately longed for back then, I felt my discomfort would be worth it. I held my breath and pressed "Share."

The response to that Instagram post floored me! Comments poured in from followers who had no idea that I had ever really struggled. Friends who had only known me in my adult years noted that since I always came off so positive, they assumed I had always been that way, even as a sick teen. One acquaintance I had known for years said she couldn't picture me ever being depressed. That day, I resolved to finally talk about what had *really* happened to me. No more glorified social media highlight reels, just the raw truth from someone who had gone through it all and had finally reached a better place.

Using my journal as a guide, I began to write my story all over again. Yet, as I did, I came to recognize that this wasn't just *my* story. The experience of my chronic illness had involved my whole family, and much of the picture was unknown to the girl writing that journal. Wanting to tell this story as completely as possible, I enlisted my mom, Dorothy, to help fill in the blanks. Throughout this book, she provides insight into everything from finding the right doctors to how helpless a mother feels in the face of her child's serious health problems.

According to the US Centers for Disease Control and Prevention, some 40 percent of school-age children and adolescents have at least one chronic illness. We don't know how many of them face fear and ambiguity in addition to physical pain as they fight for their experiences to be recognized by family, friends, and the medical establishment. I was lucky enough to have fierce advocates by my side, but not everyone is so fortunate. Some struggle in isolation, without loving hands to help guide them out. I sincerely hope this memoir can serve as a beacon of light for anyone who needs it. This is the story of my life with Lyme disease.

CHAPTER 1

She Just Sits There

Standing at the edge of the goal box, I blocked the sun with my hand and squinted, watching the soccer ball bounce around on the other end of the field. This was our second game today, and if we won, we'd play in the semifinals tomorrow. Suddenly, I saw the ball barreling right toward me, in the skilled control of player No. 15. She was easily the biggest, most intimidating girl on the opposing team, a full head taller than me. Knowing I was the last line of defense before she reached our goal, I raced straight for her and slammed my foot into the ball. Suddenly, I lost my balance and pitched forward toward the ground. As I instinctively braced my fall with both hands stretched in front of me, pain lashed through my right wrist. In the distance, I heard someone pleading for a penalty call on No. 15.

Cradling my arm, I walked off the field as my coach sent in my replacement. I made my way toward the shade of a pop-up canopy, where Mom had a folding chair and an ice pack waiting for me. Dad patted my shoulder, telling me I had played great in both games today, and other parents chimed in as well. My older brother Jeremy offered me some orange slices, left over from our halftime snack, and sat down next to me. We went back to watching the game, cheering on my team together and idly wondering how long my injury would keep me out. Just as we'd expected, later that week, a doctor declared my injury was only a sprained wrist. Nothing broken. It would heal. No big deal.

Dorothy

None of us realized how big of a deal Rachel's sprain would turn out to be. As a competitive soccer player, she had been injured before and had always bounced back without issue. After the game was over, her father, Bob, and I took her home and encouraged her to take it easy, assuming that a few days of rest, ice packs, and ibuprofen would get her back in the game in no time. But that's not what happened.

Instead, things started going haywire. The next week, she developed severe pain in her knees. Then, one ankle hurt so much she couldn't put weight on that foot at all. Something felt very wrong. But when we went for X-rays, the doctors didn't see any problem. They sent us home with a recommendation to keep up the ice and ibuprofen—which didn't help at all. Clearly, something dreadful was happening. It was as if the wrist injury had somehow unleashed a sinister process throughout her body.

After a few weeks of ice, rest, and ibuprofen, the pain in my wrist had only gotten worse. And then my knees started hurting, too. I'd dealt with knee pain for several years, which my doctors had always shrugged off as "growing pains." But this hurt much worse than it ever had before. I tried wearing elastic knee braces, which at first helped a bit. But I soon realized it was impossible to walk from classroom to classroom at school. Mom unearthed a pair of crutches from our garage, and I tried those out. They helped by taking pressure off my knees, but my injured wrist made it difficult to maneuver with them. The crutches were an imperfect solution, but what choice did I have? I had to get to six different classes throughout the day, and I couldn't do it without help.

When I got to school, students and teachers alike hounded me with questions.

"I hurt myself in soccer," I replied for the millionth time, explaining to my fourth-period homeroom teacher why I was on crutches today when I wasn't yesterday. "I fell and hurt my knees."

I broke eye contact with her. This wasn't quite true. My knees had been getting worse and worse lately, but they didn't have anything to do with my fall—only my wrist had been injured on the field. Yet somehow, here we were. Until we knew what the real issue was, blaming everything on soccer seemed like the best bet.

My friend Jessica, who shared most of my classes, carried my backpack for me while I awkwardly navigated the halls on my crutches. There was no way I could carry my own stuff—full of textbooks, my backpack weighed a whopping twelve pounds. With the crutches chafing my armpits, I slowly made my way to science class, Jessica beside me.

Although we lived within walking distance of school, Mom picked me up in the car after the last bell. Once home, I sat at my desk to crank out my math homework. With ice packs on my knees, my wrist, and a smaller one wrapped around my ankle, I struggled to focus. For no obvious reason, my left ankle had begun hurting today, too. Nothing had happened to account for it. No new injuries. Just inexplicable bone pain. And the ice and ibuprofen didn't seem to help.

Despite two weeks on crutches, my pain was out of control. Both ankles hurt all the time. Sometimes it was stabbing pain, sometimes pins and needles. My wrist had a constant ache deep in the bone.

I couldn't even use my crutches anymore, since putting weight on either my feet or my wrist was unbearable.

In the living room, I tested out the black and silver wheelchair Mom had rented from a medical supply store that afternoon. Placing both hands on the wheels, I pushed myself forward, feeling the extra strain on my splinted wrist.

"What do I say when people ask why I'm in a wheelchair?" I knew I'd be bombarded with questions at school tomorrow.

"It's none of their business why you're using a wheelchair," Mom replied. "Say it's a soccer injury."

By now, I think we both knew this was much more than a soccer injury.

Dorothy

The wheelchair made it easier for Rachel to get from one side of her school to the other, but it didn't work very well within our home. Like most mid-twentieth-century houses, it had been built with no thought to wheelchair accessibility. Thankfully, we could get her through the front door, but things became complicated from there. Our hallway was too narrow to maneuver the wheelchair, so Rachel had no way to get to the bathroom or her bedroom. We tried pushing her in a wheeled office chair, which glided well over the vinyl floors of the kitchen and family room. But the hallway and her bedroom were carpeted—rough territory for such small wheels. A couple of times, my son, Jeremy, scooped Rachel up and carried her where she needed to go, but that was not a long-term solution.

After weeks of trying to solve this logistical problem, I finally hired someone to rip out the carpet in the hallway and Rachel's bedroom and replace it with smooth laminate flooring. Now we could push her in the office chair, and sometimes she could even move herself by pressing her hands along the walls. This particular challenge was fixed within a day. Unfortunately, sorting out our other problems would take much longer.

On my first day of using the wheelchair at school, Mom pushed me all the way to my first class, which was in one of the portable buildings at the far corner of campus. Feeling everybody's eyes on me, I focused my gaze on the green backpack in my lap. My fingers grazed the insignia on it, showing I had gotten the Presidential Award for my fifth-grade physical fitness test. I had been so proud of my accomplishment that I asked Mom to sew it on my backpack in a place of honor. Two years later, it was still there.

Legs sprinted toward me from the left. "What happened?" Jessica exclaimed with deep concern.

"Things are getting worse," I replied softly.

Since my wrist injury and joint pain made it difficult for me to manage the wheelchair, Mom asked Jessica if she could push me from class to class. Fortunately, my friend seemed honored by the request.

All day, I fielded the same questions over and over. From math to science to homeroom, everyone wanted to know what specific event led from the crutches yesterday to the wheelchair today. To discourage these interrogations, I tried keeping a blank, unapproachable expression on my face.

In fourth-period geography, Harper, the girl who sat in front of me, turned around and asked disdainfully, "What's wrong with you?"

I parroted back my well-rehearsed line, to which she responded, "*Pfft*," and turned away.

By mid-afternoon I couldn't take the pressure of everyone's callous curiosity on top of the searing pain in my bones. I had Jessica push me to the office, where choking down sobs, I asked the receptionist to call my mom. Making no effort to do so, she tersely asked, "Why?"

Because my feet are on fire, I thought but didn't say aloud. Burning pins were jabbing my ankles. I let Jessica speak for me.

"We just need to call her mom," she said briskly, reaching across me for the phone, bringing it close enough to dial.

Mom picked up on the first ring, and I burst into tears.

"I'm on my way," she said.

The following week, I left school early because we had an appointment for a full-body bone scan at a hospital thirty minutes away from where we lived. Mom picked me up after science class so I wouldn't miss my end-of-unit quiz. I had missed a lot of school lately as we tried to find out what was going on. One doctor said I had reflex sympathetic dystrophy (RSD), and another thought it was juvenile rheumatoid arthritis. No one seemed certain about anything. All the tests and lab work came back with the same result: "We don't know what's wrong with you."

That morning, the phlebotomist drew nine vials of blood, which beat my previous record of seven from the last week. I was keeping track in my journal.

My pre-algebra book pressed hard against my lap as I tried to do homework in the waiting room. My math grades had plummeted lately. For starters, I didn't understand what letters were doing in my math problems anyway, or why we would ever need to know this stuff at any point in the real world. Math was stupid.

Someone called my name, and a nurse brought us back to a room where they gave me a shot to prepare for the body scan. The drug apparently needed a couple hours to do its thing, so they asked us to come back after lunch. We headed to a sandwich shop down the road, where I got turkey with lettuce and brie on a baguette, just like I did when we went to Paris the summer after fourth grade.

Before we headed back, I wanted to go to the restroom. Mom pushed my wheelchair down the hall, but as we turned the corner, we were stopped by a stack of boxes in our path.

"It's okay," I said immediately. "Let's just go back to the hospital."

"No, this is against ADA," Mom said firmly, referring to the Americans with Disabilities Act. It wasn't the first time she'd brought it up. I didn't like when she talked about ADA violations, because it meant she was about to embarrass me by making a scene. She steered my chair over to the cash register. "My daughter is in a wheelchair and needs to use the restroom. You have boxes blocking the path, and we can't get back there."

My cheeks burned as my mom announced to the whole restaurant that I had to go to the bathroom! The lady behind the cash register apologized and moved the boxes so we could pass. By then, I didn't even want to go to the restroom—I just wanted to get the heck out of there. I kept that to myself, however. After the lady went to all the trouble of moving the boxes for us, it would be rude to just leave. And I didn't want my mom to go off on another tirade about the ADA.

Back at the hospital, I changed into a gown and climbed up onto a long table. The scan would take up to an hour, they said, and I had to lie flat and completely still the whole time. I must have gone pale when they told me this. Lately, every time I tried to lie flat, it hurt like crazy. Strategically placed pillows could help at home, but there were no pillows here—they'd interfere with the scan. I didn't know how I'd be able to make it, but I resigned myself to suffering in silence.

As electronic beeping sounded around me, my rib bones felt like they were being dislodged from my spine. Tears streamed down my face. Some pooled inside my ears, while others soaked into my thin polka-dot hospital gown. Inside this oxygen-deprived vault of despair, all I could do was lie there, my whole body clenched, hoping it would be over soon.

When the beeping finally stopped, I sat up on the table and wiped my tears with the back of my arm.

"Is everything okay?" the nurse asked as she helped me down into my wheelchair. "If you needed us to stop, you could have said so through the microphone, sweetie!"

Now she tells me? But stopping wouldn't have helped anything. The scan needed to be done, and getting it over as quickly as possible was the best plan of action.

That night, with pillows propped under my back and knees, I lay in bed with my brother next to me. We played *Hydro Thunder*, a racing game, on the Playstation. He had recently moved the game console into my bedroom so we could play it lying down. It had become a great escape from my crushing reality.

Dorothy

In the weeks following her injury, Rachel's condition continued to deteriorate. This was a confusing and scary time for the whole family. Rachel's symptoms came and went capriciously. Sometimes one foot hurt, sometimes the other. Sometimes she felt electrical shocks in her elbow. Sometimes one foot felt as cold as ice, while the other felt hot to the touch. What never varied was a searing pain in her wrist, knees, and ankles. It was difficult to reassure my frightened and suffering daughter when I was frightened and suffering myself.

Back at school, it was time for my daily barrage of negative comments from Harper. "You're so lazy, Rachel. You can get up and walk; you just don't want to."

Unfortunately, Harper was in five of my six classes, and every day she loudly expressed her disdain for me. I'd known her since elementary school and until a few weeks ago, our relationship was not noteworthy. That all changed once I showed up at school in a wheelchair. Now I couldn't pass her without hearing at least one rude comment. Her verbal attacks strayed very little from their usual territory: the chair, me being lazy, or how I must be making everything up. Sometimes she called me "stupid" or "pathetic." Surprisingly, she tormented me in public places—not even trying to hide her outrageous bullying behind closed doors.

Jessica witnessed the harassment firsthand while pushing me from class to class each day. It was her idea for me to start writing down exactly what Harper said. If I got enough data, maybe the principal would tell her to knock it off once and for all. So, for the past week, I had written down every incident in my Harper notebook. Even though her words were meant to belittle me, filling my notebook with her vile comments made me feel empowered. I didn't understand what her goal was with all of this, but at the end of the day, Jessica and I had taken the high road, and I was sure that Harper's words would come back to bite her once enough of them were documented.

Pushing myself out of the classroom, I winced as someone bumped into me, trying to get through the door before I was all the way out. No surprise, it was my perpetual tormentor. I went out into the hall and pulled off to the side to document her offense. Harper had called me many things, including some colorful profanity, but today was the first time she'd ever actually touched me. And with even slight vibrations now sending pain up and down my spine, I just couldn't have some unhinged seventh grader with a vendetta sideswiping my chair. Pulling out my notebook, I jotted down a few words before continuing on to English class.

When I left the room an hour later, I felt somebody rip my backpack out of my hands. Looking around in shock, I saw Harper dumping the contents of my backpack into a trash can. Somehow, she knew exactly what she was looking for. She ripped out the pages of my notebook and tore them into tiny pieces. She turned toward me and spit out, "You're worthless." Then she raced away down the hall.

Stunned, I turned toward Jessica, who told me firmly, "We're going to the principal *right now!*"

Retrieving my backpack and binders from the trash, Jessica placed them on my lap and then pushed my wheelchair to the front office. Soon we were inside with Mrs. Clark, our school counselor, trying to keep our composure as we recounted the events leading up to today's blowup.

My mind went blank. Mrs. Clark wanted specifics, but without my Harper notebook, I could only remember the gist of her hostility toward me. I could control so little of my life at this time, and that notebook had been the *one* thing I could. My pain was worse that day than it had been all week. My knees throbbed and my ankles burned. As Jessica took the lead, explaining Harper's bad behavior over the past few weeks, I took deep breaths and examined my elastic knee braces. They were covered in drawings by Christine, a close friend who lived down the street from me. Seeing the little brown cat looking back at me from my right knee brace helped lighten this dark and dreary moment. At least someone out there cared about me.

Mrs. Clark made a phone call, and shortly after, another staff member led Harper into the room.

"Why am I here?" she demanded, glaring sideways at me.

"Why don't you tell us?" Mrs. Clark responded calmly.

"I don't know why I'm here. I haven't done anything. I was at lunch."

Like my recurring nightmare from the past few years, I couldn't make words come out of my mouth.

"Rachel says you grabbed her backpack from her and took her notebook. Did you do this?"

Harper didn't look at me. "No."

Finding my voice, I blurted out, "Yes, you did! You took my backpack and threw it in the *trash*! What have I ever done to you?"

Harper stood next to the door, refusing to sit in the chair offered to her, not saying a word for what felt like forever. Her eyes filled with tears, and her breathing staggered in and out.

"Well?" Mrs. Clark nudged.

Harper mumbled, "She just sits there."

"What do you mean?" asked the counselor.

"She just *sits* there. *All day*," Harper said louder. "She just *sits* there. Looking at me."

"You sit in front of me in nearly every class," I snapped back at her. "Of course I look at you when you turn to look at me!"

Mrs. Clark chimed in. "What do you want Rachel to do differently?"

"I don't know. She just sits there."

"She's in a wheelchair," Mrs. Clark stated bluntly. "What else can she do but sit?"

I suppressed a pathetic smile. Harper was torturing me because I *sit*?

Jessica and I were released to lunch while Harper remained behind.

"All she could say is I sit," I muttered to Jessica as we headed to our lockers. "That's it. I sit!"

Dorothy

Because the school never notified me of what had happened, and my daughter kept it to herself, I knew nothing about this at the time. Months later, when she finally told my husband and me what had transpired, I felt appalled, angry, and sick to my stomach. Rachel had been continuously harassed by this girl, the abuse had escalated to the point that school officials became involved, and nobody thought to notify me? More than anything, I felt helpless. How could I protect my daughter from something I had no idea was even going on? First a mystery illness was inflicting my child with unbearable pain, and now she was being *bullied* because of it?

In short order, I called the school to ask why I hadn't been contacted about the incident. I was told, "We find it's better if students handle such problems on their own." *Really?* Someone was physically harassing a disabled student at school, and the people in charge just blew it off like that? How exactly was Rachel supposed to "handle this on her own"? She handled it by going to the authorities, and those authorities did nothing. I was frustrated and annoyed with the whole situation. But by this point, it was a new school year, and Harper wasn't even in Rachel's classes—so there was really nothing to be done. The issue of school bullying hadn't yet achieved media prominence by this time in 2005. Since then, I've often wondered if junior high staff would take the same position today, or if they would treat the abuse Rachel suffered for weeks on end with the seriousness it deserved.

CHAPTER 2

Attention-Seeking Behavior

J eremy was graduating from high school, and in a couple of months he would leave for college. I already knew I would miss him so much. I wanted to get him a special graduation present, but I hadn't exactly been in a position to do that lately. Luckily, I had thought ahead. A couple of months before, I had stashed a box of his favorite Girl Scout cookies in the back of the freezer, which I'd gift wrapped for him today. Now, as he smiled at the box of Samoas, I felt like I had done good.

Dorothy

When we arrived at Jeremy's high school graduation ceremony at the local football stadium, we immediately realized there was a problem. At the time, the venue offered only nominal wheelchair accessibility. We would have to park Rachel in her wheelchair on the ground level in the full sun on a blistering hot afternoon, with one family member sitting next to her on a folding chair. The only available shade was high up in the bleachers and completely inaccessible by wheelchair. Our family friends Lynn and Steve were with us, and Steve saved the day. He was six-foot-seven and incredibly muscular. We stashed the wheelchair under the bleachers, and Steve carried Rachel up to where we could all sit together in the shade. Although it solved the immediate logistical problem, I know it embarrassed Rachel. It reminded me once more how the concept of wheelchair accessibility is, shall we say, imperfectly understood by the world at large.

Before Rachel got sick, we had planned some special outings for this last summer before Jeremy left for college. We had booked an August trip to Alaska and planned on visiting my mother in Southern California in July. Her health was failing, and she longed to see her grandchildren again. These plans flew out the window, however, as we tried to figure out the cause of Rachel's alarming decline.

With our family travel on hold for now, we continued to make the rounds of Rachel's medical appointments. Now that the school year was over and many of her friends were away, I knew it would be essential to find other, more positive things that could keep Rachel engaged in life. At her request, we signed her up for an acting class at the local arts center.

A week after his graduation, Jeremy, Mom, and I were in the car on the way back from my acting class. As much as I had *wanted* to go to that class, the fifteen-minute drive there and back was excruciating.

All pavement was the devil. Even with two pillows under me, one behind, and another on the car floor, nothing could make a dent in the pain I felt during that short drive. I could feel every pebble in the street, every line painted on the road, and every single raised reflector we passed over while changing lanes. Each vibration hurled lightning bolts into my bones.

Back home after acting class, Jeremy offered to play Hydro Thunder with me, and I accepted. I climbed into my bed, which was decked out in beautiful lime green sheets—my favorite color—and propped myself up with pillows. I focused my attention on the TV across the room and concentrated on beating my brother. But when my boat slammed against a rocky cliff, the controller vibrated in my hands, sending pain spiraling through both wrists. In an instant, our fun screeched to a halt as I dropped the controller and gasped for air.

Hyperventilating, I bolted upright, my chest heaving up and down too quickly for me to catch my breath. As I coughed and choked, my face went numb, and I felt a strange tingling sensation around my eyes and cheeks. Jeremy helped me into the office chair by my bed and pushed me out to where Mom and Dad were sitting in the living room. As I fought for air, Mom gently put her hands on my head, because she knew it was the only place she could touch me that didn't hurt. She calmly encouraged me to take slow, deep breaths.

Such panic attacks came more frequently now. Evenings were the hardest. Somehow, I could make it through a whole day's worth of constant pain on pure adrenaline. But once the distractions of the daylight hours passed, I'd lose my composure and couldn't get it back.

By then, my shoulders had become hypersensitive to even the lightest touch. While my clothes caused me constant low-level discomfort, if somebody placed a hand on me, the pain was intolerable. At this moment, my mom's tender caress on my head was the only kind of comforting touch I could experience anymore. I began the process of calming down to baseline by listening to Jeremy's soft voice.

"There you were," he whispered. "Hugging my dirty sock, completely unaware . . ." His words brought air to my lungs, and I cracked a smile at the inside joke. He was referring to a funny incident during a family trip we'd taken two years before, when he'd put his dirty socks next to me in bed where I'd been fast asleep. This had become a favorite memory of ours.

Dorothy

Since Rachel's fall during the soccer game, she had been seen by an assortment of specialists, who had ordered a battery of tests and imaging. But so far, nothing had shed any light on what was happening to her. At first, the doctors approached her symptoms as a sports injury, and we did, too. But although the wrist she had fallen on continued to cause Rachel great pain, an MRI showed that nothing was amiss. These results seemed to bring a shift in how the doctors viewed us. Although I didn't understand it until later, at least some of them now felt that Rachel's pain was psychosomatic—meaning it had no physical basis. They thought it was all in her head.

I dove into research on the internet. I searched many variations of "childhood pain" but found little that seemed pertinent to Rachel's condition. Then, during a chance conversation, one of our neighbors asked if Rachel had ever been tested for Lyme disease. He said he'd known someone in a similar situation who had turned out to have the potentially debilitating, tick-borne illness. I went to my computer and typed "Lyme disease" into my search engine. Some of the information I found seemed to fit our circumstances, but most was contradictory and confusing. I made a mental note to ask our doctors about it.

The first doctor I asked stoutly replied that there was no need to even test her for it, because she didn't have Lyme disease. When I asked how he knew that, he replied, "Because there's no Lyme disease around here." *That's all you got?* I thought. From my cursory online research, I knew that Lyme disease was spread by ticks infected with it, and there were, in fact, known cases in California.

"We don't spend all our time here," I protested. "We hike. We camp. We've gone to different states, even out of the country."

"It doesn't matter," he said pointedly. "There's *no* Lyme around here!"

This was my first experience with what I came to call the "Alice-down-the-Lyme-rabbit-hole" phenomenon—the weird and dysfunctional way the medical establishment approaches Lyme disease. I didn't know then how big a part this dynamic would play in our lives.

The following week, two of my neighborhood friends, Shira and Alicia, sat in my room painting with watercolors. This was our main entertainment these days because I could do it from bed, but today everything hurt too much for me to join them. They painted alone.

Shira and I were in the same grade at school. We'd been friends since forever. Alicia was six years younger than me, and I'd known her since she was born. Her older brothers used to hang out with Jeremy, and although Alicia was much younger than me, she was very mature for her age. We sort of met in the middle.

When Alicia shifted her position next to me on the bed, I felt the vibrations in every joint, bone, and muscle in my body. As I slowly released air through pursed lips, I let the infraction slide without comment. She knew the rules. She wasn't supposed to jostle the bed at all.

Music by the band Yellowcard blared throughout my room, removing any need for small talk. By this point, we were talked out anyway. Each day was exactly like the one before it. Shira and Alicia would come over, and we'd always end up painting. When we finished one, we'd lay it out to dry and start another. We had done this a thousand times before, and I was sure we'd do it a thousand times more.

But as bored as we were, I was so grateful for these two people sitting next to me. They visited me daily, knowing full well that they wouldn't be leaving the four walls of my room while they were here. But still, they came. They didn't know what it was like to be in my body, but at least they knew what it was like to be stuck here day in and day out the way I was.

Dorothy

During this time before we had a diagnosis, different doctors suggested various strategies for treating Rachel's pain. At one point, one doctor even prescribed opioid painkillers. These made her feel dizzy and nauseated but didn't lessen the pain firmly ensconced in her neck, back, knees, and ankles. We stopped that medication after only a few doses.

Rachel also developed extreme hypersensitivity in her upper back and shoulders. Even a featherlight touch felt "like being stung by a thousand bees," she told us. Ironically, the fact that the strong painkillers brought Rachel no relief undermined our position with the doctors. If her pain was *real*, they said, then the opioids would have helped.

Even though none of her doctors felt that Lyme disease could possibly be a factor in Rachel's condition—they refused to even order lab tests for it—my husband and I *insisted*. Finally, one of her doctors agreed to order a Lyme test—I think mainly to shut me up. When that test came back negative, I accepted the result. But I never gave up on my quest to find the root cause of what was ailing my daughter.

By this point, my husband and I figured that this probably wasn't Reflex Sympathetic Dystrophy or juvenile arthritis—two conditions doctors had suggested early on. Her symptoms didn't really fit the picture of either. Where could we find a team of medical detectives who would keep investigating until they found the answer?

Finally, over the Fourth of July weekend, we received a call from the pediatric pain unit of a prominent children's hospital. A spot was available for Rachel if we could be there the following Tuesday.

On July 5, after checking into the pediatric hospital, I was led by a nurse to my very own room. It was small, but all mine, and I even had my own bathroom and TV! The best part was that my hospital bed allowed me to lean back at the perfect angle. No need for hundreds of pillows anymore!

This was also a teaching hospital, so medical students traipsed through my room all day, wanting to listen to my heartbeat. It was as if that was all they knew how to do. They came in, introduced themselves, and asked, "Can I listen to your heart for a moment?"

I mean, sure, knock yourself out, I thought. But what I wanted to say was, "That's not why I'm here. Can I interest you in learning more about my knee pain?" But no. They didn't actually seem to care much about my health, other than what they could hear with their stethoscopes.

Finally, someone who seemed to know what she was doing pulled up a chair by my bed and discussed the weekly schedule with me and my parents. Starting tomorrow, I would receive physical, occupational, and psychotherapy each day. On Fridays, my whole team would get together for what they called a "care conference" to compare notes and review my progress.

Although it was overwhelming, it also felt right. In my heart, I believed that I was meant to be here. What better place to heal than in a famous children's hospital?

Dorothy

We had such high hopes for Rachel's new team of experts in pediatric pain. But there were so many unknowns. For one thing, we had no idea how long we'd be staying at the hospital or how much free time Rachel would have to fill between therapy sessions. Just in case, I brought many things to occupy our time—my laptop, a portable video player, art supplies, books, magazines, and every DVD of *Gilmore Girls* I could get my hands on.

As promised, the very next day, a young woman wearing white pants and a plain black shirt walked into my room and introduced herself as Emily, my physical therapist. After a quick hello, Mom headed to the cafeteria downstairs to give the two of us some privacy.

Emily asked me to show her how I got in and out of bed from my wheelchair. I did as instructed, but my strategy was not to her liking. She wanted me to try again—this time putting weight on my legs.

"I can't use my legs," I said. "They hurt too much, so I do it this way." I proudly showed her how strong my arms were now, and how there was really no need to use my legs to transfer myself back and forth.

I could see Emily wasn't happy with my response. She smiled stiffly, complimented me on my arm strength, and once more requested that I show her what she originally asked for.

This wasn't a great start. She seemed confused as to why I wasn't using my legs. Instead of arguing about it, I lowered my legs as if I were using them and then continued the process as normal. My little optical illusion seemed to satisfy her for the time being, and we moved on.

She took me to the physical therapy room, which was decked out with tons of games and different colored weights. She handed me a piece of paper and pointed out important dates, with notes written under each.

"Next Tuesday we will begin using crutches," she said nonchalantly, as if her words didn't have devastating consequences for me.

My eyes widened, and I felt my heart pounding in my chest. "But what if I can't walk on crutches by next week? What if it still hurts too much?"

"This is the plan, Rachel," Emily said, sounding annoyed—as if my very real concerns were the equivalent of a gnat buzzing around her head. "Your team came up with this plan, and we're going to follow it."

None of this made any sense to me. If all we were doing was trying to get me to walk . . . then why were we even here? Walking wasn't the goal. Stopping my body-wide pain was the goal. Finding answers was the goal. As soon as my pain improved, walking would take care of itself. I'd been walking my whole life! I was a year-round competitive soccer player, for God's sake. Walking wasn't the issue!

I felt disgusted. Unseen. Unheard. Uncared for. The schedule on that paper wasn't going to get me better, that much I knew. And the fact that it was already planned out, not individualized for me at all, made me feel icky inside. Because, if it were truly as simple as the paper made it out to be, I would have already done it.

At the end of the session with Emily, I returned to my room to rest. Then it was time for my first occupational therapy session. Lucy, the occupational therapist (OT), led me to a kitchen down the hall.

"How do you feel about baking in here sometime?" she asked.

"Sounds fun." I loved baking with my neighborhood friends back home. But how would baking give us any answers about my condition?

"Great!" Lucy replied. "We can start out being seated at the table, and as your legs get stronger, we can work up to standing while we cook."

Not this again! Did my file somehow mislabel me as someone in need of strength training?

I couldn't stay silent anymore—I needed to set the record straight.

"I'm not weak," I said. "My legs and ankles hurt; that's why I can't walk. We need to find out how to stop my pain. When we do that, *then* I can get back to playing soccer again."

It's not rocket science, people.

Later that afternoon, two women came into my hospital room. One introduced herself as Abby, a psychotherapist. She said she would meet with me daily during my stay here.

The other one, Charlotte, asked if Mom could leave us alone for the next thirty minutes. Then, Charlotte and Abby pulled chairs up next to my hospital bed, and Charlotte said she had a relaxation technique for us to try. It took everything I had not to roll my eyes. Forced relaxation is so stupid. I don't understand people who think that having us all sit next to each other, saying nothing, will be beneficial in any way.

"Close your eyes and picture a place that brings you peace," Charlotte said in a quiet voice that she probably thought sounded calming.

I watched as they both closed their eyes. This was ridiculous. It was embarrassing to even attempt to go along with it. But not wanting to be rude, I tried to picture myself at my big soccer tournament from last year, when my team won first place. However, that only took about two seconds, and Charlotte clearly wanted to draw this exercise out. I opened my right eye and watched Charlotte breathing deeply in the chair next to me. Was she even doing the exercise, or was she mentally going through her shopping list? Moving my gaze left, I watched Abby open her eyes and look directly at me with a faint smile. Squeezing my eyes shut tight, I waited to see what would happen next. Abby said nothing, though, and we sat in silence for what felt like forever, using up all of our allotted time.

At the end, as Charlotte and Abby prepared to leave, Abby smiled and said she would come back and see me tomorrow, and that we could spend our hour together wherever I wanted. It could be in my hospital room, on the balcony to get fresh air, or in an empty room in my wing of the hospital. She said we could do whatever I felt comfortable with.

"And I want to hear all about how you like to spend your time," she said enthusiastically.

I was excited about having someone interested in learning more about me. And I was eager to meet with her again, as long as we could leave the relaxation techniques for her to do on her own time.

Dorothy

Rachel's days at the hospital were scheduled with blocks of time devoted to physical and occupational therapy, as well as counseling sessions with a psychotherapist. During these hours, I roamed the hospital grounds for exercise and tried to figure out the most productive use of my time. I soon discovered that the hospital had a small library for patients' families—with an internet-enabled computer for their use.

This was back in 2005, and although I owned a laptop computer, Wi-Fi was not widely available. I had a cell phone, but it was only useful for talking. Facebook and YouTube were in their infancy. Moreover, there was no way to reliably stream video. This was back in the day when Netflix would send you DVDs through the mail.

My first time on that hospital computer, I sent an email update to friends and family. Then I continued the research I'd started at home, scouring the internet for anything related to pediatric pain. While there was a lot of research about children with cancer and arthritis, there was little about anything resembling Rachel's situation. But everything I *did* find kept coming back to Lyme disease.

Although I knew Rachel had tested negative for Lyme, I started reading more about it anyway. I discovered that many people felt the type of test Rachel had been given had a high rate of false negatives. *Hmm.* Something to ask the doctors about.

A few days after my therapy sessions began, I was moved to a double room. Thankfully, I was the only occupant at first, but I didn't like the change in plans. When Mom left to get us a meal that wasn't hospital food, I flipped through the channels on TV.

I'd been there less than a week, but already the pain in my back had dramatically increased. Unable to focus on the TV, I lowered my bed down until it was flat, which made my back hurt even more. This was a tactic I often used to make my constant pain feel less acute. I would temporarily put myself into a position that made my pain worse so that when I returned to my original position, my body would be tricked into thinking it was getting relief. The feeling was fleeting, but worth it.

When Mom returned, we watched *Little Women* on my hospital TV. Halfway through, shooting nerve pain set fire to my right leg, taking up all our attention. Spasms radiated through my calf, feeling like electric shocks. We were in a hospital, yet no one here could do anything except Mom, who cupped my knee in her hands. Although this didn't do anything to reduce the actual pain, it felt worse when she let go, so she kept her hands in place as we continued watching the movie. After the credits rolled, Mom kissed my cheek and headed to her motel room. Alone and in pain, I listened to the portable CD player my brother had lent me and tried to sleep.

At some point during the night, I was jolted awake by what sounded like a child screaming. There was a baby crying, too, I thought, and voices whispering in Spanish. It was dark, but thanks to the lights emitted by the various medical machines in the room, I could see perfectly. The clock by my bed read 11:15 p.m.

The sounds were coming from behind the curtain surrounding the other bed in my room. Suddenly, Elaine, my favorite nurse, emerged from behind the drape and came over to me. "You have a new roommate," she whispered, giving my arm a little squeeze before heading back across the room.

I closed my eyes, knowing that sleep was unlikely tonight. Screaming sliced through the air like sharpened knives, and the voices coming from behind the curtain were loud and unpredictable. Finally, a woman took the wailing baby out into the hallway, but I could still hear whimpering coming from my unseen roommate. Then someone entered with a cart full of syringes and alcohol wipes. The shrieking resumed in full force.

When Mom walked into my room the next morning, I shot up in bed.

"I was awake during every single hour last night," I said, not even bothering with hello. My new roommate and her entourage were gone, but they could return at any moment, so I needed to get out what I'd been waiting eight hours to say.

As I told Mom about the previous night's events, I shoveled pancakes and hash browns into my mouth from my position in bed. A nurse walked in and interrupted me mid-sentence.

"Sweetie, you don't have to eat in bed," she said cheerfully. "You can eat in your chair or on the couch!"

My mouth full of syrup-covered pancake, I looked her way and smiled. "Oh, I'm fine," I said, getting back to my story as the nurse took my vitals.

That afternoon, after my PT, OT, and psychotherapy sessions were completed, Dad and Jeremy arrived for a visit. Giving them the deluxe tour of the third-floor wing, I finished up with my favorite place in the whole hospital—the balcony.

Being cooped up in this place made me crave fresh air and sunlight more than ever, so I would come out to the balcony whenever I got a chance. Then Jeremy said he had a gift for me. He handed over a package covered in wrapping paper. Inside, a green iPod Mini sat in its box.

"I downloaded all of your music from iTunes, so everything from your computer is now on this," he said.

I beamed. What a godsend this iPod would be! Hours passed at a snail's pace in this joint. Most days, all I could look forward to was the blissful nothingness of sleep, my only escape from the suffocating boredom of being trapped here. And to top off the most amazing gift ever, Jeremy walked me through how to access the games that were built into the device. I'd no longer be forced to stare at my ceiling for hours on end—now I could play Solitaire for as long as I wanted.

After a dinner of French fries and multiple desserts at the hospital cafeteria, I said goodbye not only to Jeremy and Dad, but also to Mom. She was going home for the night and would drive back to the hospital the next morning. I pulled the covers of my bed up over myself and snuggled with my stuffed bear, playing Solitaire on my new iPod as I listened to "Boulevard of Broken Dreams" by Green Day.

Dorothy

When I left the hospital Friday afternoon to take care of some things back home, I expected to make the three-hour drive back to the hospital early Saturday morning. From Rachel's perspective, it shouldn't have been much different than the other nights when I left the hospital to stay at a nearby motel. However, when I tried to get out of bed on Saturday morning, I suddenly felt like I was on a Tilt-A-Whirl ride or George Clooney's fishing boat in *A Perfect Storm*. I tried to steady myself against the wall but quickly fell back on the bed. Overcome with dizziness, I clearly wasn't going anywhere anytime soon.

My husband and I called Rachel and told her I'd be delayed. Bob was going to take me to urgent care so we could figure out what was going on. Rachel said she'd be okay. The urgent care clinic diagnosed me with vertigo and gave me some Dramamine that knocked me out for the rest of the day.

Three days after she had gone home for a break and had a vertigo spell, Mom still hadn't returned. Luckily, she had left the cell phone with me so we could stay in touch, but I was on my own at the hospital, and things were getting ridiculous. Everyone had gone bananas.

A few days before, when the nurse had seen me eating breakfast in bed, she told my medical team, and they went ballistic. They insisted that I eat all my meals sitting up in a chair. In fact, they said I wasn't *allowed* to eat in bed. *Why do they even care?* I wondered. Originally,

I had eaten in bed because it was what felt best for my back. But now, I ate in bed just to defy them. I found the whole thing insulting.

Today, after my breakfast of pancakes and bacon was delivered, I waited fifteen minutes while my food got cold and soggy, just to see if anybody would check on me. When it seemed like the coast was clear, I placed the tray on my bed and took *one* bite of my food. Then, *bam*! Nurse Sarah appeared out of nowhere and laid it on thick, saying she was disappointed in me and that she would tell my team I was "disobeying their orders." *Their orders? Lady, you don't know me at all if you think saying that will help your cause.*

Later, during my PT session, Emily said she'd heard I was "making trouble" with my medical team. I told her I wasn't making *anything*. "This is all ludicrous," I said. "I'll eat my food wherever the heck I want to. No one else in this hospital has to sit in their chair to eat!" It was true. Not a *single* one of the six roommates I'd had so far (yes, I was keeping track) had *ever* eaten in their chair. So why did *I* have to? I had never agreed to any goal of sitting in a chair while I ate. I was not in this stupid place because I ate food sitting in bed. I was at this hospital for reasons all these idiots had yet to figure out. I thought they should stop caring about where I ate and start caring about how to get rid of this body-wide pain that was getting worse every day.

When I returned from PT, I saw a typed note attached to my door. It read: "Food will be waiting at nurses station for 16B." That was me, 16B. Did 16A have any such restrictions imposed on her? No, she could have her food delivered straight to her bed and spoon-fed to her if she wanted. But not 16B. I'd been singled out for punishment.

That sign made me *livid*. My roommate wasn't there at the moment, so I pushed the door shut with an extra *thud* and climbed into bed. I called my friend Shira in a blind rage. She calmed me down, agreeing that my medical team was being stupid. I vowed not to eat a single thing any of these nutjobs gave me anymore. Not if they expected me to admit defeat by dragging myself down to the nurse's station to eat in a chair while someone watched over me like a prison guard. My meal could rot on its tray for all I cared.

By the time night fell, I had managed to stick to the promise I'd made myself and not retrieve my tray from the nurses station for dinner. I realized I didn't have to! I still had a huge drawer filled with Rice Krispy Treats and other packaged foods left over from previous meals. I could literally go days without eating any more hospital food, and by the time my stash was gone, Mom or Dad would be there to bring me outside food.

After checking to make sure no one was coming, I grabbed a few goodies from their hiding place and pushed myself to the bathroom to eat in privacy. What a stupid world. There I was, sitting in my wheelchair behind a locked bathroom door, eating a package of Lay's BBQ chips for dinner.

Dorothy

When I finally made it back to the hospital a few days later, I discovered that the "Rachel has to eat sitting up in a chair" directive had exploded into a full-on standoff during my absence. I tried to talk to the doctor in charge of Rachel's care team about finding ways to de-escalate the situation, but she didn't want to discuss it. However, to my relief, shortly after, they seemed to drop the subject.

After I'd been in the hospital for about three weeks, the team told Mom to take the wheelchair away and never bring it back, forcing me to use crutches full-time, not just during PT as I had been doing. So now, Mom and I were trapped in my room during our many hours of downtime each day—able to wander only as far as my legs could take me. With each step I took on crutches, my knees felt like the bones were being ground together without any cartilage between them. Even just thinking about how much I would be forced to use my legs in a single day sent me into a panic. That day, I had PT at 10:00 a.m., which meant I would need to walk clear across the third-floor wing of the hospital to the physical and occupational therapy suite. After lunch I had OT, requiring me to return to the same place. My 2:00 p.m. psychotherapy session could be done anywhere, but I liked to do it on the balcony to get fresh air. That took a good two minutes of struggling. Finally, we had my care conference at 3:00 p.m., which, thankfully, was right across the hall from my room. But by then I'd have moved so much that even traveling that short distance would be hard. I'd also need to get out of bed and limp to my bathroom repeatedly throughout the day. The mere thought of all this walking made me want to scream.

Whenever I spoke up, saying it hurt too much to walk, Emily threatened me. She said that if I stopped making progress or refused to comply with my team's plan, I would be discharged from the hospital and sent home to deteriorate further. Each day, more and more was expected of me physically, but no one ever mentioned pain relief or finding out what had put me here in the first place. I had stopped expecting sympathetic comments when I was unable to push myself past my limits to please my medical team. Each day became markedly worse than the last. I slogged through on fumes, feeling more depressed with each passing moment.

Just a few weeks in this hospital had sucked the life out of me. Smiling was no longer a natural expression of pleasure. Instead, it was how I hid my dark state of mind. During my downtime, my thoughts were filled with visions of death—how and when it would happen. I would be surrounded by blissful nothingness, I fantasized, all my pain and suffering eradicated. I'd be free from the nonstop misery of my broken body.

No one here was looking for any answers. At our so-called care conferences each Friday, everyone talked about the *progress* we had made. Each team member boasted about the aspects they saw improving, backing up their statements with breezy declarations of "She moves more easily" or "She can walk on crutches to the bathroom." But I knew this wasn't an improvement! When I stumbled to the bathroom, it only showed that I had learned to push through the intense pain that no one here would even admit I had. Each day in OT, PT, and psychotherapy, I repeated how much my knees hurt—and no one cared. They always told me to focus on how much better I was getting instead of thinking about my unrelenting pain.

One day, after our weekly care conference, everyone had left the room except for me and Abby, my psychotherapist. To my surprise, she started picking up markers from the table and throwing them at the wall. The markers still had their caps on, and as she pitched them, she made a loud growling sound: "*Gggrrrr.*" She looked ridiculous. And she wanted *me* to join her, because this exercise would supposedly allow me to let my "true feelings" out. What nonsense! Whenever I did express my true feelings—about how much my body hurt—nobody wanted to hear it. These stupid people weren't helping me at all. I didn't want to be here anymore. And by "here," I didn't just mean in the hospital.

Dorothy

When we first brought Rachel to this prestigious hospital, we assumed that the goal would be to solve the mystery of what was causing her debilitating pain—kind of like an episode of the

TV show *House*. But apparently that wasn't happening. Nobody seemed to be looking for the underlying cause of Rachel's pain. Instead, as time went on, it became evident to me that the team had decided early on that her pain was psychological. If she could just grit her way through it, they insisted, the pain would subside. Mind over matter.

That wasn't going to cut it for me. I kept up my daily research on the hospital computer. The more I read, the more I wanted for Rachel to be given a Lyme test called the Western blot. I asked the care team about it. No, I was told, Rachel's prior test had come back negative, which meant she *didn't* have Lyme disease.

By this time, Rachel wasn't the only one having sessions with the psychotherapist—I was, too. The woman spent a lot of time probing to find out what terrible thing must have happened in our family to cause Rachel to "act out" like this. When I asked *her* about a Western blot test, she told me that I should "drop that line of inquiry." I told her that I'd be more likely to do that if they ordered the Western blot. Finally—and I'm certain it was just to placate me—they conceded and ordered the test.

I waited nervously for the results, and then eventually one of the medical interns on Rachel's care team told me that the test had come back negative. I asked her a follow-up question about the details of the test results, and she simply replied, "The results were negative. That's *all* you need to know." I told her that I would like to see a copy of the lab report myself. She looked at me blankly and mumbled something about checking into that. But I never did get one.

Now going on my fourth week at the hospital, I was sitting in a backless office chair in the center of the PT room, watching as an unfamiliar woman wearing glasses placed an instrument on my finger to take my pulse. Emily sat in the corner, observing quietly from her perch on a raised blue mat.

"We're going to work on desensitization," the woman with glasses said.

"Desensitization of what?" I asked cautiously.

"Of your shoulders," the woman replied. "We need to tell your body that there's nothing wrong."

My stomach turned over, and suddenly the pancake and Rice Krispy Treat I'd had for breakfast wasn't sitting so well. I didn't like the sound of this.

My heart started beating faster, and it was hard to catch my breath. "Well, we can't touch my shoulders—"

"We need to desensitize them," the woman said bluntly. "To do that, we need to touch them."

I glanced at Emily, and she smiled back. The monitor on my finger showed my pulse steadily increasing. My chest tightened too much to get an adequate amount of oxygen through.

"I—"

Without warning, the woman placed her hand on my shoulder, rubbing it slowly back and forth. Her touch felt like an electric shock. I lurched forward, straining away from her.

"No!" I raised my hand in protest.

I was so weak by this point that my core couldn't hold me upright any longer. I slumped over in my chair.

"It's okay," the woman tried to soothe me. "Just keep breathing." She moved her hand to my other shoulder blade. *When would this torture stop?* I tried to block out the pain by clenching my whole body. It didn't work.

For the past few years, I'd had a recurring nightmare where I couldn't call out for help, even though I was about to be murdered. Until today, I thought it had just been a bad dream, and I always awoke with the knowledge that it would never happen in real life. But now, as I was stunned into silence, I held my breath and willed my heart to stop beating. This was no nightmare. I was *awake*.

Dorothy

During the fifth week of our hospital stay, Rachel's doctors called me into a private conference. They told me that my attitude was contributing heavily to Rachel's situation. They said that my *misguided* belief that something real was causing Rachel's pain was preventing her from "getting past it." They said I could best help her by recognizing that there was nothing physically wrong with her, and that she had developed a psychological need to be in a wheelchair. Enabling her by allowing her to continue using that emotional crutch would be destructive. They told me I shouldn't "give in" or "coddle" her in any way.

Their words hit like a punch to the gut. *Was this my fault?* Practically overnight, my daughter had gone from being healthy, happy, and athletic to a state of constant pain. And now these doctors said that my efforts to help her were actually *hurting* her? It didn't make sense. Rachel had been suffering—our whole family had been suffering along with her—for five long months. Five months of her pain and my dogged determination to leave no stone unturned in our efforts to fix whatever this was. Now they told me that my desire to help my daughter was making it worse. How could this be?

I was aghast, confused, and wounded by their words. I tried not to burst into tears right there in the conference room. Could I have done something differently? Was I not *supposed* to look for answers? They were right about one thing: I did believe that something real was causing Rachel's pain. But at that point, after two negative tests, I had accepted that it wasn't Lyme disease. Now these doctors said my very search for answers was impeding her progress.

Clearly, the care team was finished dealing with this case. They said they would discharge Rachel from the hospital and transfer her care back to our local medical group. They recommended that she continue twice-weekly physical therapy back home and meet regularly with a psychotherapist.

After five weeks in this wretched place, we left the hospital, discharge papers in hand. By this time, I could hobble short distances without the use of crutches, and I staggered down the halls of the hospital for the last time. I was in no way better. My medical team's official diagnosis was that the problem with me was *me*. I wasn't sick; I wasn't injured. They said I just needed to go home, do psychotherapy and physical therapy, and stop my attention-seeking behavior.

A heavy, flat expression pressed like a ten-pound weight on my face as I stood by the hospital entrance. Once, I had naively sat in this very same spot, filled with hope that this place would be my salvation. But now, after a crash course in how the real world worked, I knew that help was not coming. Help was *never* coming.

CHAPTER 3

Kryptonite

M y first week home from the hospital was disorienting
to say the least. No longer constantly surrounded by
nurses, doctors, and therapists, I spent all day in bed,
alone. My friends came over from time to time, but I was rarely in
the mood to socialize. Mom and Dad wanted me to see a therapist,
so I started having sessions with a woman named Taylor. She was
nice enough, but it all seemed pointless. She couldn't do anything
about all the pain I was in, and I figured it was just a matter of time
before she'd ask me to start throwing markers at the wall, too.

And then, Jeremy had an idea. "I want to show you something,"
he said one day, while doing a pull-up on the bar attached to the
frame of my bedroom door. Another reminder of my old life.

"All right, show me," I said almost inaudibly.

"You need to come to my room." He motioned for me to follow
him. "It's on my computer."

I didn't want to get up, but I was intrigued. Slowly, I walked
with painful steps from my room to his, and then plopped on his
bed.

"I just did this real quick," he said, opening a program I'd never
seen before. He tapped the mouse, and suddenly I saw a video of
our previous dog running in the backyard, destroying his new

chew toy, and then sitting in his bed. It had all been edited together like a professional movie.

Astounded by what I'd just seen, I asked, "How did you do that?"

He pointed to a FireWire cable that transferred the video footage from his camera to the computer. I stared with fascination as he walked me through the process. Using the iMovie program that came with his Mac Mini computer, he showed me that I could not only do smooth edits—I could also add music and create special effects. I could even make it look like it was pouring rain!

Over the past few years, my friends and I had made a lot of videos. But we'd always needed to film all our shots in sequence, since we had no way to edit individual moments together. Now, Jeremy was showing me a way to up our game considerably. Gone were the days of rewinding the tape each time we made a mistake so we could redo it. Instead, we could film several takes and choose the one we liked best. Just like real filmmakers do!

In yet another surprise, Jeremy told me I could *keep* his computer. He had bought himself a new one for college and said his old one was all mine.

My jaw dropped. "Really?" I couldn't believe it!

I sat down at his desk and he demonstrated how to line up clips and trim them to fit the tempo of the music. I already knew what song I wanted to use for my very first professionally edited video. I couldn't wait to get started.

Over the weeks that followed, I learned that editing videos helped me lose track of time, in a good way. Instead of focusing on how much my body hurt, I'd concentrate on the video clips coming to life before my eyes. The one bright spot in my otherwise dismal world was that FireWire cable from my brother—and all the possibilities that came with it.

Dorothy

Once we were back home, we followed the hospital's treatment protocol to the letter—at first. Per the doctors' instructions, Rachel's wheelchair was banished. Twice a week, I carted her to physical therapy. Twice a week, she saw her psychotherapist. When eighth grade started that fall, I drove her to school and dropped her off as close to her first class as possible. It was a huge ordeal for her to walk haltingly from one class to another. She'd arrive late for each class, exhausted, her increasing pain distracting her from learning math, English, or anything else. At PE time, she sat alone in the school library.

Soon, even the most limited amount of what Rachel called "pretend walking" was too much for her. At home, we reverted to the wheeled office chair to push her from bedroom to bathroom. We knew the doctors wouldn't approve, but it seemed prudent to save her energy for walking at school. Soon enough, though, even walking only at school was too difficult. Eventually, all of Rachel's pain, anger, and frustration boiled over. She began to have frequent emotional outbursts—screaming fits directed mostly at her dad and me. As I looked at my daughter's beautiful face distorted in agony and heard the animal-like howls that seemed to come from somewhere deep within her, I wanted to shriek too. But I tamped down my own fears—that Rachel might never get better, that our family might never emerge from this dark and painful place—because I had to stay strong.

As Bob and I struggled to figure out what to do next, the words of Rachel's doctors reverberated in my head: "Don't enable her psychological crutch." Was it a crutch to help her go to the bathroom? "Nothing real is causing her pain." I just couldn't accept that. The doctors and the PTs didn't see her laboring more and more each day just to accomplish the ordinary tasks of living. They didn't see how much she longed to go to school, to be with friends and carry on with her life. They didn't see her anguish when she couldn't manage the simplest things. They didn't see how much she suffered.

But the doctors were right about one thing: More than ever, I believed that an insidious invader had taken over my child. I just didn't believe that invader was only psychological. I knew we had to keep searching for answers. By this point, we'd invested a tremendous amount of time and energy in her medical team's perverse combination of tough love, physical therapy, and psychological counseling. Even though we had done everything they'd told us to do, things weren't better. In fact, they were markedly worse.

After a series of gut-wrenching discussions, my husband and I finally decided to break with the doctors' advice and rent another wheelchair. Abandoning the plan laid out for us at the hospital and admitting we'd lost faith in so-called experts felt like a point of no return. Looking back, I see it as the pivotal moment when we reclaimed our decision-making power for the health and welfare of our child. But at the time, I was awash in conflicting emotions. My heart pounded as I drove to the medical supply store. Was I making a mistake? Were the doctors right? I half expected somebody from Child Protective Services to jump out of the bushes and arrest me for child abuse.

After a couple months of hell following my discharge from the hospital, Mom and Dad unexpectedly told me that I could start using a wheelchair again. This made my life easier and released me from being held captive inside my bedroom. My friends and I began venturing outside after school and on the weekends, picking fruit from my neighborhood's edible landscaping as we went, enjoying our extra freedom. With the burden of painfully hobbling from class to class lifted from my hypersensitive shoulders, I could enjoy school once more. I even organized a knitting club, which now met every Tuesday at lunch. Would you believe that my junior high didn't already have one? I was shocked, too.

Dorothy

Getting another wheelchair solved a logistical problem, but we still didn't know what to do next. It seemed pointless to consult more of the same kinds of doctors, offering more of the same tests and theories. Must we reconcile ourselves to having Rachel imprisoned by pain? I couldn't accept that. It dawned on me that all the doctors we had seen had operated within the same medical mindset. They read one another's notes and seemed to always reach the same conclusions. We needed a fresh pair of eyes—someone to look at it from a different perspective. But who could that be?

I tracked down an alternative practitioner in our area who specialized in acupuncture and herbal remedies. Did he know anything else we could pursue, a rock we hadn't looked under? He listened intently and suggested I bring Rachel to see him. When I did, he asked lots of questions and examined her gently. Then, he turned to me and said, "I think she might have Lyme disease."

I was floored. *Lyme disease?* All the specialists we'd seen had dismissed that idea out of hand. They used the negative results of the Lyme tests as proof I was barking up the wrong tree. I told him that I'd abandoned that theory months earlier, after our previous doctors convinced me that it was wildly out of the question.

He nodded and stroked his beard. "Even so, I think there's a good chance it's Lyme disease." He added soberly, "I don't know how to help you. I don't even know who to refer you to. You need to find somebody who can diagnose it and knows how to treat it."

Emboldened by this new opinion, I started researching again with a vengeance. I found out more about the medical controversy that surrounded Lyme disease, and how few California doctors would even consider the diagnosis. I learned that lab tests for Lyme disease were unreliable, and that you needed a doctor who could make what's called a "clinical diagnosis." This means the doctor would diagnose you based on your symptoms, your physical exam, and your medical history—rather than relying solely on the results of a lab test. However, due to heated debates in the medical world—often called "the Lyme Wars"—few doctors were willing to go through that process.

But I discovered that there were a handful of physicians who diagnosed and treated Lyme outside of the medical mainstream, often with good results. Our challenge was going to be finding one such doctor and getting Rachel in to see them. That's when I came across an online article from the *Washington Post* about Amy Tan, author of *The Joy Luck Club*. A few years before, out of the blue, she had started experiencing bizarre physical symptoms that were so debilitating that she couldn't finish the book she was writing. None of the many specialists she had consulted could figure out what was wrong. Finally, a doctor in San Francisco diagnosed her with Lyme disease. With treatment, she was able to resume writing. I called the office of the doctor named in the article and found he had a six-month waiting list. Finally, through connections on the online support group CaliforniaLyme, I found out about another Lyme specialist, about a two-hour drive from our house. He had a waiting list too. But finally, we got a phone call. Due to a cancellation, there was now a spot available for Rachel at 4:00 p.m. on the day before Thanksgiving. It was another turning point in our lives, the beginning of unlocking the mystery surrounding Rachel's dire condition.

As usual, I felt every bump in the road during the car trek to Dr. Landers's office. Yet, despite my discomfort, I felt a hint of optimism about this appointment. Jeremy, home from college for Thanksgiving, accompanied us on the trip and we amused ourselves by playing Twenty Questions. Before too long, we had arrived at our destination.

A nurse ushered us from the lobby into one of the examination rooms. While taking my blood pressure and temperature, she made no mention of the wheelchair, but instead commented that I looked like an athlete. *I am an athlete,* I thought. Just that one, simple comment from her perked me up and made me feel validated.

"I'm a soccer player," I said proudly, leading us into a conversation about her own love for the sport. None of my PT or OT therapists had ever talked to me like that. To them, I was weak. To her, I was an athlete. My good feeling about this appointment only grew stronger.

Soon, Dr. Landers came in, introducing himself as he sat in a big brown chair across from me. Mom retold the saga of the past eight months, with me interjecting now and then to emphasize how badly my knees, back, and shoulders hurt.

Mom talked about the hospital and how the people there had decided pretty early on that I was making up the pain. I watched Dr. Landers as Mom spoke. He was listening—like, *really* listening. He took notes, and after Mom mentioned my hypersensitive shoulders, he promised me that he would never touch them.

I believed him.

This was the longest appointment I'd had to date, and so far, he hadn't let out even one condescending put-down, nor had he questioned a single aspect of our story. Right there, that put this doctor in a different category from all the others I'd seen.

As we neared the two-hour mark, Dr. Landers turned to me with a sympathetic smile and uttered the best sentence I'd heard in a long time.

"I want to run some tests, but I strongly suspect you have Lyme disease."

Dorothy

We felt jubilant on the two-hour drive home from the doctor's office. After months of spinning our wheels, we finally felt a spark of hope. And that night, Rachel slept seven or eight hours straight through—perhaps her longest stretch of uninterrupted sleep since this all began eight months before. As we gathered the next day for a Thanksgiving meal with family and friends, I felt truly blessed. In the back of my mind, I could hear the new doctor's warning that there could still be rough seas ahead. But I batted that thought away and focused instead on my smiling loved ones around the holiday table. Alas, our family's Thanksgiving euphoria would soon evaporate.

Additional tests from a specialty lab confirmed the doctor's suspicion that Rachel had Lyme disease. (Months later, further testing would show she also had two co-infections—*Babesia* and *Bartonella*—which can complicate the diagnosis and treatment of Lyme disease.) Lyme disease is caused by bacteria, and so Rachel started taking antibiotics in early December. The doctor strongly advised us to eliminate sugar from her diet and give her probiotics daily to help ward off a candida infection. Candida is a type of yeast found naturally in the body in small amounts. Unfortunately, both antibiotics and dietary sugar can make candida grow out of control, causing a host of problems. Rachel wasn't thrilled at the idea of giving up her favorite sugary treats, but she agreed to try.

For about a week after starting antibiotics, nothing seemed to change. Then, suddenly, Rachel's pain skyrocketed and her mood plummeted. Surely these were the "rough seas" the doctor had warned us about. Since winter break was coming soon anyway, we kept Rachel home from school and tried our best to keep daily life on an even keel. Soon enough, however, there were even more worrisome developments.

That winter, our family learned a new term: *Jarisch-Herxheimer reaction*, or *herx* for short. It indicated that the Lyme was being killed off by the antibiotics. As the bad bugs died, they emitted a poison that made me feel worse than ever before. What it *really* meant is that I felt like I was dying. Everything hurt ten times more, if that was even possible. Pins and needles stabbed into me all over at random times. Everything seemed foggy, as if my thoughts were on the other side of a transparent curtain, where I could see but not access them. I missed my friends at school.

The herx added new symptoms and at the same time made the existing ones worse. When I lay down flat or sat up straight, I struggled to breathe, and the pain in my spine hurt so badly I sometimes thought I could *hear* it. Mom had rented an adjustable hospital bed that allowed me to get in the best position possible for breathing. There was now nowhere safe for me to spend my days except in bed at my reclined angle—not until we could fix my breathing. Sadly, this meant I could no longer sit at my brother's computer to edit videos. Instead, I had to entertain myself from bed, by either playing a game on Mom's laptop or on my PlayStation.

Dorothy

With all of Rachel's breathing problems, we finally dropped the twice-weekly PT sessions. We'd been at it for months, they didn't appear to be helping, and Rachel despised going. But we kept up the psychotherapy sessions with Taylor. I was grateful that Rachel seemed to be developing a strong connection with her therapist. My increasingly sullen daughter needed a supportive adult with whom she could share her inner turmoil—someone with the training and experience to help her navigate this agonizing time.

One day in December, I dropped Rachel off at her appointment with Taylor and went to the farmers market. I bought oranges from Jo, a favorite vendor of ours, who asked about Rachel and sent good wishes. Then I collected Rachel from the therapist's office and loaded her and the wheelchair back in the van, which was always a bit of production. Wary of her obvious moodiness, I reached for something cheerful to talk about as we headed home.

"Guess who I saw at the farmers market?" I asked brightly. "Jo—and I bought some of her wonderful oranges."

"Jo!" Rachel replied with delight. "I haven't seen her in a long time. How is she?"

We talked about that for a moment, and then she asked what else I had bought at the market. I listed off several items. "Is that all?" she asked.

"Well, and oranges, of course," I said. "I already told you about the oranges I bought from Jo."

Rachel looked at me in complete surprise and said, "Jo? You saw Jo? How is she?"

I tried to mask my startled reaction. Was Rachel pulling my leg by acting like she couldn't remember something we'd just discussed two minutes before? I stole glances at her as I drove. It didn't seem like she was joking.

"Jo's fine," I answered quietly. But inside, I knew *nothing* was fine.

Could antibiotics break your spine? I wondered absurdly. Because my spine felt broken. I bet if we did an MRI, it would show cracks all up and down my back; that had to be the reason why everything hurt so much more since I started antibiotics. *Sponge-Bob SquarePants* was on TV, but I ignored it. Instead, I listened to Dad and Jeremy in the next room, gearing up to go get our Christmas tree.

This wasn't right. I had *always* helped pick out the Leland family Christmas tree. Each year, we examined every seven-foot noble fir on the lot, and we decided together which one was the best. But since I couldn't leave my bed and we needed a tree, Jeremy and Dad would go without me.

As the door shut behind them, I turned my focus back to the TV perched on top of my bookshelf across the room. I endured the rest of *SpongeBob* until it finally switched to *Rocket Power*, a show I greatly preferred. I liked that the characters were always doing something fun outdoors, like surfing or skateboarding. *Rocket Power* kept my attention off my broken spine better than other cartoons did.

Eventually, I heard Jeremy and Dad hauling the new tree into the living room. Mom helped me out to the recliner by the couch, where I watched as they set it up in its usual spot. Mom turned on Nat King Cole in the background as Dad retrieved our ornaments from the garage. We each had a special box filled with our own unique ornaments collected through the years. Usually, we'd each put our own decorations on the tree. But this year, Jeremy and I tag-teamed it—I unwrapped them, and he hung them up.

Every day it was getting harder to pretend like I was okay. This recliner was at the wrong angle for my back, and its hard leather upholstery irritated my shoulders. I wanted so much to enjoy this time with my family, but I couldn't focus on the music, the scent of the tree, or the fact that it was my favorite time of year. Instead, I thought only of how difficult it was to breathe and how every inhalation shot pains throughout my body. I wanted to crawl back into bed, but I didn't want to be alone in my room. And I thought about how this might be my last Christmas ever.

Dorothy

Rachel's pain escalated daily that dismal December, and as her pain rose, her mental state declined. I feared she was suicidal, though I couldn't be sure. There had been hints in some comments we'd overheard. She had also apparently sent some dark emails to people at school, which a counselor had alerted us to. My husband and I soldiered through our holiday festivities, hoping somehow that our family traditions would buoy Rachel's spirits despite her physical and emotional anguish. Yet, even as we made

Christmas cookies, decorated the house, and had friends over to visit, I was faking a cheerfulness I didn't feel. Lucky for us, Jeremy was home from college for the holidays. Having his playful energy back in the house was a comfort to us all.

Rachel's junior high gave eighth graders a special assignment every winter break: to interview an older person about what life had been like when they were young. Jeremy had done it when he was in eighth grade, and now it was Rachel's turn. Two days after Christmas, I set her up with a speakerphone and tape recorder, and she had a nice long chat with my eighty-seven-year-old mother. A few hours later, Grandma called back, saying she had thought of something more she wanted to tell Rachel. While I was on the phone with her, the line suddenly went silent. When I tried calling back, I got a busy signal. Although I didn't know it for some time, my mother had had a massive stroke while I'd been on the phone with her. By the time I learned what happened, she was hospitalized and in a coma.

My natural inclination would have been to catch the next available flight and rush to see my mother at the hospital, but I made the heartbreaking decision not to leave right away. I was out of my mind with worry for Rachel, and we had a follow-up appointment with the Lyme doctor the very next day. I chose to accompany my family on our two-hour drive to the doctor and have them drop me off at the airport on their way home. It tore me up that I could not go immediately to my dying mother's bedside. But in my heart, I firmly believed that attending to my daughter's precarious physical and mental health was the right call. It's what my mother—a loving and ever-practical woman—would have wanted me to do. I was sure of it.

Sitting in the waiting room for our next appointment with Dr. Landers, Mom told me that she and Dad would meet with the doctor first without me, and then I would join them. *What?* I thought. *No way!*

"We'll finish off the rest of the appointment with you," she reassured me, as if allowing me to attend my own appointment was some kind of favor. This was *my* life we were talking about here. *Mine.* Anything they wanted to say to Dr. Landers, they could say in front of me.

Lately I had become skilled at listening in on phone calls if I thought I might be the topic of conversation. This was back in the time of landline phones, which made a slight clicking sound each time an extension phone was picked up. Thus, anytime my therapist's number popped up on caller ID, I tried to pick up the bedroom phone at the exact moment Mom answered the office phone, thereby disguising my presence on the line. It wasn't a foolproof strategy, though. One time Taylor and I were sitting alone on the line together for a few seconds, as she repeated "Dorothy? Hello? Dorothy?" into the silence until Mom finally picked up the office phone. They chalked it up to a bad connection before diving in and discussing Taylor's concerns about my declining mental health.

However, there was no phone to help me listen in on the private conversation my parents wanted to have with the doctor. Unacceptable! When Dr. Landers was ready, my parents brought me back to the main treatment room and parked me in the green reclining lounge chair that used to belong in our backyard. We brought it to all of my doctor's appointments these days, because it was too hard for me to breathe sitting upright in my wheelchair, and most offices didn't have furniture to accommodate the position I needed. The lounge chair was bulky and took up space, but it did the trick. It allowed me to lean back with my feet up at the same angle of my bed at home. We tried to use the wheelchair as little as possible because it had become so uncomfortable for me. Alone in the treatment room, I played Solitaire on my iPod while Mom, Dad, and Dr. Landers went to a different room across the hall to tell secrets about me.

Dorothy

Rachel was furious when we told her we needed to speak with Dr. Landers alone. But she was angry with us most of the time those days, and we absolutely had to impress upon the doctor how serious things had become. Her intensifying pain had completely overridden every coping mechanism Rachel had once possessed. Now, there were only crying fits, episodes of rage, and on one occasion, she even kicked a hole in the drywall of her bedroom. She glared hatefully at her dad and me if she looked at us at all, and she sent emails to friends saying she didn't want to live anymore. Out of deep concern for Rachel, those friends had let us know privately what she'd written.

After we'd conveyed our concerns to Dr. Landers, he left the room for a moment. When he returned, he handed me a piece of paper with a name and telephone number written on it. It was contact information for a family therapist in Connecticut who specialized in helping families coping with Lyme disease. "I think she'll be able to help you," he said. I stared at the paper in front of me and then back at the doctor. I didn't say it aloud, but I remember thinking, *Is that the best you can do?*

When Dr. Landers and my parents finally finished talking in the adjacent room, he sat down in his brown leather chair and looked at me solemnly.

"Rachel, I want you to know that you will get better from this. I *know* you will. You just have to give it time and believe it yourself."

A crack in the wall behind him suddenly required all of my attention, but I nodded my head ever so slightly so he'd know that I had heard him. Tears stung my eyes. I didn't believe him when he said I'd get better. We all knew there was no coming back from the place I now found myself in. Why did we even keep trying?

Dorothy

As planned, Bob and the kids dropped me off at the airport on the way home from Dr. Landers' office. After landing in San Diego, I took a shuttle from the airport to the hospital, where my two brothers sat vigil at our mother's bedside. Our sister arrived from Hawaii soon after. The four of us huddled together in the presence of the woman who had been our rock for our whole lives. The doctors explained that there was no hope of recovery and said that they expected her to pass away soon. This was different from our dad's sudden, fatal heart attack ten years earlier. That had been over and done with before any of us even knew it had happened. Now, we could gaze at our mom, hold her hand, and speak softly in her ear, hoping that on some level she could pick up our loving thoughts. Yet, throughout it all, part of my mind remained back home with Rachel—worrying, fearing, and not knowing what we should do.

After Mom flew to San Diego to see Grandma, I received a surprise visit from Julianne and Tenaya, neighborhood friends who were both a few years older. They were basically the coolest people imaginable. Hanging with them always felt like I had made it to the big leagues! Ever since I got sick, they'd tried to find fun ways to lift my spirits. The last time they had come around, we'd gone on a field trip to the kitchen to make pancakes!

Tenaya walked in, holding a bag bulging with makeup. Julianne followed with a hair straightening tool.

Tenaya grinned slyly and said, "Julianne and I want to give you a makeover!"

My heart raced! I was fourteen, and I'd never had a makeover before! But then, like always, reality set in.

"I can't get out of bed. How can you do a makeover if I can't sit up?"

"We'll figure it out," Tenaya said with a shrug.

"I think we should start with your hair," Julianne chimed in, playing with it as she spoke, careful not to touch my shoulders.

We tried several positions that didn't work. Then Julianne said, "What about if I get behind you in bed, and I don't move at all, and I don't touch your back or shoulders? We can prop you up just a *bit* with pillows when I need to get the back of your hair."

This ended up being the best solution. With multiple pillows to hold Julianne in place, and an extra pillow behind my neck, we got started on my makeover.

As Julianne gently straightened my hair and Tenaya applied makeup to my face, I closed my eyes and listened as their happy voices filled my room. I wanted this to last forever. Tenaya took a picture of the finished product and turned the camera around to show me. I looked incredible—like a supermodel!

I changed into a black tank top—the chicest blouse I could muster from my closet—while the girls tacked a sheet to the wall for a backdrop, preparing for a photoshoot to document the experience. Knowing I couldn't sit in an upright position for long, we wasted no time. I scooted over on my office chair, positioned myself in front of the backdrop, and tried out different expressions. I attempted to make my eyes pop—just like the contestants on *America's Next Top Model* were told to. In less than a minute, I was back in bed.

We gave my lungs some time to rest before changing outfits and going for round two. I didn't want this to stop. I didn't want Julianne and Tenaya to ever leave my bedroom. For reasons I didn't understand, I only felt happy and calm when I had friends over. As soon as Tenaya and Julianne left, it was like a volcano erupted inside of me. Minutes after their departure, I was screaming, sobbing, and feeling like I wanted to end it all. I hated it. The makeover today had been the most amazing experience. I never wanted this day to end, but just like everything good in my life, it did.

Dorothy

My mother passed away on New Year's Day, and I immediately flew back home to check on Rachel. Jeremy returned to college, and although junior high classes resumed that week as well, Rachel stayed home. She was glum at the prospect of not seeing her friends, but she seemed calm enough that I felt I could return to San Diego to help prepare for the memorial service scheduled for January 7. Bob took some days off work to be with Rachel while I was gone, and we arranged for family friends to stay with her so Bob could fly to San Diego for the day to attend the service with me. Then he and I would return home together.

It was the first week of the New Year, 2006, and I wished I had cancer instead of Lyme. If I had cancer, then people would *get* it. They would instantly know how bad things were, and they'd understand that there was no way I could continue living like this. If I had cancer, then maybe it would kill me on its own. But in my case, it looked like I would have to do it myself. I didn't want to do it myself.

Things were bad. Most days I lay in the dark, listening to "Kryptonite" by 3 Doors Down. As I stared at the wall across from my bed, I kept the song on repeat and let the lyrics reverberate in my head.

Usually, time dragged for me. But today was different. Today, I wasn't just languishing in the dark. Today I was on a mission.

Using markers and computer paper, I made a booklet titled *Cancer vs. Lyme* for my therapist, Taylor. In it, I spelled out exactly why my biggest desire was to swap out my Lyme for cancer. I wanted someone to know how I felt. Although I couldn't bring myself to say "Taylor, I want to kill myself," I could tell her all the reasons cancer would be the better option, and maybe she would put it together.

Hiding my book under a stack of papers littering my dresser, I began drawing a picture of a cloud with rain coming down from it. It had been pouring rain for over a week now—normally, my absolute favorite kind of weather. But I'd been too sick to go outside even once to feel it. Each day I told myself to make the effort—to go out and feel the rain one last time. But each day ended with me never having left my bed.

Dorothy

Two days after Bob and I returned from my mother's memorial service, we received word that our dear friend and next-door neighbor Craig, the father of two kids Rachel had often played with for the past seven years, had lost his battle with cancer.

His funeral would be the following weekend. News of his death seemed to bring Rachel new levels of pain and agitation. In frantic phone calls to her doctor, I pleaded for something—anything—that could offer a modicum of relief. Finally, he prescribed a pain medication recently approved by the FDA that worked differently than the opioids that had failed to help the previous summer. I raced to the pharmacy to get it.

The clock on my dresser showed 11:43 p.m. Inching back and forth, I once again tried to find a comfortable position, but it was a lost cause. And the new medication made it even harder to breathe than before. My throat just didn't let air in the way it was supposed to anymore, and it felt like I had a weight sitting on my chest.

I turned on the lamp by my bed and reached for my headphones, being careful not to jostle the ten-foot cord that connected them to the TV across the room. I didn't want to have to get out of bed to plug it back in tonight.

Most people had nightmares when they were asleep. But mine started when I woke up. Every night around midnight, I found myself starring in *Operation: Make It till Morning*. It usually went like this:

> **Step One:** Flip on all the lights in my bedroom.

> **Step Two:** Turn on the TV. Anything involving happy people would do the trick.

> **Step Three:** Grab Mom's laptop from my dresser and open up Solitaire.

Step Four: Begin playing Solitaire.

Step Five: Once boredom set in, switch to handheld Tetris device.

Step Six: Repeat steps four and five until Mom got up at about 6:00 am.

On a good night, I might get four hours of sleep. But most nights were not good.

Dorothy

The new medication, for which I'd had such high hopes, ultimately did nothing for Rachel's pain. Perversely, it seemed to exacerbate her breathing difficulties, which quickly segued into panic attacks. I stopped giving her the medicine after two days, but she continued to spiral out of control. As the day of Craig's memorial approached, it seemed less and less likely that Bob and I would be able to attend. With Rachel toggling between moments of calmly watching TV and having hysterical outbursts, I knew her situation was too volatile to leave her with someone else, even for a little while. Bob said I could go, and he'd stay back with Rachel. I was dubious about that, too, and suggested we wait until the day of the service to decide.

Shooting, throbbing, paralyzing pain! It never quit! *I can't live through another day of this hell!* I sat up in bed, slamming my arm against the side of my dresser, hoping my wrist would shatter into tiny pieces on impact. But then I realized that if I wanted to die, smashing my arm wouldn't get me there. Forcing breath into my lungs, I wiped my tears. I needed to look calm if I was going to make it out to the kitchen without my parents getting suspicious.

I paused to regain some composure, then cautiously moved from the bed to my office chair. I wheeled out of my room, scooted down the hallway and turned into the kitchen. Mom sat at the table and looked up as I entered. Scanning the counter as nonchalantly as possible, I spotted the knives resting in their block next to the stove. Then, I headed directly for them.

Dorothy

As soon as I saw Rachel reaching for the knives, I lurched toward her. Gripping her by the shoulders—her painful shoulders!—I pulled her back from the counter, while Bob grabbed the block full of knives and put it up out of her reach. Rachel erupted like a wild animal. Still in the office chair, she thrust herself toward the plastic bin of medicines that also sat on the kitchen counter. Once again, I dragged her back far enough that Bob could seize the container and place it on top of the refrigerator. Screaming, Rachel escaped from my grasp, furiously propelled herself back to her bedroom, and slammed the door.

As the door banged shut behind me, my eyes darted around the room, looking for anything I could get my hands on—pillows, blankets, computer . . . Then I saw it. Sitting on my bookshelf was a red, two-pound weight I had once used for arm exercises. I reached for it and felt its coarse rubber against my palm. Then I smashed it against my head.

Dynamite exploded down my face. Pain-infused anger fueled my rage as I slammed the dumbbell into my bedroom door. Dropping it with a thud, I reached for my mattress and yanked it off the bed, harnessing power I didn't know I had.

This all needed to end. *Now.*

Dorothy

We found Rachel on the floor of her bedroom, her mattress half off the bed, the rest of the room in shambles. To my horror, she was pounding an exercise weight against her head. We dove down, trying to stop her, and she heaved against us with surprising strength. The three of us rolled around—first halfway under the bed, then halfway into the closet, as our daughter somehow managed to elude our efforts to contain her. Why couldn't two able-bodied adults overpower our child? We finally managed to wrestle the weight from her hands, but she continued to fight us.

Somehow, I extricated myself from the jumble of arms and legs on the floor and stepped out of the room to retrieve my phone. Taylor, Rachel's therapist, picked up immediately. After hearing my terse explanation of what had just transpired, Taylor replied: "If you believe she's going to continue to harm herself, call 911." When I told Bob what the therapist had advised, he looked at me with equal parts of fear, despair, and resignation. We both knew we were about to pass the point of no return. He called 911 while I tried to contain Rachel. Soon, we heard sirens approaching.

My tiny bedroom quickly filled with police and EMTs. A female officer stepped forward with handcuffs and asked me to place my arms behind my back. I was speechless. *Why was I being handcuffed like a criminal?*

As instructed, I placed my arms behind me as she tightened the cold metal cuffs around my wrists. I couldn't breathe at this angle.

"Can we put the handcuffs in front instead of behind my back?" I choked out through struggling lungs.

"No." Her response was ice cold. "It's for everyone's safety that they stay where they are."

Everyone's safety? Did I murder someone or something?

Two EMTs lifted me up onto a black-and-yellow gurney and strapped me to it.

One of the EMTs leaned down and whispered, "If you stay calm, we can take those off once we get you loaded up." He offered a weak smile.

"Loaded up where?" I asked.

"The ambulance."

I was going somewhere in an ambulance? As we wheeled out to the living room, I saw Mom and Dad talking to a different officer. I was outraged at the sight of them, comfortably uncuffed, while I was tied to a stretcher, struggling to get enough air to my lungs. If I'd had it my way, I would have flipped this gurney over, cracked my head open on the hard floor, and ended this once and for all.

Dorothy

Bob and I arrived at the emergency room right after Rachel did. There was paperwork to fill out and medical personnel to talk to. The ER was busy that day. After a quick checkup in one of the exam rooms, Rachel and the wheeled bed she occupied were pushed to a hallway and parked there for what turned out to be

> hours. She wanted nothing to do with either Bob or me, so we stationed ourselves down the hall where we could at least see her from a distance. As we waited for whatever the next step would be, I called Taylor to update her on our situation. I'll be forever grateful that she came to the hospital to sit and talk with Rachel. It tore me up to see my daughter stuck in the hallway alone. At least here, the head of the bed could be raised up to allow her to be in as comfortable a position as possible, given the circumstances.

I had been parked in the hallway of this godforsaken emergency room for hours. Every once in a while, Mom and Dad briefly resurfaced, but mostly they kept their distance. Taylor sat to my right, quietly explaining what would happen next.

She told me that eventually I would be transported to a psychiatric facility. That is, if an available bed could be found for me, which wasn't looking so good at the moment—hence the wait.

"No matter where you go, they should have phones for you to use," Taylor said. "So, let's write my cell phone number on your hand so you've got it with you, okay?"

I made her write it on the back of both hands just in case one got smudged.

Pictures of what life at the psychiatric facility could be like flashed through my mind. Would I be tied to a bed in a straitjacket? Gagged and left alone for hours, unable to breathe? What if they saw I had a phone number on me and scrubbed it off against my will?

I stared at the numbers written across my hands, silently repeating them over and over until they were etched into my brain. They could handcuff me, lock me up, and rub off the ink, but I would never forget that number.

Dorothy

Ultimately, medical staff at the ER found a place for Rachel at a psychiatric facility. It had taken some time because she could only be admitted to one that could accommodate adolescents, of course, and those were in short supply. After another long wait in the hallway, we were notified that she would be sent to a facility about twenty-five miles from our house. It could have easily been one hundred miles away or more, so we were thankful for that. An ambulance transferred her there, while Bob and I followed in our car. In all, we had been at the emergency room for twelve grueling hours. We reached the psychiatric hospital at about 11:00 p.m.

Once at the psych hospital, I was put through what seemed like a never-ending list of safety procedures. "Take off any strings longer than this," a tired old lady said, holding up her fingers to show me three inches as she started backing out of the room.

"Why?" I struggled to keep my voice steady.

"Because someone could use it to strangle themselves," she said curtly, shutting the door behind her.

Alone, I looked around at the tiny room. A single bed. No windows. Nothing on the walls. It looked like a jail cell. I didn't belong in jail. My hands shaking, I removed my beaded necklace and pulled out the drawstring of my pajama pants. Luckily, they were still held up by an elastic waist band.

As I left the room through its heavy door, I saw Mom and Dad off to the side, quietly talking to a staff member. Part of me wanted to demand that they immediately take me away from this terrible place. But then, remembering that they had called the cops on me this morning, my hatred for them flared up again. I turned my wheelchair to face away because I couldn't even stand to look at them. I wanted my parents gone more than I wanted my freedom.

Dorothy

Throughout the intake process, Rachel spoke little and avoided meeting our eyes. Anger and hate seemed to emanate from her tense body, silently communicating what she wouldn't or couldn't put into words. After a long while, an attendant took her away, pushing her wheelchair down the hall.

When they reached the door of what was to be her new room, she looked inside and started to shriek, "Mom! Mom!"

I ran toward her, afraid someone might try to stop me.

"The bed is flat!" she cried out in horror.

My husband and I then spent the next fifteen minutes insisting to those in charge that she simply could not tolerate a flat bed. I don't think they believed me, or maybe they just didn't care. But Bob and I stood our ground. It turned out there was indeed a hospital-type bed in the unit and eventually, they agreed to place Rachel there. Once that point was settled, Rachel went back to refusing to acknowledge us, and Bob and I drove home.

After talking with Mom and Dad, a man in a black jacket showed us to my real room, demonstrating how to raise and lower the hospital bed with a button on the side. All other inmates got a roommate, but because I needed the hospital bed, I'd be stuck in here alone.

The man ushered my parents out the door, and they waved good-bye. I ignored them. As their footsteps faded, the man informed me that my door would be locked. If I needed anything, I could knock and someone would come to check on me.

As the key turned, caging me in for the night, I dissolved into tears. *What was happening to me?*

As I crawled into bed, the mattress felt like cement to my pain-riddled body. My hands cupped the side of my head where the dumbbell had made its mark that morning. It seemed like a life-time ago. Clutching tightly to my special bear that Mom and Dad had placed in my suitcase, I spotted a device mounted in the upper corner of the room—it looked like a camera. I slid under the covers to hide from it, pulling my sweatshirt free from around my waist. My sweatshirt—I had forgotten to remove the drawstring from my sweatshirt! I kicked it down to my feet, terrified that time would be added to my sentence because of my honest mistake.

Sobbing into my pillow below the covers, I gasped for air that wasn't coming. No one was coming.

Dorothy

Bob and I somehow made it home from the hospital, stunned and horrified by the day's events. Well after midnight, we collapsed into bed and wept bitterly, holding each other in the dark. It was the bleakest moment I had ever experienced in my life. I felt par-alyzed, seeing no way out of this impossible situation. At that moment, my family's future seemed to be teetering on the edge of a sharp precipice, soon to plunge into a pitch-dark abyss.

Misgivings and self-incrimination tortured my brain, alternat-ing with images of Rachel shooting looks of pure hatred at me.

Had calling 911 been a mistake? Had we irretrievably alienated our daughter in her time of greatest need?

Taylor seemed to think we made the right choice, but what would Rachel think? She was angry now, and afraid, but when she calmed down, would she understand that we had been desperately trying to protect her? Would she forgive us? The uncertainty I'd felt about letting Rachel resume using a wheelchair against medical advice paled in comparison to what gripped us now. The stakes were higher, but here we were again, entering uncharted territory, hoping the boldness of our choices would ultimately heal—not harm—our daughter.

CHAPTER 4

I'll Put You Down for an 8

The lock turned, and a woman entered, telling me it was time for breakfast.

Transferring to my wheelchair, I followed her. My chest still felt tight, and it was hard to breathe.

Around the corner, two girls about my age sat on a couch facing a TV. They eyed me as I approached, and one said, "You're new."

"Yeah." I scooted forward in the wheelchair as far as I could, which let me recline my back ever so slightly. It didn't really help.

"Why are you here?" she asked bluntly.

"I wanted to die. Guess it didn't work." Two could play this game.

She laughed. "I'm Addison."

After breakfast, everyone was locked in their rooms for thirty minutes of "quiet time" so the staff could get a break. Crawling under the covers, I located my contraband sweatshirt drawstring with my foot. There was a knock at my door, and soon a man in a white lab coat introduced himself as Dr. Yarow.

"How are you feeling today?" he asked.

This was it: my moment to shine. No one had told me how long I would be exiled here—whether it would be days, weeks, months, or years. All I knew was that my new acting role had no room for error.

I smiled with both sides of my mouth as well as my eyes. "I'm good. How are you?" I said, using inflection while making appropriate eye contact.

"I'm fine; thank you for asking. Can you tell me about what happened yesterday?"

"Oh," I said, faking a small laugh. "I was just having a rough day. But I'm doing much better, and I'm definitely ready to go home now."

He had such a punchable face.

"Can you count backward from one hundred by sevens for me?"

My mind went blank.

"Um." I bit my lip. "One hundred . . ." I had issues with concentration even on my good days, and today was not a good day.

He saw me struggling and said I could count backward from one hundred by ones if that was easier than doing it by sevens.

"One hundred, ninety-nine, ninety-eight, ninety-seven . . . ninety-eight, ninety-nine." Wait . . . what happened? I had been counting backward—and then, somehow, I had turned around and went back up to ninety-nine.

"Try again," he urged.

I counted louder this time, pointing carefully to each finger as I went. "One hundred, ninety-nine, ninety-eight, ninety-seven, ninety-eight, ninety-nine." Why couldn't I count backward?

He wrote something down on his clipboard.

"Seven from one hundred is ninety-three. Start from ninety-three."

"Ninety-three, ninety-two, ninety-one, ninety, fifty-six, fifty-seven." I stopped, and my cheeks burned with embarrassment. I had no idea what number I was supposed to be on! Why couldn't I do this?

Dorothy

During Rachel's late-night intake at the psych hospital, I had given the attendants several bottles of medications prescribed by Rachel's Lyme doctor. I emphasized how important it was to continue her treatment uninterrupted. They'd looked at me dubiously and said the staff doctor would decide that in the morning. So, early the next day, I phoned the hospital with an urgent message for the doctor to call me, which he did.

Dr. Yarow listened to what I had to say, and then, in measured tones, he told me that he had previously lived in Connecticut and thus knew a lot about Lyme disease. He said Lyme was virtually unheard of in California, and besides, Rachel's symptoms didn't sound anything like Lyme disease to him. Alarms started ringing in my brain at his words. Here was yet another so-called specialist making a snap decision—based on very little information and without any formal experience with Lyme disease—saying that Rachel couldn't possibly have it. Besides, our Lyme doctor had told us that the infection could manifest in many different ways throughout the body—that there was no "typical" case of Lyme disease. Furthermore, "virtually unheard of in California" was flat-out wrong. With a concerted effort, I kept my voice calm. I said that Rachel had a long and complicated medical history with which her doctor of record was most familiar. At this stage, we wanted to follow her doctor's instructions. I told him I'd be happy to arrange a phone meeting for the two of them if that would help. By the end of our conversation, to my relief, Dr. Yarow agreed to let Rachel keep taking the antibiotics.

When Dr. Yarow finally left my room, a woman entered and announced that I was late for "group," whatever the heck that was. She even said it like it was my fault. As if being locked in a jail cell with a dimwitted doctor was somehow my own doing. As if *any* of this was my own doing.

When she offered to push my wheelchair down the hall, I gave a firm no. I didn't want these creeps anywhere near me. I would do it myself. She opened a door to a room filled with many more kids than I had seen at breakfast.

I settled in next to Addison, the only person I was remotely familiar with.

"Rachel, we're glad you could join us," the counselor said. "We're going around the circle, telling everyone why we are here and what our goals are to be able to go back home safely. Addison, I believe it's your turn."

"I'm Addison, and I'm here 'cause I'm a *bad* girl." She said "bad" with emphasis, moving her head back and forth like a snake gearing up to attack. "And I'm gonna sit on my ass and do *nothing!*" She folded her arms across her chest and leaned back, clearly signaling that she was done.

"I'm Joanna, and I hurt my sister so much she had to go to the hospital," said the girl next to her. She smiled slightly as she paused for effect. "So, I guess . . . I'm going to try to not do that."

These people may have had their own problems, but they weren't in pain like I was. They could walk and sit and do other stuff I couldn't do. I didn't belong here. I didn't deserve this.

Then everyone looked at me.

"I'm Rachel," I started slowly. What the heck was I supposed to say? "I've been unhappy lately . . ." *Now what?* "So, I'm here to work on that . . ."

This was bullshit, as Addison would say. Addison said a lot, actually, and I was paying close attention. Earlier today I'd said "shit," too, followed by "fuck" and "bitch." All new vocabulary words for me. In fact, the new Rachel had said all those things before 8:00 a.m., and I was just getting started! Since Mom and Dad chose to lock me up in this hellhole, well then, they could kiss their precious little girl goodbye. She died the second the cuffs went on.

After everyone got a chance to talk, we were forced to watch a presentation on how drugs were bad. I tuned everything out. What a waste of time. My back was killing me, and I couldn't get enough air. I needed to be in bed with my back reclined, not sitting here listening to this garbage.

Lifting my legs up onto an empty chair in front of me, I scooted forward a few more inches to relieve my back and lungs. Addison nudged my arm and pointed to her paper. She'd drawn a crying girl, and I gave her a quiet thumbs up. She pointed at me and leaned over.

"It's you," she whispered. "The girl is you. I *see* you."

Addison handed me the paper, and I took a closer look. This was the nicest thing, and she didn't even know me. I offered her a genuine Rachel smile—the first in a very long time.

I'd made a friend.

Dorothy

After Dr. Yarow assured me that Rachel could continue with her course of antibiotics at the psychiatric hospital, my next phone call was to Sandy Berenbaum, the Connecticut therapist who'd been suggested by our Lyme doctor three weeks before. At the time, I'd been frustrated with Dr. Landers's response. A referral to someone on the other side of the country seemed like an inadequate solution for what Rachel was going through. But life had been an emotional roller coaster since I'd stashed that crumpled scrap of paper in my purse. Even though I still couldn't imagine what some faraway counselor could do for us, I had nowhere else to turn. I left a phone message for the therapist summarizing our situation: My fourteen-year-old daughter—in a wheelchair and being newly treated for Lyme disease—was on a seventy-two-hour psych hold. I needed help figuring out our next move. Sandy called me back immediately. She was sympathetic, knowledgeable, and eminently practical. "You need a plan," she stated firmly. "Let's make one."

After group, we were allowed back into the lounge area to wait for our next session to start in an hour. I didn't know what the counselors would talk about this time, but I knew it would have no relevance to my life.

"Rachel," a staff member called from across the way. "You have someone here to see you."

My stomach muscles clenched, but I rolled my eyes and played it cool for Addison's benefit. I didn't want to see Mom or Dad, and visiting hours weren't even until tonight, so whoever it was could just leave. I peered down the hall anyway. Soon, a short woman with curly brown hair emerged, towing my green recliner behind her. It was Taylor!

Oh, thank *God*. I rolled my chair over to her and flung my arms around her waist. Relief flooded my system as I released the tension I had been holding since arriving late last night. Someone actually cared about me! I wasn't alone!

The hospital had granted Taylor permission to see me because she was my therapist. Although they wouldn't allow my parents to give me the green chair sooner, they'd let Taylor do it. We headed to my room for privacy and shut the door behind us. I climbed into bed, feeling the immediate comfort of my back being in its best position. We couldn't visit for long, so I wasted no time telling her everything that had happened since we had parted ways the previous day.

"I want out of here," I said. "But I don't want to go back home with my parents. They are horrible. This is all their fault." The very thought of their betrayal made my rage boil over again. "Adopt me. Please," I pleaded.

Taylor smiled sympathetically and gave my hand a comforting squeeze. We talked for a while, and I showed her the stubby pencil I'd found in the drawers by my bed this morning. I'd been using it to write entries in my new makeshift journal, made up of random sheets of paper I'd also found in the dresser. My real journal was at home, of course, but I had no idea how long I'd be here, and I had to document everything. It felt so good to see Taylor. I was glad she'd come.

I watched forlornly when she left, wondering what would happen if Taylor demanded they release me into her custody. Would they put her in handcuffs, too?

Dorothy

During that first phone call with Sandy, the therapist, I asked about finding an in-patient facility where Rachel could continue with Lyme treatment while getting the psychiatric support she obviously needed. Sandy was blunt: "Doesn't exist."

"What?" I responded. "What do you mean?"

"I'm not aware of any psychiatric facility in the whole country that will allow a patient to continue long-term antibiotics for Lyme disease," she said.

Over the past few months of internet research, I'd figured out that chronic Lyme was a controversial diagnosis. Now, Sandy filled in the big picture for me. The use of long-term antibiotics for Lyme disease was a major bone of contention in the medical world. In some parts of the country, doctors who prescribed them had been hauled before medical boards and stripped of their licenses. And even though there was growing evidence of a strong connection between Lyme disease and psychiatric symptoms, mainstream psychiatry was slow to recognize this. Sandy was personally aware of several cases of teens with Lyme disease who had gone into psychiatric facilities and been much worse off for it. "Don't go down that road," she cautioned.

"So, what do we do instead?" I had already explained in detail the events leading up to Rachel's hospitalization. Going back to how things had been before seemed out of the question.

"Your house must become the hospital," Sandy explained. "You have to set up a safe environment and make it possible for Rachel to get the help that she needs. It's a tough job, but you can do it."

After Taylor left, I wheeled myself back to the common area and found everyone milling around the line of phones on the wall. Grabbing an available receiver, I instinctively dialed my home number.

"Hello?" Mom sounded tentative.

"Hi." I would only give one-word answers. She didn't deserve more. I didn't even know why I'd called.

After a pause, Mom said, "We're coming to visit you tonight."

"Okay." I kept my tone rigid, unlike my usual self. She no longer got the privilege of hearing my normal voice. She needed to suffer for what she had done.

"Do you want us to bring anything when we come?"

"No."

The real answer was yes—I wanted her to bring French fries. All day, all I'd been hearing about was how everyone's families always brought them French fries during visiting hours. But Mom shouldn't even have had to ask. She should've just *known* they were expected.

"Okay, I love you," she said quietly.

I didn't answer. Instead, I hung up, hoping she heard that click and knew this was all her fault.

Dorothy

We got to the facility early, allowing time to meet with a staff member. A young psych tech led us to a room with two chairs, and then leaned against a table facing us. He kept his arms crossed tightly over his chest. "Your daughter is conning you," he said brusquely.

"Excuse me?" I responded. "What are you talking about?"

"She's faking," he continued, "and both of you have swallowed it hook, line, and sinker."

"Faking what?" I asked cautiously.

"The pain, needing a wheelchair, the whole thing. She's pulling the wool over your eyes. It's a snow job, and you guys are totally falling for it."

I was flabbergasted. Rachel had been on the premises for less than twenty-four hours and this guy thought he already had everything figured out? Was this merely his personal opinion, or was it the party line at this place? I wondered if he'd been told that by the doctor who'd insisted earlier that Rachel's case "didn't look like Lyme." I kept my cool because I wanted Rachel out of here when her seventy-two hours were up. I didn't know whether they could keep her longer, but at this point I was convinced they wouldn't do anything to really help her.

After our evening group session, we were confined to our rooms to wait for visiting hours. Why didn't they just let us sit on the couches and chat? I would've appreciated the company. And everyone else had a roommate when they were locked up—except for me. I was stuck here alone all the time, and I hated it. With no iPod, no books, no distractions of any kind, I was held captive in silence for hours each day, in pain and loathing every minute of my life.

Eventually, someone unlocked my room to say that Mom and Dad had arrived, and I followed reluctantly. I could smell French fries when I entered the visitation area and wheeled myself over to the table where my parents were seated. I looked around at my fellow convicts, all of whom had visitors who actually gave a damn and had shown up bearing gifts.

A war raged inside of me. Part of me wanted to hug my parents and beg them to take me home. The other part wanted to tell them to fuck off and never return. These battling emotions were too much for me to bear. I pushed back from the table and wheeled frantically toward the door.

Mom and Dad followed me to my room.

"I hate you!" I screamed, my lungs burning as much as my face. I didn't care if people could hear me. I didn't care if they saw me at my lowest and threw me in the panic room. It couldn't be worse than the hell I already lived in. I was done acting. I was done with this shit.

"You're horrible people! Leave me alone!" I yelled at them with such hatred that I even startled myself.

A staff member ran in, speaking over my cries, and pushed my parents out the door.

There they went, leaving me yet again.

"Nooo!" I shrieked long and loud, shredding what was left of my vocal cords. "Come back!" I sobbed, slamming my hand against the metal bed frame. The pounding pain reverberated up my arm, giving me extra strength to scream through this moment.

I felt like I'd been on the verge of drowning for months. As I fought to keep my head above water, I'd been calling out for someone to throw me a life preserver. But no one ever did. Instead, doctor after doctor had placed their foot on me, pushing me deeper into the water. I was cold and fatigued from swimming, and I'd finally accepted the fact that I wasn't meant to be saved. And that was *okay*. But this whole time, I'd had two people next to me, no matter how hard I was being pulled under by the violent current. Although they had never found a way to get me up into their boat, they had followed me the whole time, and had even gotten in the water so I wasn't swimming alone.

Two days ago, exhausted by the struggle, I had finally stopped swimming. But instead of being there next to me like they always had been, they'd handcuffed me, gotten back in their boat, and sped off in the distance. Now I was alone, sinking deeper and deeper below the surface with my hands cuffed behind my back, wondering what I had done to deserve *any* of this. And now, once again, Mom and Dad were leaving me alone in these terrifying, unsafe waters.

I climbed under the covers, hugging my bear tightly. Her wet fur pressed hard against my face as I writhed on the bed, howling at the unrelenting pain shooting everywhere all at once.

Dorothy

During my conversations with Sandy, we strategized ways to help Rachel get through this difficult period without relinquishing her to a system that was likely to make things worse, not better. In retrospect, one of the best things we did was to arrange for Sandy to regularly consult with Taylor by telephone. Taylor was a young, energetic therapist who had a great rapport with Rachel and a lot of experience working with teenage girls. But she knew little about Lyme disease and the many ways it could manifest, both physically and psychologically. Sandy, on the other hand, was a seasoned family therapist who also had personal and professional experience with long-term Lyme disease. In fact, her bustling therapy practice now focused exclusively on helping families dealing with tick-borne illnesses. Sandy told me that sometimes other therapists were open to working with her in such cases—other times, not so much. To my relief, Taylor said she was more than willing to do anything we felt could help Rachel.

I had been home from the psych hospital for two days now. After the trauma of my stay there, the pain in my body had increased astronomically. I didn't have the strength or desire to do anything except lie in bed and watch TV alone in the dark. My friends called, but I didn't want to be with anyone. I let it ring until Mom picked up and told them I wasn't up for company. Dad hadn't gone back to work, but I didn't want him or Mom to be with me, so they stayed away. I would never forgive them for their actions this past week. Everything that was wrong in our lives was because of them, and they knew it.

Dorothy

I believe Rachel's suicidal outburst was the result of a perfect storm of factors: a Herxheimer reaction from starting antibiotics (herxes were known to exacerbate both the physical and psycho-logical symptoms of Lyme disease); the ill-fated introduction of a pain medication that made it harder for her to breathe, under-standably increasing her sense of panic; the death of my mother and the fact that I was subsequently gone for several days, giving Rachel the message that if my mother could disappear sud-denly, maybe her mother could, too; the death of our friend and neighbor Craig, which was incredibly sad for our whole family; Rachel's unrelenting pain; and her inability to sleep more than a few hours each night, which robbed her brain of the rest it needed to function properly. None of these elements had been resolved by her trip to the psych hospital. And now, there was a new ingredient in the mix: Rachel's total animosity toward her dad and me.

After Rachel's release from the psych hospital, she allowed us to transfer her to the van. But she wouldn't talk to us or even meet our eyes. She nodded almost imperceptibly when we asked if she'd like us to drive through Jack in the Box for French fries. If we'd hoped the treat might soften her angry demeanor—it did not. At home, Rachel stayed in bed, listening to the TV with head-phones on, leaving her room only to use the toilet. She tolerated my presence when I brought her food but made it abundantly clear she wanted nothing else to do with us. We saw no point in fighting her and kept in the background as much as possible.

This was such a bleak time for me. Though Bob took time off when he could, he still had to work most weekdays and often had meetings at night. This left me to deal with Rachel's volatile epi-sodes alone. While I had several good friends I could have called on for emotional support, I found myself unable to reach out to them. It took every ounce of strength I could muster just to get through the challenges and uncertainties of each day. The mere thought of trying to explain our complicated situation to somebody else exhausted me, even if that person was a dear friend with my best interests at heart. My telephone therapy sessions with Sandy became my lifeline. I felt she was the only person who truly understood where I was coming from.

Unfortunately, our lack of communication about Rachel's circumstances also extended to Jeremy. Bob and I told him about Rachel's stint at the psych hospital, but for the most part, we were so swamped with her day-to-day care that we didn't talk to him much at all. It was easier to just assume he was doing fine during his first year of college and leave it at that. But Rachel's illness affected her brother in ways we didn't realize at the time. As I would learn years later, Jeremy worried very much about Rachel, Bob, and me while he was away at school. He felt disconnected from what was happening at home and reluctant to burden us with any problems in his own life. Furthermore, when he came home to visit, he found that our household dynamics had radically shifted to revolve around the needs of his sister, and he felt excluded.

About a week after I'd come home from the hospital, the phone by my bed rang, and Taylor's name popped up on the caller ID. Mom grabbed it from her office before I had a chance to even lift my arm, but the call turned out to be for me. *What?* Taylor never called to speak to me.

I picked up the receiver to hear a very excited therapist. She wanted to know if I was free to come in for an extra appointment outside of our normal Tuesday/Thursday sessions.

"I have some really good ideas that you'll like, Rachel. I don't want to wait until next week."

Mom, Dad, and I packed up the van and rode downtown in silence, since I still had no desire to talk to them. However, I was curious about what Taylor had in mind.

Mom lugged the green recliner into Taylor's office and set it up. I said nothing until after my parents left.

I looked at Taylor as she settled into a chair across from me.

"I have an idea," she said with a mischievous grin. "I think we should say what we really feel about all of the horrible doctors you've met with over the past year. Say anything we want. Completely unfiltered."

"Like what?"

"Like . . ." she thought for a moment, and then half-smiled as she said, "I think Dr. Morse from the children's hospital last summer was a shitty doctor."

My mouth dropped open. Taylor had just sworn. She had never, ever used a bad word in our sessions before!

"Do you have something you'd like to add?" she asked.

I hesitated. Up until a week ago, I had never used swear words. And now my own therapist wanted me to say them here with *her!* I paused and then said, "I think Emily, the physical therapist, was an idiot."

Taylor tilted her head and looked straight into my eyes like she always did when she felt she wasn't getting the full truth. "You can do better than that. Come on. Tell me what she *really* was."

I bit the inside of my lip. "She was a *fucking* idiot."

"She *was* a fucking idiot," Taylor agreed.

A smile emerged as I formulated my next insult. "Every doctor except for Dr. Landers is a fucking psychopath who doesn't know shit."

Dorothy

When Bob and I returned to Taylor's office to pick up Rachel, we practically fell over in surprise. She looked very different from the sullen girl we had dropped off an hour before. Her face seemed more relaxed, and her body language didn't scream, "I hate you guys." She even met our eyes when we greeted her. What magic had Taylor wrought?

It would be a long time before I learned precisely what had transpired during that therapy session. The idea had grown out of Sandy and Taylor's first phone consultation. In Sandy's view, Rachel had been traumatized by her hospital stay the previous summer, as well as the months of having her pain and suffering discounted by doctors. Her recent stint at the psych hospital had brought her anger into sharp focus. Sandy felt Rachel was displacing her long-simmering rage at her doctors onto me and Bob, and she needed a way to redirect that anger to more appropriate targets. Sandy theorized that using profanity to help Rachel recognize and channel her true feelings might shock her into viewing her situation differently. All I can say now is, it certainly helped!

Although Rachel never externally acknowledged any change in herself, from that point on, the tension between us eased. She was still obviously engulfed in pain and moodiness, and still lashed out at times. But mostly, she seemed to accept that her dad and I were firmly committed to Team Rachel and always had been. As a result, ideas I proposed to her didn't automatically become heated battles.

Since I'd gotten home from the psych hospital, I hadn't much felt up to socializing with friends, so I had lots of time for *Gilmore Girls* while lying in the new reclining bed we had recently acquired. I'd seen many episodes twenty times already and could recite much of the dialogue by heart. And I liked it that way. I found it soothing to know exactly what was going to happen in each episode.

One afternoon, Mom walked in with a shower cap filled with dry shampoo that she had bought at the drugstore. I hadn't bathed for two weeks, since before the psych hospital. My breathing was still labored, and I avoided any extra effort. Bathing—a complicated process that involved getting in the tub and using the handheld shower attachment—had been out of the question. But my hair was greasy and gross, and I felt disgusting.

"I don't know how well this will work," Mom said, "but let's try it."

I helped Mom push my hair into the cap as she read the instructions, which said to slowly massage the dry shampoo into the scalp, moving around the hair to get it clean. When we were done, Mom pushed me out into the living room, where my old hospital bed now resided, so she could put clean sheets on the one in my bedroom. Soon I was back under the covers, my newly laundered Care Bear pajama pants brushing against fresh, crisp linens. I hadn't felt this clean in a long time.

Mom brought me a heaping bowl of fruit salad, which was all I ever wanted to eat these days. She took off my old socks and replaced them with fresh ones—a simple task I hadn't been able to do for myself in recent weeks. Movements like that just hurt too much. Then, she parked herself next to me as we finished off the rest of my *Gilmore Girls* episode.

Dorothy

Like most insurance companies, our health plan would not pay for appointments with the Lyme specialist, Dr. Landers. We discovered this kind of refusal was par for the course in a long, complicated battle that many members of the Lyme community are still fighting to this day. However, our health plan actually did pay for most of the drugs prescribed by our doctor—but with a troublesome requirement. For some reason, when our doctor switched Rachel to azithromycin, the insurance would only pay for three days' worth at a time. They didn't deny us coverage—they just made us go to the drugstore every three days for a refill. I never understood the issue but had neither strength nor patience to contest it. Blessedly, my friend and neighbor Jill agreed to make regular runs to the pharmacy for us. I remember her saying, "You can tell me what's going on—or not—but please let me know if there's any way I can help you." And I took her up on it.

A couple weeks after my first dry shampoo experience, Mom and Dad entered my room, bearing a gift of fresh peach slices.

"Last night was so nice," Mom commented as she sat down in the office chair next to my bed.

"What do you mean?" I asked.

"I mean with Dad massaging your feet. I'd love to do that again today."

I wracked my brain for a memory of what she was referring to. Massaging my feet? "What are you talking about?"

"After Shira and Julianne left, you were having a rough time, and we found that massaging your feet helped calm you down."

What in the world? "Julianne and Shira were here yesterday?"

Mom glanced at Dad. "Yes, they were both here. After they left, you were very upset and crying. But Dad got some lotion and massaged your feet. After that, we all had a nice evening."

My throat tightened. "I don't remember that."

When my parents recounted the events of yesterday, it was as if they were making it all up. None of that had really happened—had it?

When Mom and Dad were out of the room, I opened the journal file I now kept on my computer and scrolled to the bottom. Nothing from yesterday.

Dorothy

Rachel's memory issues became more dramatic. One afternoon, two staff members Rachel knew from school stopped by to drop off a gift for her—a little green teddy bear. Since she was awake and amenable to visitors, I invited them in to give it to her in person. They stayed for twenty minutes or so, and Rachel seemed delighted to see them. After they left, she propped the little bear on her bedside table and dozed off, while I went to the kitchen to make dinner. A few minutes later, I heard Rachel calling me urgently. "Mom! Where did this bear come from?" When I told her who had brought it, she wailed, "Why didn't they come see me?" When I told her they *had* stayed for a visit, Rachel looked frightened and confused. A while later, she called out from her room again, "Mom! Where did this bear come from?" It was as if our earlier conversation hadn't happened at all. Again, she was distressed at my answer. After that, I stashed the bear out of sight.

After I'd been home from the psych hospital for a few weeks, I finally felt up to seeing my friends occasionally—even if I didn't always remember that they'd been there. Shira came over often enough that we talked openly about my memory problems. She even came up with a new way to deal with it.

Pointing the video camera at me, she said, "Rachel, you won't remember what we did today, so let's record it. Tell me what's going on!"

I looked at Shira before turning away, mumbling that my life was boring.

"No, it's not," she pressed. "Tell the camera what you want to remember. What are we doing right now?"

"We're just looking at pictures," I said quietly, pointing to the computer screen, which showed a recent photo of Jeremy at college.

"You need to make sure you write in your journal about this, so you remember to watch our video," Shira instructed and turned the camera around to face herself. "I'm here too. See?" She waved.

To my knowledge, this was the first video diary entry we'd made. I had been overwhelmed by other people telling me things I didn't remember, and Shira thought it might be less upsetting for me to hear it from myself. We uploaded the footage to my computer, placing the file in the center of my screen and titling it, "RACHEL WATCH THIS NOW!"

Dorothy

Given Rachel's depression, mood swings, and memory problems, Dr. Landers ordered a single-photon emission computed tomography (SPECT) scan, a type of imaging that identifies areas of blood flow in the brain. He told us that certain patterns of blood flow were highly associated with Lyme disease and other infections and that the SPECT scan could help him determine how much the illness was affecting her brain. I could see the benefit of such information, but I was doubtful that Rachel would cooperate enough for us to complete the procedure.

I didn't think any medical interventions would help me at this point, but Dr. Landers wanted me to have a special scan, and I agreed to do it. That was easier than resisting, since I had precious little energy anymore. I pushed myself through the door of the imaging center, and Mom carried in my green recliner and set it up in the waiting room. As soon as I had finally gotten situated, a man in scrubs called my name and asked us to follow him to the back room. So, it was back to the wheelchair for me again.

The man inserted an IV into my arm and then started jabbering about some other test I needed to take before they could perform the scan. I had no idea what he was talking about, mostly because all my attention was on trying to breathe while sitting at this angle. I needed my lounge chair back.

He pointed to the computer, where letters randomly appeared on the screen. "Push the spacebar for everything except the letter X, okay?"

X? What? Opening my mouth wide, I struggled to get enough oxygen into my body while sitting up straight at the desk. My tongue was dry, and I felt feverish. *What exactly was in this IV?*

As letters floated across the screen, I pushed the spacebar mostly at random, focusing more on my dizziness and the pressure crushing my temples than this test or his instructions.

"Don't push the spacebar when you see the letter *X*," he reminded me.

I couldn't care less about the letter *X* right now. Tears burned my eyes as I bent forward, using the table as support. What would happen if I passed out? Would he let me sit in my green chair then?

After I finished with the world's dumbest test, we moved to a different room. Mom explained to the attendant that I couldn't lie down flat once in the machine. He offered me some pillows, which didn't help. Each time I leaned back to try them out, my lungs constricted and pain shot down my spine.

I sat up on the table, flopped my legs over the side, and announced, "I'm done. Get me my wheelchair."

"Just hold on a minute," Mom said.

"No." I was making a scene in front of the stupid man operating this stupid machine, and I didn't care. "Give me my wheelchair *right now*, or I will fling myself off this table!"

Without another word, Mom pushed the wheelchair toward me. I toppled down into it, disregarding the painful jolt from my rough landing. Panicking, I tried to figure out my next move. I wanted to roll out the door and escape. But there was nowhere to go, and I couldn't leave without my reclining chair.

My lungs felt like they were covered in gauze, preventing me from getting enough oxygen. My face tingled as I quietly hyperventilated in the corner. Mom continued to arrange pillows on the table, determined to do the impossible and find an acceptable position for me. Recognizing that my breathing would only get worse from here, and that we weren't leaving without the brain scan, I gave up, defeated.

"Okay," I whispered through tightened vocal cords that didn't want to let air in or out.

I climbed back up onto the table, the last bit of air forced from my lungs as I leaned against the pillows.

"It's just fifteen minutes," the man told me. *Does he have any idea how long fifteen minutes is?*

He put a white cloth over my eyes, shielding me from the machine that was spinning just inches from my face. With a clenched jaw and my eyes squeezed shut, I watched the pain play out in visuals against the back of my eyelids. Red lightning bolts shattered the bones of my rib cage, and razor blades sliced through my spine from top to bottom. My arms and legs went numb as the machine spun around me.

Imagining the beautiful blackness that would inevitably surround me when I died was the only thing that kept me going during the longest fifteen minutes of my life. The sheer joy I would feel, knowing that within moments I would be free, no longer bound by the agony forced upon me by this cruel illness.

When the ordeal with the machine was finally over, the man told us to return in two days for the second part of the test. I looked away, ignoring his words. *Second part? There's not gonna be a second part.*

Dorothy

We never went back for the second test. Rachel wanted nothing to do with it, and our Lyme doctor said the first one had given him most of the information he was looking for anyway. Dr. Landers told us he was actually relieved the brain scan showed that the damage to Rachel's brain was not as serious as he had feared. "We can handle this," he said.

We found ourselves running on parallel tracks in terms of Rachel's care. First and foremost was Dr. Landers, providing guidance on medications, tests, and supplements. Next came the combined forces of our therapists, Sandy and Taylor, who gave essential support to both Rachel and me as we worked through the trauma of the past year. But we still needed help addressing Rachel's unremitting pain. To that end, we secured an appointment at a well-known pain clinic, hoping they could offer something—anything—that would bring her some relief.

Mom, Dad, and I left bright and early for the appointment with the new pain doctor. At 7:15 a.m., we stopped to pick up Diane, a family friend, who would come with us to the doctor's appointment and stay with me when Mom and Dad needed to talk to the doctor alone.

We had to sit in the waiting room a long time before we were finally called back. Diane stayed behind with her magazine as the nurse led the rest of us to an exam room at the end of the hall. After taking my blood pressure, the nurse asked a question I'd come to dread, "Can you rate your pain on a scale from 1 to 10?" *Why bother? These guys always ask this question and then totally ignore my answer.*

"It's a 10," I replied curtly. I didn't make eye contact with her and instead focused on a still life hanging on the wall, depicting an empty vase. No flowers . . . just the vase. Stupid painting.

Her smile seemed condescending. "No, dear. A 10 is reserved for the worst pain you can imagine, like childbirth. I'll put you down for an 8."

Yeah, I was fourteen years old, but somehow I was supposed to know what childbirth felt like? I didn't waste my breath saying that aloud. It was hard enough to breathe in this stupid little room. The nurse left, and Mom and Dad set up the green lounge chair for me, wedging it into the space between the exam table and the other furniture in the room. I put on my headphones and listened to my iPod, focusing all my attention on Good Charlotte's "I Just Wanna Live." I liked the song, but I wasn't so sure I agreed with the sentiment.

Dorothy

The wait for the pain doctor seemed endless. Rachel had started out the day in reasonably good spirits, even though I knew she despised meeting new doctors. After this long wait, punctuated by the nurse's clueless comments about pain and childbirth, I feared Rachel would lose patience altogether—and who knew what might happen then?

I didn't know if I could handle a repeat of what had happened during the SPECT scan. The search for answers about what was wrong with my daughter was already grueling, but now each new avenue we pursued seemed to bring Rachel fresh misery. Bob and I discussed the relative merits of putting Rachel through more pain with the nebulous hope of bringing her relief in the future. For now, we agreed to keep trying, but our resolve wore thinner with each new callous encounter we had with the medical establishment.

After we'd waited for two excruciating hours, the pain doctor finally came in, accompanied by another guy in a white coat. The head doc reached out to shake my hand and said, "So, what's stopping you from walking out of here today?"

What a dumb thing to say! Hadn't he read my medical records? Feeling utterly defeated, I replied quietly, "My knees hurt too much to stand. I feel sharp, shooting pains up my spine all the time, and my shoulders are hypersensitive, so no one can touch them."

"All right, let's see here." He leaned forward, his arm outstretched toward my shoulder. Before he could make contact, I heard Mom's voice, strained but clear.

"Doctor, can I speak with you for a moment, out in the hallway, right now?"

Dorothy

I feared this appointment would go down in flames if this doctor started off on the wrong foot with Rachel. We couldn't afford to have yet another opportunity closed off to us because of this man's poor bedside manner. If he wasn't going to take the time to figure out an effective means of approaching Rachel, I would simply have to tell him. I briefly recapped recent events and stressed the importance of *not touching her shoulders*. Rachel was psychologically fragile, and we'd already used up most of her energy reserves for the whole day just waiting for the appointment to begin. As I briefly made my case with the doctor, my husband followed us out to the hallway. In retrospect, that was a big mistake. When the three of us stepped back into the room, the other doctor—a resident, I assume—had brought Rachel to tears. *Angry* tears.

Once my parents and the main doctor left, I found myself alone with the other one. To my horror, he immediately reached out for my shoulder. Stunned, I tilted back, blocking his hand with my own. Again, I told him that he couldn't touch my shoulders because they hurt too much.

"I just need to see something," he said. Pushing past my hand, he placed his own firmly on top of my shoulder, sending what felt like an electric shock reverberating through my body. It also conjured up every time I'd told someone *not to touch my shoulders* and had been ignored, suffering the predictable—and *avoidable*—agony when they did it anyway. Like back at the children's hospital, when their efforts to "desensitize me" had only inflicted more pain. Those horrendous therapies had done nothing to fix my hypersensitivity, instead causing it to explode in all directions. Now, the top half of my back was untouchable as well, thanks to them.

"You keep touching the same spot!" I hissed.

"I know," he said nonchalantly, pulling his hand away. "I'm waiting for you to say it doesn't hurt anymore."

What?! Another psychotic doctor accusing me of faking my pain! How could I have ever held even the slightest hope that this clinic could help? How dare he say he would keep touching my shoulders until I gave in and confessed that I wasn't really in pain? How *dare* he? We came here because we were out of options. I couldn't keep living in this awful situation—it just wasn't possible. Why continue fighting to stay in a body I didn't want anymore?

Dorothy

I knew how upset Rachel was, as our friend Diane escorted her out of the building to wait for us in the van. I was disheartened, too. But we'd come this far, managing to secure an appointment with this highly regarded pain specialist. I still hoped against hope that if I could just make him understand what Rachel was going through, he might find a way to help us. If we could sit down with him alone and go over the medical records we carried in a big binder, then, surely, he'd have some suggestions for something we could try.

As Bob and I sat in his office, it soon became clear that this doctor had no interest in anything we had to say. He barely looked at the SPECT scan results I handed him. He told us without any discernable compassion that he didn't accept the Lyme diagnosis.

"Okay, so let's say it's not Lyme," I said, sidestepping that argument for the moment. "She's still in intense pain all the time. Can we work on *that?*"

He shrugged my question away. "We don't know what's going on with your daughter, so it would be irresponsible for us to treat her." First do no harm, *blah, blah, blah*. But the status quo was doing her plenty of harm, I protested. I might as well have been talking to a stone wall. He offered no new lines of inquiry or action. He just insisted there was nothing to be done. His unspoken message came through loud and clear: "Don't let the door hit you on your way out."

Diane and I waited in the van for a while before Mom and Dad came back. Mom climbed in and slumped against the seat. "We aren't going to any new doctors, Rachel." She buckled her seat belt as Dad started the engine. "These people can't help us."

I listened to my iPod on the thirty-minute car ride home, hoping to stave off what I knew would be a truly terrible evening ahead. Harnessing every ounce of power within me, I delayed my panic attack until Diane was safely out of the vehicle.

Once home, I cried in my room for hours. Leaving the light off, I sobbed in bed, soaking the top of my shirt with tears. The change in texture of the now-wet cotton set off my shoulders, making it feel as if that awful man's hands were back on me again, touching me when I'd told him not to. Like he wouldn't let go of me.

In a blind rage, I hurled myself off the bed. My shoulder slammed against the hard floor, shooting pain down my spine. At least now I knew why I was screaming. Like all the doctors said, *I* was the problem.

Mom came running and found me crumpled on the ground. She tried to speak, but I drowned her out with my shrieking, not wanting to hear anything she had to say. My throat burned and my lungs gasped for air. Without a further word, she handed me a pillow. I put it under my head and curled up on the floor. I felt the electric bed's power cord underneath me, inflicting an extra layer of pain. Mom reached down and cupped my knees with her warm hands. Soon my cries trailed off to whimpers.

Lying on my bedroom floor, all energy siphoned out of me, I silently pleaded for it all to end. Why couldn't it just end?

Dorothy

I realized once we were back at home that I had pinned unreasonable hopes on our appointment with the pain specialist. When that encounter blew up in our faces, it left me feeling even more angry, abandoned, and emotionally depleted than I'd been before. Despite my exhaustion, and Rachel's, I knew we had no choice but to keep marching through one predictably awful hour after another, our own miserable version of the movie *Groundhog Day*.

Shortly after Rachel's stint in the psych hospital, our family doctor had finally persuaded a local psychiatrist to take her case, even though we'd previously been told there was a long waiting list. This was after I'd called every psychiatrist in the area with no luck. (As I write this, seventeen years later, the critical lack of mental health professionals who treat adolescents has only gotten worse.) The new doctor tried various psychiatric drugs to treat Rachel's mounting feeling of hopelessness, but nothing made any difference.

Sundowning is a term usually associated with Alzheimer's disease and other forms of dementia. It refers to the phenomenon wherein patients with the condition often become more confused, anxious, and agitated in the late afternoon and evening. No one really knows why. This appeared to be the case with Rachel. Despite her continuous pain, she seemed more capable of keeping her composure during the mornings and early afternoons—especially if her friends were able to spend time with her. But even when it was just the two of us, she often managed to stay calm throughout the day while we watched TV, listened to music, or read stories. But come evening, everything changed. The slightest comment might set her off. My husband and I had a code name for what happened next: Hurricane Rachel. We also had a hand signal, so we could discreetly communicate to each other without further agitating our daughter. When Bob came through the door after work, he'd look to see if I waggled my fingers in a certain way. If I did, it meant "Danger! You're walking into a volatile situation."

CHAPTER 5

A Visit to Rachel's House

Recently, my parents had solved one of my problems by acquiring a hospital table that swung up and over the bed. We put Jeremy's computer on it. This gave me a work surface I could use while reclining in a position that allowed me to breathe more easily. With a wireless keyboard on my lap and a mouse sitting next to it, I could now edit videos again—my favorite activity. When my friends weren't in school, they came over to film videos with me in my room. Editing seemed to be the only mental capability that was still under my control. It was like editing accessed a part of my brain that was unaffected by Lyme.

Since I was too sick to leave the house, Taylor now came to me for our therapy sessions. Today we were doing something special! She was filming me for a documentary we were making about my health journey.

"Tell us a little about yourself," she suggested, holding my Panasonic video camera.

"I . . . I'm . . ." My mind went blank. "Shoot. Start over." Adjusting the green and silver soccer jersey I was wearing, I began again. As soon as my mouth opened, it was like someone had erratically erased the whiteboard that made up my brain. Parts of what I wanted to say were still visible, but the rest was wiped clean. After a few takes, I managed to say, "Hi, I'm Rachel, I'm fourteen years old, and I have Lyme disease." Eventually we got enough footage for me to edit together, but as someone who enjoyed being in front of the camera, it was beyond infuriating to be dragged down by a brain that couldn't stay focused on what it was trying to do.

As Taylor was leaving, she stopped to talk with Mom in the living room. What were they saying? Were they talking about me? Was Taylor telling her we filmed our video? Holding my breath, I tried to make out even a few of their words. I hated the thought of people talking about me when I wasn't there to hear exactly what was being said. Once Taylor was gone, Mom walked in, asking if I had any desire for a change of scenery.

It had been thirty days since my last doctor's appointment, which meant it had been a whole month since I'd been anywhere other than my bedroom and the bathroom. Mom and I decided to mix things up and take a quick excursion to the living room. When I looked around, it seemed like I was in a different house. I realized that I hadn't seen my own kitchen for a month now. It even smelled unfamiliar—like someone else's house. After a few minutes, Mom helped me back to my bedroom, where she turned on *Gilmore Girls*. We watched the show, ate fruit salad, and waited for Dad to return from work.

Dorothy

It was March of Rachel's eighth grade year. She hadn't attended classes at her junior high since before Christmas vacation. School officials didn't like this. Early on, they had insisted she either return to the classroom, study with the home/hospital teacher, or enroll in the district's independent study program. We tried the home teacher option, but it didn't work for us at all. With Rachel's pain, insomnia, fatigue, and memory problems, any schoolwork was simply beyond her capabilities.

Our Lyme doctor wrote a letter explaining this, which school officials disregarded. They didn't accept that she was too ill to do any schooling at all. They acted as if I wanted my child to fall behind academically and it was their job to change my mind. Several times, they told me about a local boy who had graduated at the top of his class, despite having chemotherapy during his senior year. They kept repeating, "And he had *cancer*." Their message seemed clear to me: "He was worse off than your daughter, and he still went to school." His case had nothing to do with us, I told them, and Rachel was too sick for school right now. For the moment, they stopped hectoring me about it.

Meanwhile, Rachel's brain continued to do strange things. One evening, while watching TV in her bedroom, she let out a blood-curdling scream. When Bob and I came running, her eyes had a wild look to them. "The jellyfish!" she rasped. "It's after me!"

Jellyfish? We looked around her bedroom, seeing nothing that might trigger such a fear. Bob switched off the TV. Had something there alarmed her? Despite our efforts to calm her down, Rachel's body shook, her voice trembled, and she seemed to be in a trance that nothing we said or did could penetrate. She kept crying out that the jellyfish was after her. She looked terrified.

Trying to break through whatever barrier separated us, I put my face as close to hers as I could, without bumping the bed or touching her sensitive shoulders. "Rachel," I said loudly and firmly. "Mommy is right here. I won't let the jellyfish get you."

Finally, this seemed to register on some level. She murmured, "You won't? Okay . . ." Her breathing grew calmer, and she closed her eyes. I stayed by her bedside until she fell asleep. The next morning, she made no mention of the jellyfish, and I sure wasn't going to remind her of it.

One afternoon in March, Alicia and I were in my bedroom playing *Crash Team Racing* on the PlayStation. The doorbell rang, and soon my neighbors Tenaya and Julianne waltzed into my bedroom with big grins on their faces. "We have something to show you," Tenaya said.

"But you need to come outside," Julianne added.

That was mysterious! I moved to the office chair, and Alicia pushed me out to the living room, where I transferred to my wheelchair. It was hard to breathe, so I slouched down as Alicia steered the chair out the front door. Both of us winced as we went over the threshold and reached the driveway.

Tenaya retrieved an odd contraption from behind the car and pulled it over to me.

My mouth gaped open. There in front of me was my green reclining lounge chair, fastened to a wheeled, wooden platform. They'd made me a new kind of wheelchair!

"We wanted to find a way for you to come outside again," Tenaya said with pride.

With help, I climbed up onto my throne. Leaning back, with my face tilted up to the sky, I took a deep, satisfying breath in. How about that? I was outside, *and* I could breathe.

"Let's go for a spin!" I squealed in delight.

The warmth of the sun felt good on my skin, but its light blinded me. I covered my eyes with my arm until Mom handed me my sunglasses.

Tenaya began pulling my new chariot, and we slowly lumbered forward. It was heavy, so she and Julianne took turns pulling me every few minutes. I looked at my surroundings in fascination, as if I'd never seen a spring day before. I marveled at how the trees were exploding with green buds, and how the air smelled clean and new.

"We asked your parents if we could use the reclining chair a couple days ago," Tenaya said, walking backward while she pulled me. "And my dad helped us make it."

Surprised neighbors stopped in their tracks when they saw our parade heading down the bike path.

"Hello, Rachel!" my neighbor Stephanie's mom called from across the grass. She walked over to inspect the chair up close.

"Tenaya and Julianne made it for me!" I explained.

"Is that Rachel I see?" another neighbor yelled from their front yard with an enthusiastic wave.

"Oh my goodness, hello there!" someone on the greenbelt called, throwing a ball for his dog.

Julianne muttered to Tenaya, "Wow, it's like we're chauffeuring a celebrity."

Mom pulled out the camera and everyone crowded around me for a picture. They smiled. I beamed.

About a week later, I heard Shira's footsteps coming down the hallway toward my bedroom. I pretended to be interested in something on my computer screen. The door creaked open, and after a short pause for effect, I feigned surprise at the camera in her hands.

"Oh, hi there! You startled me! Come on in!" I said to the camera.

Shira and I were filming a video titled *A Visit to Rachel's House* for our group of friends at school.

"It's good to see you guys!" I said to the camera.

Each Friday at lunch, the aides at school would call me and pass around the phone so that I could catch up with my friends. I waited all week for that phone call—longing to shoot the breeze about surface-level topics with people who had no clue how horrible things were at home these days.

It was Shira's idea to take this lifeline of communication one step further and make a video as if they were here with me. I couldn't wait to burn it onto a DVD for Shira to take to school the next day. I wished they could make a video to send to me, too.

Dorothy

Our Lyme doctor recommended that Rachel begin hyperbaric oxygen therapy (HBOT), which he said had been shown to offer many benefits to people with Lyme disease. Basically, HBOT involves breathing 100 percent oxygen while staying in a specialized chamber with increased air pressure. This moves more oxygen throughout the body, enhancing blood flow, reducing inflammation, and helping the immune system to function better. Many Lyme patients have reported that it helped clear up their brain fog and fatigue, as well as reduce pain and other symptoms.

The FDA had approved HBOT for many conditions, including carbon monoxide poisoning, decompression sickness, and various infections. However, the use of HBOT for Lyme disease and some other conditions was not approved by the FDA, but rather merely considered "investigational." There are two practical implications to this. First, while many hospitals owned hyperbaric chambers, they wouldn't use them to treat people for Lyme disease. Second, even if you found a place that would treat you, your insurance probably wouldn't pay for it. (This was true in 2006 and is still true as I write this in 2023.)

Our doctor suggested an HBOT clinic not affiliated with any hospital, which was about two hours from our home. We immediately applied to go there.

It didn't take long for a spot at the hyperbaric clinic to open up. Since we were leaving for two months, Mom suggested we throw a little going-away party. Dad bought pizza and chips for us, and my neighborhood friends Shira, Alicia, Christine, Kate, Julia, and Stephanie all played a card game called Apples to Apples with me. They sat in a circle around my hospital bed in the living room.

Then Christine suggested, "Let's make a movie!"

Everyone started talking at once. I let them hash out the details while I lay back, enjoying the happy voices bouncing around me.

We decided to make commercials. For mine, I played a character who was dealing with the aftermath of a vending machine accident. Shira tied a cloth napkin around my head like a bandage. Because of my brain fog (and a few laughing fits), I kept stumbling over my one line. But after a few tries, I managed to get it out: "I am a victim of falling vending machines."

After everyone left, I felt both exhausted and replenished. Mom finished packing, making sure to include all of my pills, ice packs, and heating pads. Then, in the morning, Dad waved goodbye as we headed down the road.

Dorothy

We rented a furnished apartment near the hyperbaric center, along with a hospital bed so Rachel could be at a reclined angle. The only place the hospital bed fit in our new apartment was in the living room. We brought a portable TV with a VHS player and a separate device to play DVDs on the big TV set that came with the apartment. Some family friends lent us what turned out to be a treasure trove of entertainment: a boxed DVD set with all ten seasons of *Friends*. That comedy became a mainstay of our days. Now, more than seventeen years later, we still recite lines from the show to each other. ("What's a MOO point? It's a cow's opinion—it just doesn't matter. It's moo.")

The apartment was our weekday home-away-from-home for the next two months. Rachel was scheduled for daily hyperbaric "dives," as they were called, Monday through Friday, and we'd drive home to see Bob on weekends. The treatments are called dives because the pressure in the chamber is equivalent to what a scuba diver experiences forty feet under the ocean's surface.

The hyperbaric chamber looked like a mini submarine. It had a sturdy metal exterior and was long enough to fit several people inside. An adjustable stretcher sat on one side—that was for me, so I could keep my back at an angle during the session. The three chairs across from it were for my dive companions. Each of us wore a plastic bubble over our heads, with a skintight rubber seal around the neck. The bubbles were attached to tubes poking out from pipes in the walls that would administer 100 percent pure oxygen during the dive.

The HBOT center was very strict about what you could wear inside the chamber. Only cotton clothing was allowed because it doesn't carry a static charge. Synthetics could theoretically generate a spark—and nobody wanted that with 100 percent pure oxygen all over the place! So, we all wore either pajamas or scrubs. I wore my green-and-white pajama pants, with my "I need a hug" Winnie the Pooh sweatshirt. An ironic fashion choice, since it had been more than a year since anyone had been able to give me a hug due to my hypersensitive shoulders.

Of the three windows in the chamber, two were covered with pictures of fish swimming in the ocean. Mom's head popped into view through the only window visible to the outside. She gave me a thumbs-up and waved goodbye before heading to the lobby.

Even though I was stuffed in this tank with three other patients and a nurse, I was the only kid, and I felt out of place. Two men and a woman sat across from me. I knew the woman had Lyme, but I wasn't sure about the man next to her. However, the guy sitting on the end had an elaborate metal gadget screwed into his jaw. If I'd had to wager a guess as to why he was here, I'd bet it had something to do with that.

"It was a piece of chocolate," said George, the guy with the metal gadget. "Everything was hunky-dory, then I bit down, and the damn thing broke my jaw."

I smiled slightly, assuming he was trying to lighten the mood.

He shook his head. "No, I'm serious. I bit down on a tiny piece of chocolate, and it broke my jaw."

Unsure of how to respond, I just said, "Wow."

Nurse Kate sealed the door closed and handed each of us a blanket, telling us, "It will get cold in here."

After one last reminder to frequently pop our ears as the pressure in the chamber lowered, a loud whooshing sound roared around us. But powerful, high-pitched hissing didn't stop Michael, another one of my dive companions, from shouting conversation to George over the pandemonium. I snuggled under my blanket, breathing in the oxygen blowing into my face as I listened to Michael's drowned-out voice hollering to the man two inches from him.

Yawning to open my jaw, I popped my ears as I would on an airplane. Except this was different than an airplane. As soon as I popped my ears, they needed to be popped again. And again. It had been just a few minutes, yet my jaw was already exhausted. How did George do this with his mouth wired shut?

When I leaned back against my pillow, the plastic bubble around my head pushed forward uncomfortably. Eventually, after some trial and error, I found a position I could live with for the next two hours. A few minutes in, Joyce, the woman with Lyme sitting across from me, put her hand in the air, pointing toward her ear. Soon, the whooshing sound stopped, and an eerie silence filled the faux submarine.

"My left one won't pop," Joyce said matter-of-factly. She'd been doing this for two months now and knew the drill.

Nurse Kate adjusted the pressure a little, giving Joyce's body extra time to get with the program.

"This happens sometimes," she told us. "If anyone else has difficulty, just put your hand up like she did."

Once Joyce was ready, we continued on down until we finally reached the desired pressure. With the chamber quiet once more, we voted on which movie to watch. With a plastic bubble around my head, pure oxygen blowing in my face, and a blanket covering me, I settled in for the long haul as *Independence Day* began to play on the TV screen across from me.

Dorothy

Our time at the hyperbaric center started a new round of *Groundhog Day* for us. Rachel was in the chamber for two hours each morning, and the rest of the time we spent at the apartment. We used our VCR timer to record episodes of *ER* that ran daily during her treatments. It became our routine to watch that show as soon as we returned from her dive. The rest of the time, we watched Netflix DVDs and worked our way through *Friends*. Luckily, the apartment had Wi-Fi service, so she could also use AOL Instant Messenger on my laptop to converse with her friends when they were available.

We lived a limited life in our temporary home: hyperbaric sessions, TV shows, and staring at the walls of our apartment. My only break came during Rachel's two-hour dive, when I might buy groceries, take a walk, or swim laps at a nearby health club.

Looking for things to distract Rachel and keep her occupied, I suggested she plan a dream vacation for the family. With internet access, she was able to find a place for us to stay, things for us to do, and restaurants where we could dine. The idea captured her imagination, and she planned two vacations for us, one on each coast: Myrtle Beach, South Carolina, and Pismo Beach, California. She even printed out photos of the locations she'd found on the internet and pasted them on poster boards we hung up on the walls of our temporary home.

One day, for some reason, Rachel was scheduled for a different dive group than usual. As I sat in the waiting room with a magazine, I noticed a woman I'd never seen before, and we struck up a lively conversation. It turned out that she and her son both had Lyme and both went to Rachel's doctor. They were staying at the Holiday Inn while her son did HBOT. I immediately invited them to our apartment the next day for dinner and to play a game. She answered with hesitation, "We really don't want to inconvenience you—"

"Inconvenience us?" I countered. "You'd be doing us a favor! We're going bonkers with no social contact! Please come."

"But I have so many foods I have to avoid," she said. "It would be hard for you to cook for us."

"Try me!" I whipped out a notepad and pen. "Tell me precisely what you can eat, and I'll fix it. What about roasted organic chicken?"

"I can eat plain chicken," she answered slowly. "But it can't have anything on it—not even salt."

"I can make chicken without salt," I said. "Now, what else?"

This afternoon, like every other since Mom and I had moved into the apartment near the hyperbaric clinic, I used Mom's laptop to message with Christine and Shira. As I chatted with my friends, Mom bustled around the kitchen, preparing for our guests.

I waved as Daniel and his mom entered our apartment. In honor of our company, I sat at the dining room table in my green recliner.

It was the first time I'd eaten anywhere other than my hospital bed since we'd moved here.

Daniel was twenty-two—a few years older than Jeremy—and he kind of reminded me of my brother. It was a relief to hear him speak about his day-to-day life with Lyme disease. Here was someone who got me, plain and simple.

After eating, we left our moms at the table and returned to the living room so I could climb back in bed. Daniel sat on the sofa.

"People don't understand how hard it is to leave the house and try to be normal," Daniel said. I nodded, and he went on. "If I go out with friends, then I come home and crash for like three days. I can't leave the couch. Even eating is too exhausting." He shook his head. "They just don't get that."

I nodded again, feeling so heard even though I wasn't the one talking. Until now, I didn't really know there were people out there like me. I'd thought our family's ordeal was unique, but I saw now that it wasn't. Daniel wasn't in a wheelchair, but like me, he was housebound most of the time, in constant pain, and struggling with crushing fatigue. He was missing out on his twenties, just like I was missing out on my teens.

After they left, Mom couldn't stop smiling. She kept saying how great it was to meet people who understood our lives. "We should invite them over again soon," she said, loading up the dishwasher. "I can get another chicken."

Dorothy

If a problem arose in the middle of a hyperbaric session, you couldn't just stop and fling open the door. Much like a submarine deep in the ocean, you first must "resurface," depressurizing as you go. Opening the chamber without doing this would spell disaster. Thus, as a safety measure, every dive group also included a staff member trained to handle potential emergencies in the tank, as well as a technician monitoring the process from the outside.

Once, in the middle of one of Rachel's dives, an older woman who was new to HBOT had a panic attack. While the staff member on the inside focused on helping the distraught woman calm down, another potential emergency unfolded at the same time. Two other patients in the dive group—a man and woman—turned to Rachel and started proselytizing to her about their religious beliefs. They exhorted her to accept Jesus Christ as her Lord and Savior, declaring that it was the only way she could ever get well. The woman chided Rachel for having a "bad attitude," which could only be helped by turning to God. The man accused Rachel of faking her pain to get attention.

Unfortunately, you couldn't have devised a more effective way to send Rachel off her emotional rails. Here she was, trapped in a pressurized tank, being badgered by two adults who claimed she really wasn't sick after all. The one person she might have turned to for help—the staffer on the inside—was consumed by the needs of the panicking woman.

Laura, the technician monitoring the session from outside, witnessed the two ganging up on Rachel and how it was clearly upsetting her. She halted the dive and started the slow process of depressurizing the chamber. Laura then alerted another staffer, who in turn reached me on my cell phone as I stood in the middle of a grocery store. I left my shopping cart in the produce aisle and drove back to the hyperbaric center immediately.

The door to the tank finally opened, and I watched the attendants transfer Rachel from the stretcher to her wheelchair. I recognized the hard expression on her face. I'd seen it often over the previous year, whenever she felt attacked and betrayed. Though I tried to keep a calm demeanor, I was furious and disgusted by the two people who had ambushed my emotionally fragile child. I couldn't even look at them. I helped Rachel into the car, and my heart sank when I heard her fiercely whisper, "I'm not coming back—ever."

Yet, remarkably, things cooled down. The hyperbaric center reassured us that the offending patients would be transferred to a different dive group, and to my relief, Rachel agreed to resume treatment.

I was glad not to have to see those two idiots from my dive group again. Now, I had something more important to focus on. First, I used Mom's laptop to search "finding an acting agent" on the internet. Then, every day, in the hours between hyperbaric treatments and watching *ER* reruns, I planned my future in Hollywood. I wanted to be famous like Miley Cyrus. I wanted to act in TV shows and movies. If I could just do that, I knew I would finally be *happy*. My darkest moments each day were when I was by myself with nothing and no one to distract me from the constant pounding up and down my spine. Miley Cyrus wouldn't have time to feel the way I did. She was always busy and constantly surrounded by the people on her team.

For the moment, I was stuck here while all my friends were off living their lives—but it wouldn't always be that way. It just couldn't. I wouldn't let it. I'd wanted to become an actress for ages now, and I was done waiting. I just needed to get healthy enough to sit up straight without difficulty breathing. As soon as that happened, I was outta here.

When I was a celebrity, the feeling of a drill grinding into the center of my knees would fade into the background. My days would consist of rehearsals and interviews on *Ellen* and *Oprah*. My manager would plan so many thrilling things for me to do that I wouldn't have a moment to feel anything but excitement.

My personal assistant would be like my best friend, hanging out with me anytime I wanted, day or night. When I was a famous actress, I'd never be lonely again. These days, I spent hours waiting for Christine and Shira to get home from school just so we could instant message online for an hour before they had to do homework, or go to tennis practice, or eat dinner with their families. When I was famous, they'd have to wait for *me* to have time for *them*!

Dorothy

Nights at the apartment took on an eerie sameness. We'd have dinner, maybe play a game, and then watch TV until Rachel fell asleep, usually about 10:00 p.m. I'd tiptoe away from the living room, trying not to make any sound as I got into bed. But by midnight, she'd be wide awake and stay that way until morning. She'd barely get two hours of sleep in a twenty-four-hour period, night after night after night. Blessedly, she typically let me sleep, though I knew she hated being alone. She'd listen to music through her headphones or watch overnight infomercials on TV. But sleep deprivation took its toll. As extreme fatigue permeated her days, Rachel's ability to keep her emotions on an even keel severely diminished. In consultation with our various doctors, we tried such sleep aids as melatonin, Ambien®, and Lunesta®, but nothing made any difference at all. When we met with the hyperbaric center's doctor and begged him for something else to try, he suggested trazodone. Taken at a high dose, this generic drug was an antidepressant. However, he said, when taken at a very low dose it could help you sleep. We tried it and—wonder of wonders—it helped. Soon, Rachel was sleeping at least five or six hours a night, a huge improvement on so many levels.

Four weeks into my new treatment regimen of hyperbaric oxygen therapy, things were worse than when I started. My breathing was the most noticeable difference—sitting up for even a few seconds made me more winded than it used to. It was more important now than ever for me to keep my back in a reclined position. When would things get better?

Dr. Landers thought it was time to hit the Lyme with something harder. So, today we were at a different medical office near the hyperbaric center, getting a PICC line inserted. Meaning, they were going to snake a thin tube into a vein in my arm so I could get IV antibiotics. Unlike a normal IV, a PICC line would stay in long-term. Yikes! It was a big deal, so Dad had driven up for the appointment.

A nurse walked in, pushing a cart filled with supplies. "I'm going to stick this in your right arm, okay?"

Mom always encouraged me not to look at the needle as it went in. Following that advice, I held out my arm and turned my gaze to a painting on the wall. I felt the tube scrape the inside of my vein as it worked its way up toward my heart. This definitely hurt more than a blood draw. But soon the pain faded to numbness as the nurse placed a clear bandage over the insertion point.

She left, and a technician came to wheel me across the hall to the X-ray room. Mom and Dad stayed behind.

"Sit right here for me, okay?" The technician patted a tiny stool in front of me.

"I can't sit up straight," I told her. "I need to keep my back reclined."

"It will only take a minute."

I didn't like this woman. I wanted the other one back—she had let me stay in my lounge chair.

"Sweetie, I need you to sit here so we can make sure the PICC line is in the right spot. Please sit here." She motioned toward the stool again.

Continuing to argue would only make it harder to breathe, so I gave in. Switching over to the little black X-ray chair, I sat up as straight as I could, feeling lightheaded and woozy.

Then the awful woman placed her hand on my shoulder. "Ahh!" I yelped in pain, lurching forward. "Don't touch my shoulders!"

"Sweetie, you keep moving, so I have to place you in the right position."

As she reached toward me again, I leaned away from her and nearly fell off the chair.

"Stop moving!" she ordered. "Stay still, or I can't take the image."

I frantically looked around for my wheelchair and saw she had moved it across the room. There was no way out. Where were Mom and Dad? Shaking, I insisted again that she *must not* touch my shoulders.

Ignoring everything I had said, she planted her hand firmly on my shoulder blade, pushing me forward as she hissed, "Don't move," before running across the room to take the X-ray.

The skin on my shoulder burned, feeling like her hand was still pressed against it. I wanted to scream. I wanted to slam my elbow directly into her face, breaking as many bones as I could with one blow. I had told her not to touch me. *Repeatedly.*

Once I was back in the safety of the first room, the floodgates broke open.

"That X-ray better be good enough," I said through sobs, "because I am *not* doing that again!"

Mom held my hand, coaxing me to breathe as the first nurse entered again.

"So," she began, "unfortunately the tube went in the wrong way, and we need to adjust it."

Pulling out nearly the entire line, she tried again, pushing it back up through my now-bruised vein. I sat in my recliner, staring at the wall as hot pain shot through my right arm.

The evil technician returned once more, forcing me back into her dungeon for X-rays. When she told us that the PICC line was *still* not in the correct place, I snapped and erupted into the kind of outburst that had become my only way of coping with the mounting feelings of powerlessness I had come to expect in medical settings.

Dorothy

Despite Rachel's meltdown, we somehow left that appointment with a properly placed PICC line and, miraculously, a daughter who still seemed on board with the plan. Now we had a new activity to fill some of the hours not taken up with hyperbaric treatment: figuring out how to give daily infusions of IV antibiotics.

Here's what we learned from our experiences during this new phase of Rachel's treatment:

A peripherally inserted central catheter (PICC line) goes through a vein in the arm in order to reach the larger veins near the heart. It delivers intravenous medications without having to poke the patient with a needle each time, making the process quicker and less painful. Once a PICC line is installed, the patient is left with a tube sticking out of their arm at all times. It was almost like a little extension cord, always ready to have something plugged into it.

Each premeasured dose of Rachel's antibiotic came encased in a plastic device about the size and shape of a tennis ball, called an elastomeric pump. The ball pumps were already connected to tubing, which then connected to the PICC line. Delivered weekly to our door in an insulated pack, the balls had to be kept refrigerated, then brought out to reach room temperature before infusion. We had to go through a process that included flushing the lines with saline and heparin, an anticoagulant, before we connected the ball of medicine to the PICC line. This became a daily ritual.

One week after getting the PICC line installed, Mom and I were home for the weekend, and Christine came over for a visit. She sat in the office chair by my bed, holding up a little mirror as I adjusted the blonde wig on my head. I *loved* this wig. When I wore it, I could be a different person. With the wig on, I was April. April was older, successful, and could do anything she wanted. She wore makeup, carried herself with confidence, and had no stress or worries whatsoever. April didn't need to go to hyperbaric or to doctor's appointments. She didn't have PICC lines or medicine. She could walk and run and sit in a normal chair for as long as she wanted. April's life was perfect. Some days, I chose to be April all day.

While my real life—Rachel's life—was as far from perfect as I could imagine, it was getting more tolerable by degrees. By June, my hyperbaric treatments ended, and we officially moved back home. My pain remained untouched, but my brain seemed to work better. I could now comprehend information more easily, and the whiteboard of my memory didn't get erased as often. But I was mostly just grateful to be back in my own bed, with easier access to my friends.

Every Tuesday, a different home health nurse came to change the dressing on my PICC line. After a few weeks, a rash had broken out under the bandage, which continued to grow bigger and bigger each day. The nurses tried different things, but nothing seemed to help.

"Not getting any better?" The nurse, a balding man with a friendly demeanor, was referring to the rash on my arm and not my overall health status, but the answer was the same.

"No." I peered down at the angry red bumps crawling across my arm. "It's getting worse."

"Hmm," he said, furrowing his brow. "Let's just put gauze on it today. Gauze and hypoallergenic tape. Maybe the Tegaderm™ is causing it."

My friends were over during my at-home nurse visit today, and they continued the work of documenting my day-to-day experiences. Alicia picked up the camera in the corner, filming as the nurse carefully ripped off the old bandage and began to methodically clean my arm with rubbing alcohol. Alicia quickly lost interest in the process, turning the camera on Shira, then on herself as she made faces in the mirror.

The taste of saline filled my mouth as he flushed out the line. Heparin had an acquired taste as well, but the saline instantly turned everything to salt. The liquid wasn't actually going into my mouth, but for reasons I didn't understand, I could taste everything that was put into my line. One time, I'd been chewing cinnamon-flavored gum while flushing out the line with saline. Instantly, the wad in my mouth turned into a disgusting blob of gooey saltiness that never regained its original flavor. I didn't make that mistake again!

My at-home nurse visits weren't the only thing I spent my time videoing. I churned out clips about other aspects of my day-to-day life, such as taking pills, playing computer games with my friends, and making music videos. One of my favorite activities was perfecting my ability to lip-sync.

I'd become quite good at lip-syncing. Some people might see it as just mouthing along to someone else's voice, but those people would be wrong. Lip-syncing is a real skill that takes time to learn. You need to know not just every single word to a song, but also every pause, every breath, every sigh. To be great at lip-syncing, you need to be expressive with your eyes, and it's best to look directly into the camera to really grab your viewer's attention. While everyone else was in school every day, I was alone in my room, honing my lip-syncing and video-editing skills.

The best thing about making videos was that there were so many fun parts involved. Filming was great, because I got to become someone else and take my mind off my depressing reality. But then, once I was done filming, I could move on to the next step, which was editing the footage. I loved creating music videos and watching the whole thing come together. After the video was finalized, I got to watch it over and over to relive the experience. I'd show it to Mom and Dad, to my friends and Taylor. And when I was done with that, I'd make another one, and then another one. Because what else was I going to do?

CHAPTER 6

Soon It Will All Be Okay

When we entered the wheelchair store, Mom carried in my reclining lounge chair as per usual, but the man behind the counter said there was no need for it. He pushed out a black wheelchair, telling me to hop on. I was hesitant at first—it seemed like adults were always telling me there was "no need" for things that I actually did need just to be able to breathe. But I soon saw what he meant. The man pulled some levers behind the wheelchair and miraculously, the back reclined! Through some trial and error, we found the best angle for me, and he locked it into that position.

Wow! This was the most comfortable wheelchair I'd ever sat in! Since the back reclined, I could breathe without a problem, and the seat was so soft. It was also easy to maneuver. I spun around a few times and then pushed myself around the store, looking at all the different kinds of chairs on display. They came in every color, wheel type, and padding you could imagine.

Dorothy

We learned about reclining wheelchairs from the mother of one of Rachel's schoolmates. She was an occupational therapist and one day asked me if we have ever considered getting a reclining wheelchair for Rachel. A reclining wheelchair? I hadn't known such a thing existed. At that point, we were doing our best to minimize the time Rachel had to spend in her rented standard wheelchair because it was so uncomfortable for her. At home, she spent most of her time in the reclining hospital bed in her room. In the van, she always sat in the front passenger seat, which also leaned back. And if we went anywhere else, we carted along the patio lounge chair. A reclining wheelchair sounded like a gift from heaven.

Our family doctor prescribed it for her, and to our surprise and delight, the insurance company agreed to cover it. Out of pocket, it would have cost us about five thousand dollars.

"Rachel, come feel this," Mom said, pointing to a squishy pad. "It's cut-up pieces of memory foam."

I pushed myself toward the back table, still in awe that I could breathe while moving from one place to another. The memory foam was interesting, but not my favorite.

"The one I'm sitting on is better," I replied. It was a gel seat—squishy, fun, and very comfortable.

"Do you want to look at color options?" the man asked with a grin.

"No! I want green!"

But see, he already knew this. The first thing I'd asked when we had entered the store was if they could make me a lime-green wheelchair.

"You sure you don't want to look? You could get bright pink!" He was toying with me good-naturedly.

"Nope! Green!" I pushed away from the table, leaning against the headrest of the wheelchair as I took a long, satisfying breath.

We ordered a custom wheelchair with green legs, a gel pad to sit on, and a cushion with special air pockets to lean against.

"This will be ready for you to pick up in about a month," the man said.

"A *month*?!"

That felt like *so* long now that I knew freedom was out there.

Dorothy

For more than a year now, my days had been engulfed by caring for Rachel's specific needs—transporting her to medical appointments, sorting and delivering medications, preparing food, etc. Whenever she slept or was engaged with friends, I spent hours online searching the internet for anything that might prove useful. Even the websites of patient-oriented Lyme organizations didn't have much information to offer. I'd set up Google Alerts for any news articles mentioning Lyme disease and a few other related terms. At that point, such notifications showed up in my inbox about once a week or so.

The two online sites that proved most helpful to me were a chat board called LymeNet and a Yahoo group called CaliforniaLyme. Via these channels, I discovered the Lyme community—a loosely organized collection of patients, family members, advocates, and support groups. One day in June 2006, I read on LymeNet about *Under Our Skin*, a documentary about Lyme disease then in production. As someone who used to work in television news, I was immediately captivated by the idea.

This was precisely what we all needed—a way to cogently illustrate how the medical establishment continued to deny a huge threat to public health, basically abandoning patients and their families to search for their own way forward. Surely, a well-made documentary could garner national attention from the media and policymakers. Could it galvanize the Lyme community to bring about real change?

The more I thought about the film, the more convinced I became that such a project was critically needed. Open Eye Pictures, the production company, was fundraising to complete the project, and I sent in a donation. But I longed to do something more. How I wished I could somehow go to the Bay Area to help work on this documentary. Alas, given my current circumstances, that was only a pipe dream. But as I mused about the situation, I wondered if there was any small way I could contribute. I emailed Andrew Abrahams, director of *Under Our Skin*, and offered him my assistance. "I have some experience in writing, publishing, and publicity," I told him. "And I'm pretty good at tracking down info on the internet. I have a computer, phone lines, and a fax machine. Is there any task I could do for you (long-distance) to help get this project where it needs to be?"

Abrahams replied right away and gave me a research task. I was thrilled! He wanted to find copies of TV and newspaper coverage from the 1970s showing how Lyme disease had been reported by the press. I threw myself into the project one night after Rachel fell asleep, and soon located several troves of information. One was Vanderbilt University's Television News Archive, which billed itself as the world's most extensive and complete archive of television news. Using that source and others, I worked on the project for about a month—always when Rachel was asleep for the night—forwarding what I found to one of Andrew's assistants.

I loved this. For so long, I had been mired in the quicksand of my family's misery, and it had been hard to see myself as part of anything larger. Doing this research helped me shift my perspective. I learned more about the issues involved and took satisfaction from contributing to a larger cause. It expanded my world.

Two weeks before my new custom wheelchair was scheduled to arrive, Alicia and I were in my bedroom playing *Marble Blast Gold* on my iMac. Unlike most of my computer games that let you pick whatever level you wanted to play, *Marble Blast Gold* didn't offer that flexibility. You couldn't move forward until you'd beaten the previous level at least once. Sometimes Alicia and I played this all day and were lucky if we could advance even one level.

Mom walked in with a plate of fresh fruit and chicken drumsticks, which she set on the desk to the left of my bed.

"Thanks," I mumbled, not looking away from the screen.

Alicia reached for grapes, and I bit into a drumstick. The warm meat barely made it down my throat before I felt as if I was choking. It was like there was suddenly no oxygen around me. I coughed and forcibly inhaled miniscule amounts of air. Alicia dropped the grapes and ran out of the room, calling for my mom.

Dorothy

Rachel's food allergies came on suddenly and ferociously. A mere bite of something that had never troubled her in the past could make her throat close up, restricting her breathing and throwing her into a panic. Her reaction to almonds was especially strong. She couldn't eat them—or even be *around* them. One day I'd eaten some almonds right before walking into her bedroom. She started choking and gasping, apparently reacting to the almonds on my breath.

The attacks occurred randomly and inconsistently, so it was hard to get a handle on what was causing them. We started eliminating any food she reacted to—and soon, there was hardly anything she could eat. Her Lyme doctor prescribed antihistamines and an inhaler, which helped some. We had her tested for food allergies, with inconclusive results. And then, after a few months, much of the problem cleared up. She went back to eating most of the foods she'd been able to eat before—except for almonds. She continued to react badly to almonds and almond milk. For the longest time, I couldn't even bring them into the house.

It wasn't just my body's reaction to food that had us stumped. The rash on my PICC line arm continued to torment me. The at-home nurses had tried every type of dressing, every brand of medical tape, all to no avail. The red bumps now reached all the way to my wrist, torturing me 24-7. Nothing helped except numbing the area with ice packs.

Then there was another problem.

"*Umph*," I groaned. "It burns."

My PICC line had been fine that morning, but when I hooked it up to my IV, I felt a nasty stinging sensation as the fluid went in.

"I think it's punctured," the home health nurse said with a frown. "We need to take it out today."

She pulled back the bandage and began pulling on the line. Slowly, the blue tube emerged from my arm, feeling icky as it slid out of the vein it had been shoved into just a few months before. I was glad it was broken. With the PICC line gone, maybe I'd finally be able to make it through the night without scratching so deeply that I bled.

Yet, three days after my PICC line had been removed, we were already at a hospital to have a new one inserted.

"Put your arm out like this for me," a nurse in pink scrubs said, extending her own arm. "We're going to put the new one right here." She pointed two inches above where my first one had been placed. The same rash-covered arm but a different insertion point.

"We find that when the line is in the crease of the elbow, it's more likely to break. That's why I prefer using this vein right here."

She threaded the PICC line painfully up my arm like last time, then sent us down the hall for X-rays to check its positioning.

Mom set up my lounge chair in the X-ray waiting room. She and Dad read magazines while I listened to my iPod. I wanted to leave—I already knew it was in the wrong spot. I knew that was the only possible way this could go down, because we were talking about *me* here. I was Murphy's Law incarnate: Everything that could go wrong would go wrong.

After we'd been kept waiting for more than an hour, the overwhelming need to slam my head into a brick wall came roaring back with a vengeance. Enraged at the world, I wanted to scream at the top of my lungs just to communicate even a hint of the pain I felt on the inside. With all my heart, I wanted to find an elevator to the roof, climb up to the edge, and jump off. And I wanted every single doctor who'd ever said I was making this up to be there to witness my last moments so they could see what they'd done to me.

"I want to go home," I snarled at Mom.

She walked to the front desk and asked how much longer the wait would be.

"We have a number of patients ahead of you, so it will be a while."

After two hours of waiting in this godforsaken X-ray lounge, my name was finally called. Climbing into my wheelchair, I arranged my face into the most pissed-off expression I could manage as I followed the nurse to the back room.

After the X-rays, I waited in my lounge chair for someone to come tell us it was in the wrong spot. Finally, the nurse slinked over with a somber look in her eyes.

"Unfortunately, the PICC line is in the wrong position," she said, looking from my parents to me. "We need to remove it and insert a new one."

Of course they did.

Scrambling back into my wheelchair once more, we followed the nurse to an empty exam room.

"I am not doing this again," I said forcefully to Mom and Dad when the nurse left for new supplies.

"Sweetie," Mom started. "We're both right here."

"No." I opened the door, heading out into the hallway. "I'm leaving. I'm done."

Mom grabbed for my chair, but I pulled out of reach. "I'm *done!*" I yelled in disgust.

With my heart beating out of my chest, I looked around frantically. Where was the elevator? Mom and Dad stepped forward to speak with the doctor who had come to inquire about the commotion. I sat in the middle of the hall, frozen as I weighed the pros and cons of making a break for it.

"Rachel," Dad turned toward me, interrupting my plans. "Come back and sit in the lounge chair so you can breathe more easily."

"No!" I didn't want to breathe more easily. I didn't want to breathe at all! I wanted to stay feeling horrendously awful in the middle of this oxygen-deprived hallway because that was the only thing I could control. I felt my face start to tingle as my fingers turned numb.

Dorothy

Hospitals and medical offices aren't set up to deal with pain-ridden, emotionally volatile teenagers. If we could have gotten swiftly into the building, had the PICC line inserted, and then left immediately—things might have been different. Rachel could usually hold her composure for a certain amount of time, perhaps up to an hour. Frustratingly, our long wait in the lobby had exhausted her reserves before they'd even called her name. Then, when the procedure went awry, Rachel had a meltdown in the hospital corridor. I remember staring at the train wreck unfolding in front of me and wondering if we'd even be able to get out of that building in one piece. Yet somehow, we did. In the end, she had an intact PICC line in her arm, and we went home to lick our wounds.

A few days after my new PICC line had been inserted, I finally felt ready to take on another challenge. At least this wouldn't be in a doctor's office, thankfully.

"Are you ready?" Mom called from the bathroom.

We both knew I could only tolerate being out of my bed for a short time. Moving quickly, I transferred myself to the office chair and propelled down the hall to the bathroom by pushing against the wall.

Three chairs sat in a line leading up to the bathtub. I knew that lying flat across them would send extra pain rippling down my ribs and spine, but I did it anyway. I also knew that in just a few minutes, the reward of clean hair would be oh-so-worth it.

Mom wet my hair with the handheld showerhead, lathering me up with flower-scented shampoo, rinsing off the suds, and wrapping my head in a towel—all with the speed of a timed athlete. She then held the towel away from my shoulders as I got back onto the office chair.

This was the worst part, but I was prepared and knew it was coming. As soon as I sat up, the piercing pain of barbed wire wrapped tightly around my ribs, expelling all the air from my lungs. Mom swiftly returned me to my room. Then, as in a choreographed dance, she held the towel as I pulled myself up and into bed.

For a minute, my ribs remained on high alert, but soon the pain eased back to its regularly scheduled programming, and I could appreciate the glorious sensation of clean hair.

My patience was rewarded with more than clean hair, as it turned out. We learned that my new reclining wheelchair had finally arrived! As much as I'd been anticipating it, however, the reality didn't quite live up to expectations. For starters, this contraption was *huge,* and going out with it in public made me self-conscious. Mom wanted to celebrate the freedom of being able to go wherever we wanted now, so she and Dad took me to our favorite Mexican restaurant. But I felt awkward and embarrassed.

With my head leaning back and my legs sticking way out in front, it was like I was in a big stupid boat that kept getting in everybody's way. Any time the waiter led us to a table, we found my chair was blocking the aisle, preventing anybody else from getting past. When, for the third time, he said, "Maybe we should try this one over here," I just wanted to disappear and never come back.

I winced as someone bumped me from behind.

"Sorry!" a woman said as she headed to her table.

I shook my head and sighed. It wasn't her fault I was in the way.

The first week with my new wheelchair took a lot of getting used to. Because sitting in my previous wheelchair had made it hard for me to breathe, I'd never been up to pushing myself. But this new chair offered me the chance for some self-sufficiency. I immediately set a goal of propelling myself around the paved walkway that looped throughout our neighborhood.

My arms were weak at first, so it would take some work, but the athlete within me was giddy at the idea of a physical challenge to crush. And each night this week, I had slept all the way through without waking up. Mom thought all the exercise I'd been getting with my new chair was tiring me out.

The weather was quite warm—normal for August. But it wasn't too hot for a quick jaunt outside. I made it halfway around the loop before my arms gave out. Mom took over as we passed the grapevines and fruit trees that dotted our neighborhood. We stopped to taste the grapes, which sadly weren't quite ripe yet. Soon they would be, and our neighbors would get together for the annual harvest festival to celebrate and press them into juice.

As we neared the greenbelt by our house, I took back control of the wheels, determined to finish on my own. But then I ran into an unexpected obstacle.

"Yuck!" I stopped pushing and looked down. My right arm was covered with squished figs.

Our neighbor's fig tree had dropped purple fruit all over the walkway, which now coated both my wheels in a thin, mushy layer.

"This is so stupid!" I spat out. "Look! These stupid figs got all over me and my wheels!"

I was ticked and decided that the walk was ruined. We made it home and did our best to clean off the tires with water and rags, but I was empty inside once more. These days, it didn't take a lot to discourage me. Nothing ever went the way it was supposed to! I finally had something I cared about and wanted to work toward, but all I got was sticky crap all over me, just like everything else in my life.

"Maybe wear long sleeves?" Mom suggested.

I shot down that idea immediately. "Too hot." And we'd still have to clean both the sleeves and the wheels. I was annoyed, but not yet ready to give up. The next day, we tried our loop once more. As we rounded the greenbelt, I saw our neighbor standing outside his house, throwing a Frisbee for his dog. He waved at us, and we waved back.

"I cleaned up the figs for you," he said with a smile.

I looked down at the newly fig-free sidewalk in front of me. I didn't know it yesterday, but he must have heard me complaining about how his figs were ruining my life. And being a great guy and a good neighbor, he de-figged the path. For the first time in a long time, I felt listened to.

When the doorbell rang that Tuesday at 8:00 a.m., I knew who it was. And I was ready.

"I've got it!" I yelled, already wheeling to the front door. I flung it open and sang out, "Let's go on our tour, Taylor!"

Now that I had my new wheelchair, I would finally get to show Taylor all my favorite neighborhood places.

"Okay, we're leaving! Bye!" I called out to Mom, who had stayed in the house, as instructed. This was *my* time with Taylor, not hers.

Taylor walked next to me as I pushed myself down the path, telling her which of my friends lived in each of the houses we passed. I pointed out the redwood trees I used to climb as a kid and showed her my favorite fruit trees to snack on.

Taylor had become one of the most important people in my life, and I loved showing her around my neighborhood. And I appreciated that she was willing to hold our sessions at my house. She'd recently moved to a second-floor office in a building that didn't have an elevator. So, even with my new wheelchair, I wouldn't have been able to go there.

She'd been with me from the beginning, and unlike most other medical personnel I interacted with, Taylor was always on *my* side.

A day didn't go by without me jotting down something to tell her about in our next session. She knew each of my friends from the videos I showed her, and when I made a new movie, she was always eager to see it.

I didn't have to explain things to Taylor. She knew who my doctors were, and she'd even spoken on the phone to some of them. With her, I didn't have to put on a fake smile, like I did with every other adult outside of my family. I didn't have to pretend everything was okay—she knew it wasn't.

In fact, she knew I didn't have any hope that things would ever get better in the future. She always said, "I'll hold your hope for now, and you can have it back when you want it." It was cheesy as heck, but it took the pressure off me in a way. I could just exist and know that she was holding my hope that things would be better down the line. And that was good enough for now.

Dorothy

The reclining wheelchair widened Rachel's world in many ways, and the recently prescribed sleep medication allowed her to get a decent night's rest. It had been a while since she'd exhibited any memory lapses, those terrifying moments when she'd forget conversations shortly after they occurred. Was this due to her improved sleep? To the hyperbaric treatment? To the IV antibiotics we put through her PICC line every day? Or maybe it was the combination of all three? Though I didn't know the cause, I was gratified to notice that *something* about Rachel's condition seemed to be improving.

From Rachel's point of view, however, nothing had changed. Excruciating pain still wracked her body every moment of the day—period. She seemed most able to stay calm when she had friends around to keep her company. The neighborhood girls checked in with her when they could, but it was summertime. Tennis lessons, sleepaway camps, and family vacations filled their days, making them less available to hang out with Rachel. Jeremy had a summer job hours away, so he wasn't around either. It seemed like an auspicious time for Rachel to consider returning to school, which would start in the middle of August.

"Baby steps," advised Sandy, the Lyme-literate therapist I still regularly consulted by telephone. "See if you can start in the afternoon. Maybe just take one or two classes, at first?" Following Sandy's suggestions, we looked through the schedule and found two classes Rachel wanted to try—drama and Spanish. They were the last two periods of the school day, so we didn't have to grapple with early-morning start times. And they were right after lunch, so if Rachel wanted to, she could go early to eat with her buddies.

My junior high was only a short walk from our house, but it was still too far for me to negotiate on my own, even with the new wheelchair. Therefore, Mom pushed me to school each day at lunchtime. It felt good to see my friends again. My group ate at the same exact table we always had two years ago in seventh grade. I found my spot by the grass just as the bell rang, releasing hordes of students out into the halls like ants.

Shira dropped her backpack to the ground and took the seat next to me. Before long, our whole table was full. Lunchtime passed too quickly, as always, and soon Shira was pushing me to our drama class as we played our favorite game of "don't ram into students in the packed hallway." When we arrived, the classroom was locked. I situated myself in a corner, so I was less likely to be jostled from behind.

Jason, a guy we'd known since seventh grade, walked toward us. For God knows what reason, he reached out and planted his hands firmly on my shoulders, pressing down hard. It felt like shards of glass slicing through my skin! I bolted upright, pulling away from his hands. I desperately tried to keep from bursting into tears in front of all my classmates.

"Jason," I said as calmly as possible, while my hands shook uncontrollably. "Remember, you *can't* touch my shoulders. They *really* hurt."

He shrugged. "Come on, that didn't hurt you."

"Yes, it did. I've told you before, you can't touch my shoulders *even lightly.*"

"Uh-huh," he said as he wandered off toward a pack of boys across from us, clearly over this conversation.

I couldn't get a full breath in. It just stopped somewhere in my throat, and everything hurt ten times more than it had moments before. My shoulders, my back, and my spine felt as if nails were being hammered into them, splitting my bones into tiny fragments.

"Are you okay?" Shira asked.

I shook my head and whispered, "I need to go home."

Dorothy

Bizarrely, people seemed to go out of their way to touch Rachel's shoulders. Not just junior high boys acting like idiots, either. Some of the worst offenders were adults who probably thought they were being supportive—teachers at school, folks in the neighborhood, even strangers at the grocery store. When they saw a sweet young girl in a strange-looking wheelchair, they were suddenly gripped by an urge to give her a friendly pat on the shoulder—or die trying. Once, when Rachel and I were out for a stroll, a woman we didn't know greeted us with a kind word and a friendly smile. As I saw her hand reaching toward Rachel's shoulder, I stepped in to block her access. Keeping my tone pleasant, I said, "Excuse me, I have to ask you not to touch my daughter. That would be very painful." Even as the woman sputtered excuses and apologies, she kept reaching out her hand toward Rachel! I shifted my position to thwart her efforts, and we managed to extricate ourselves. In retrospect, it's funny. At the time, it was disturbing.

A week later, in the back of my drama class, Shira sat by me as we watched a silent movie that was supposedly a comedy. My heart started to pound as I took in the horrifying scene. The man on the screen was getting hurt—over and over—and his friends just stood by laughing. He was clearly injured, but no one even noticed his pain.

Looking over at me, Shira whispered, "Are you okay?"

It was hard to breathe. "I have to get out of here—now!" I sputtered.

She grabbed my backpack from the floor and walked to the front of the room. Leaning down, she whispered something to Mrs. Jones, the drama teacher, who looked back at me and nodded.

"I told her you don't feel well and I'm taking you to the office," she said once we were out in the hallway.

Visions of that man writhing in pain flashed through my mind as I waited for Mom to come get me. He was obviously hurt, but no one cared. I bet his doctor had even told him he was making it all up.

Dorothy

Many early silent films, such as the Charlie Chaplin classic *The Tramp*, included a lot of exaggerated physical comedy. These devices—such as pratfalls, tripping, and characters getting bonked on the head with heavy objects—became the hallmarks of early slapstick comedies. These movies were supposed to be funny and were routinely shown to student actors as part of film history classes. But this was exactly the wrong thing for Rachel to watch at that time. Although she'd started ninth grade anticipating that drama would be her favorite subject, the experience was tainted now. Rachel withdrew from the class.

After dropping drama class on the heels of my traumatic experience with Charlie Chaplin, I was back at school only for Spanish now.

Señora Lopez walked around the room. "Okay," she began, "I am assigning new seats, so please listen carefully." She started telling each student where they should move.

My friend Jenny sat beside me, and I met her gaze with a slight smile as our teacher walked over to us and whispered, "You two can stay where you are."

At the beginning of the year, when Señora Lopez had tried to move me away from Jenny, I told her that because I was in a wheelchair, I needed her close by to help me. That actually wasn't true, seeing as Jenny did nothing except make me happy—which was no small thing these days. But our teacher took the bait and, considering this was the third reseating arrangement of the year when Jenny hadn't moved, I thought it was safe to say we had Senora Lopez trained to our satisfaction.

After school, my friend and neighbor Christine pushed me home, giving Mom a break. I went straight to bed, put my computer, keyboard, and mouse in the right position, and turned on my music. I browsed through unused video clips in search of something to edit.

Lately, none of my friends had time to shoot new videos. Luckily, editing was something I could do on my own. It let me create my own reality and escape into a different world. Sure, going to school helped break up the day, but it was all an act, even after I dropped drama class. I put on a fake smile and played the role of a kid who remained positive even when dealt a bad hand of cards. But it was all a lie.

Scrolling through movie files on my hard drive, I opened an untitled folder and stumbled upon clips from our old camera—the one we'd used before I got sick. Opening a video I'd never seen before, I saw a girl playing in the snow at the Grand Canyon. Jeremy was filming her, and I watched as she slipped and slid on the ice. Twirling around like a dancer, she smiled and stuck her tongue out to catch the falling snow. I restarted the video and watched her twirl again and again. Staring at the screen, I studied the girl in the snow. She was wearing my clothes, but she wasn't me—this girl had disappeared long ago, before she'd had to endure any pain or suffering. I was grateful for that, because as I could see in this video, she was *weak*. She wouldn't have made it this far.

Dorothy

Since the onset of Rachel's health problems, our family hadn't traveled anywhere except to medical appointments. Occasionally, Rachel wistfully said that she wished we could go to the beach again, but that always seemed out of the question. Then, one day, I happened to see an article that mentioned beach wheelchairs. They were specially outfitted with wide wheels that could maneuver on sand and in the surf. It turned out that many beaches in California made them available for free or at a nominal cost. One of the places offering such wheelchairs was central California's Pismo Beach—not far from Jeremy's college in San Luis Obispo. In fact, Rachel had made a "dream vacation" poster about Pismo during those dreary times between hyperbaric appointments. Now, it seemed like this was one wish we could help make come true. Bob and I packed up, alerted Jeremy we were coming, bundled Rachel and her friend Christine into the van, and headed off on the first family vacation in what seemed like forever. We were all exhilarated.

Panting heavily, Christine tried her best to shove the wheelchair across the dry sand and finally gave up. It wouldn't move.

With wheels the width of hefty watermelons, this contraption was supposed to roll easily over the sand. But today it didn't.

Dad tried next, managing to propel us forward a whole inch. When I was not in the chair, they could easily push it across the sand. But with me in it, it wouldn't budge.

"Here," Jeremy interjected, handing Christine his bags filled with snacks and beach towels. "I've got this."

Grunting, he pushed with all his might, and the wheels began to turn slightly. He kept the pressure on, and the chair moved a bit further. And then a bit more.

"We need to keep it moving," Jeremy said with authority. "Once we have momentum, it's not that bad."

I was happy he was here, and not just to push the wheelchair. I missed him when he was at school.

His plan worked, and we made it across a big expanse of sand without too much trouble. He pushed the chair straight into an oncoming wave, and though the water was only a few inches deep, the wheels lifted off the ground and floated. For a moment I panicked—envisioning myself being pulled out to sea in my floating wheelchair as sharks circled below.

"Let's get out right here," I said, scooting out of my chair onto the wet sand.

The chilly water lapped over me, numbing my whole body—which actually worked to my advantage. I knew I'd pay for this over the next few days, with extra pain and fatigue, but it was worth it. Jeremy pulled the wheelchair back to safety, leaving it with Mom and Dad as he grabbed the video camera.

Playing in the sand at the water's edge, Christine and I created a family of sea people out of the kelp strewn along the beach, while Jeremy captured our actions on video. As we focused on our little creatures, a big wave crashed into us from behind, knocking us both over.

My arms slammed into the hard sand. Luckily, my vacuum-sealed PICC line protector did its job—the catheter appeared to be undisturbed.

Later in the day, at a beachfront restaurant, I ate clam chowder out of a bowl made of deliciously warm bread as we watched surfers just beyond the window. Months ago, when I'd planned this dream vacation, I'd chosen this exact beach, down to the very hotel we were staying in. I had even specified the bread bowls we were enjoying right that moment. Back then, I had never really thought it would've been possible for me to experience such things again.

Yet here I was.

Dorothy

The trip to Pismo was a magical respite for us all. However, too soon, we had to return to regular life. I pushed Rachel over to school for her Spanish class every day, we did daily infusions through her PICC line, and we watched a lot of Netflix. But one situation continued to worsen, no matter what we did. The skin around the catheter's insertion point got itchier and more inflamed with each passing day. Was she allergic to the adhesive on the bandages that were changed weekly? The IV nurses tried many different kinds— no change.

It had been four weeks since my dream vacation at Pismo Beach, and since that time things had only gone downhill.

My hands shook as I typed into my keyboard, "How much air in PICC line will kill you?"

The top link brought me to a forum where a bunch of people had already asked this very question. Skimming the page, I did my best to nail down specifics. What happened *after* I did it? How long would it take?

This horrible rash on my arm had been torturing me for months. No matter what we did, it wouldn't go away. Waking up throughout the night, I scratched uncontrollably until it bled—unable to return to sleep due to the ghastly raised bumps covering my entire right arm that were too painful to ignore.

Clicking on another link brought me no closer to answers. Would it hurt? Would it take hours? Would it be instantaneous? I wanted someone to sit here and tell me how this would play out, to tell me that this would finally make everything the way it should be.

Even with the help of antidepressants, I'd been in a downward spiral for a while now. What was the point of anything we tried? Nothing was working. There would be no happily ever after for me, and we all knew it.

I heard the faucet turn on in the kitchen—Mom was cleaning dishes, then. Dad was at work. Jeremy was away at college. I was here in my bedroom, alone.

Sitting up in bed brought on the familiar stabbing of barbed wire tightening around my rib cage as I reached over to my dresser. Feeling around for my hidden syringe, my hand located it under a napkin. I had planted it weeks ago after one of my IV infusions, preparing for the day when I'd need it.

Today was the day.

The hard plastic of the syringe pushed against my hand as I crawled back under the covers. Inspecting my arm, I saw that by coincidence, my PICC line happened to be covered with my repurposed dark-green soccer sock. The last team I ever played on. *Fitting,* I thought.

Silent tears fell as I attached the air-filled syringe to my PICC line. Everyone was right—*This too shall pass.* We just hadn't known that this was how it would happen.

Closing my eyes, I took in what it was like to be me one last time. Looking back, I thought my life hadn't been *so* bad. There were good parts, lots of them. But everyone had their time to go, and I had long surpassed mine.

I'd made it to fifteen.

Forcing breaths in and out of my lungs, I slowly pushed in the full syringe of air. Unhooking it from my PICC line, I gently placed it on the dresser next to my bed. No one would think anything of the syringe being there—no one would know how it happened.

As air bubbles passed through my chest, I felt sick and dizzy.

Bolting upright with the realization that I hadn't written a last entry in my journal, I reached for the keyboard. But as fast as I picked it up, I put it back down. I didn't want the last thing I did to be writing in my journal, alone. I wanted to be with Mom.

Transferring to my office chair, I used both hands to push off the wall, giving me momentum to reach the door. *What if I can't get out there in time?* I leaned forward, grabbing the handle, pulling myself toward the hallway. Pain screamed from my spine as I made my way down the hall and around the corner into the living room. I climbed into the hospital bed there and watched Mom preparing food at the kitchen counter.

"Hey, sweet girl," she greeted me cheerily.

I didn't usually come out here, but she didn't question it. In fact, I think she liked it. I watched Mom move around, washing vegetables at the sink and then moving over to the stove. All anxiety faded away, and the constant, pounding pain that I'd lived with for longer than I could remember dissolved into the background. I felt lighter than I had for so long as Mom's soothing voice described what she was making for dinner.

It was going to be okay. Soon it would all be okay.

CHAPTER 7

Just a Fluke

It didn't work. Holy *fuck*, it didn't work. I was still here—alive—in the hospital bed in the living room. The weight of this realization hit me like a boulder to the stomach. *What do I do now?*

I burst into tears and screamed, "I want this *gone!*"

Mom spun around from her position at the kitchen counter, blindsided. I'd gone from zero to sixty in record time.

"I want my PICC line out now!" I sat up straight, fueled by the added pain.

"I know, sweetie," Mom said, rushing over to me.

"No! You do *not* know!" My mind raced as I tried to get a handle on how to fix this. For *months* I'd kept this plan. I'd had an *out*. All this pain was supposed to *end*. And now it just didn't.

Hurling myself off the hospital bed, I purposely missed my office chair and fell straight to the ground. My knee slammed hard against the floor as the weight of my body collapsed on itself. Every rib exploded in pain. I wanted the world to see on the outside just how bad I felt on the inside. I let out an earsplitting shriek.

Mom ran into the office and shut the door behind her. Between screams, I heard her telling Dad that he needed to leave work and come home immediately.

"I want my PICC line *gone*! I will pull it out myself!" I shouted at her through the closed door. "I don't care anymore! I will pull it out myself right now!"

My throat and lungs burned. Breathing only fanned the flames. I looked desperately around for something to break. There was nothing but a piano, a couch, and a hospital bed in our living room. I scooted over and slammed my arms into the piano stool. It crashed down, spilling sheet music as it fell.

Mom came out of the office and took in the wreckage. She stood by the couch and sobbed. If my plan had worked, she wouldn't be crying right now. This would be over for her, too. I hated being such a burden to her. It hurt me more than my rib pain to see how hard this was for Mom.

This shouldn't be her life. She didn't deserve this.

Seeing her face knocked the wind out of my sails. "I want my PICC line gone *now*!" I whimpered.

"I know."

Dorothy

I had no inkling of what was actually going through Rachel's mind at that moment, of course. But as I watched her lurch around the living room, hurting herself and knocking over furniture, the whole situation just seemed too hard—for all of us. I had no clue what our next move should be. I'd previously held such high hopes that IV antibiotics would be Rachel's way out of this mess. In hindsight, we should have pulled the plug on them much sooner.

It had been seven days since I'd pushed air into my PICC line—and absolutely nothing had happened. Well, except my skin continued to itch like crazy, requiring me to scratch it 24-7. At night I couldn't sleep due to the insistent itch, and throughout the day I could think of nothing else.

Using my fingernail, I broke through the thin, sticky Tegaderm™ dressing, pressing into the irritated skin below. Fear of contaminating this sterile space didn't haunt me like it had my home health nurses. Interestingly, I saw blood seeping out from my PICC line. Well, that wasn't normal.

"Mom! My PICC line broke!"

Soon, we were crowded into my primary care physician's tiny white office that smelled strongly of antiseptic. Dr. Caddel leaned over me, examining the leaking catheter and pulling back the adhesive, exposing the line as he gently guided it out an inch.

"Just like this, nice and easy." He handed the line to me.

I met his gaze. "Wait, I can pull it out myself?"

"Yeah, go for it. Be gentle."

I pinched the narrow tube with my left hand, pulling sideways carefully so as not to snap the already weakened silicone line. Going in, it had felt painful, but coming out, it just felt like I was pulling a long worm from my body. Dr. Caddel brought up my chart on his computer, noting that he was sending us home with a medicated ointment for my rash. There was no mention of anything suspicious.

"These things happen," he said with a shrug. "It could be because you move your arm so much, pushing your wheelchair. Or it could just be a fluke."

Yeah, or it could be the full syringe of air I forced through its tiny circumference a week ago, I thought but said nothing.

Over the next few days, I watched with satisfaction as my rash diminished in both color and size. With no incessant itching keeping me up at all hours, my sleeping pills could finally do their job, allowing for uninterrupted, desperately needed sleep.

Dorothy

I had braced myself for some new, awful thing to befall us after we stopped Rachel's IV antibiotics. But, in fact, that's not what happened. Instead, our Lyme doctor switched Rachel to a couple of different oral antibiotics, and without the constant irritation of the PICC line, the fiery rash on her arm cleared up. Rather than being worse after stopping the IVs, it seemed as if Rachel got a bit better—a little calmer, a little more tolerant of each day's challenges. She had wanted the PICC line gone—and that had happened. Did she feel more in control of her life?

It would be years before we finally figured out what had caused such severe skin inflammation on her arm. It turned out that Rachel had developed an acute allergy to rubbing alcohol—one that continues to this day. The nurses used rubbing alcohol liberally every time they changed her IV dressing. The possibility that she was allergic to it hadn't occurred to anyone. I don't know how it might have changed the timeline of her treatment if we'd made the connection sooner.

My Lyme doctor, Dr. Landers, said I needed to visualize myself walking and living a pain-free life. I thought that was complete crap, and here's why: I didn't remember what it felt like to live without pain. How could I visualize something I couldn't even comprehend? What did a person feel like when their body wasn't bombarded by a constant stream of pounding, burning, throbbing sensations?

I was also royally offended at his insinuation that if I just imagined a better future, it would magically come true. What complete bullshit. Screw him.

Dorothy

Several years before she got sick, Rachel had watched the film *The Miracle Worker,* about the life of Helen Keller and her teacher, Anne Sullivan. As a result, she had become fascinated by the idea of communicating with her hands and had asked Jeremy to help her find the American Sign Language alphabet on the internet. After printing out an ASL chart, she'd spent the rest of that day teaching herself to fingerspell. Because of her enthusiastic interest at that time, we had tried to find an ASL class for her, but nothing was available. We did arrange a few sessions with a Deaf woman who offered private tutoring, but that all fell by the wayside at the onset of Rachel's health problems.

Fast-forward to November 2006. The PICC line was out, Rachel was on different medications, and she seemed to have gotten some of her old spark back. One day, out of the blue, she said, "Mom, I want to take an ASL class." After a brief internet search, I discovered a church across town that had a Deaf ministry and offered free weekly ASL classes to anyone in the community. We signed her up right away.

It was the second week of my American Sign Language class. After Mom pulled the van into the church parking lot, my eyes flitted from car to car, checking to make sure no one watched as I transferred into my wheelchair. Today was going to be different than last week, when I'd attended class with Shira. This time I would be flying solo, since Shira's new schedule of tennis lessons conflicted with ASL from here on out.

Mom opened the door, and I pushed myself through, being extra cautious not to scrape the wall as I entered the building. Energetic voices rang out down the hall from people gathering in the adjacent room.

"I'll be right here," Mom said, motioning to a chair in the hallway. She knew I didn't want her in the classroom with me.

"Hello there!" the teacher called out. "It's Rachel, right?"

"Yes! Hi!" I replied. He remembered my name!

Sheila, a woman about Mom's age, whom I'd met last week, headed straight for me.

"Hello again! So happy you can join us!" She handed me a paper with the list of signs we'd be learning today.

As I positioned myself out of the way so people could pass by without bumping me, a clicking noise caught my attention. I turned and saw a woman using a walker. Oh, thank God—I wouldn't be the only person who was different here!

"Maggie! Great to see you!" our instructor said with a wave.

Maggie smiled at him, turning briefly to wink at me. She parked her walker right beside me, asking my name as she took a seat.

Maggie, Sheila, and I worked together on the day's assignment. We were learning family signs, so I told them I had a mom, dad, and a nineteen-year-old brother named Jeremy. I asked them similar questions about their families. To my relief, my new classmates didn't inquire about my health or ask why I was in a wheelchair. Instead, we focused on learning this thrilling secret code that allowed us to communicate without speaking. The time flew by, and soon class was over.

Reluctantly, I said goodbye to my new friends and headed back to the hallway to find Mom. "I'm ready!" I said enthusiastically.

"Was it fun?"

"It was amazing!"

Dorothy

Rachel's weekly ASL classes marked a turning point for our family. She seemed energized and excited about learning this new language—a level of enthusiasm she'd never shown for ninth-grade Spanish. The class also provided some friendly interaction with people of various ages in a low-key setting. This was a far cry from the often-oppressive social hierarchy so prominent in junior high.

The class was held across town from us, which made it impractical for me to return home after dropping Rachel off. I needed to occupy myself nearby for about an hour, so I took to shopping at a neighboring market and treating myself to a cup of hot chocolate at the in-store café. Soon, my husband joined me on these weekly "grocery store dates," and all three of us found ourselves looking forward to Monday nights.

On Christmas Day, we celebrated together at my godmother Mary's house. A crisp wind pierced my jacket as Jeremy steered my wheelchair down the uneven sidewalk. Mary's twelve-year-old son, Brendan, came with us, pushing the new dirt bike he'd found under the tree that morning. Brendan's dad and my dad walked at the tail end of our parade.

When we reached the deserted parking lot of the nearby library, Brendan climbed on his bike and sped away, engine roaring. As I watched him go, a pang of longing rippled through my body. I wanted what he had! *So* badly! Nearing the end of the lot, Brendan turned around, barreling back toward us, the sound of his vehicle reverberating as he approached.

With calm conviction, I turned to Dad. "I want to ride the dirt bike."

"What? Oh, I don't know about that," he replied as Brendan screeched to a halt in front of us.

I *needed* this. "Please! I really want to! I can do it!" I pleaded, "I can sit up on it! And the controls are all with my hands! *Please*, Dad?"

He looked at the bike, and to my complete surprise, nodded his head slowly. Brendan handed me his yellow-and-black motorcycle helmet, which felt unexpectedly heavy when I placed it on my head. Kicking off his shoes, Brendan stood barefoot on the cold concrete as he bent down to put them on my feet. I hadn't worn anything more than socks for nearly two years, and I was taken aback by how bulky the shoes felt.

Jeremy held my wheelchair steady while I made the move to Brendan's bike. I lifted my leg over the black padded seat, grabbed the handlebars, and scooched onto my new ride. Once in place, I wiggled my toes in Brendan's shoes with a smile. I felt *cool*. I *was* cool.

As Brendan explained which gears did what, a car drove past us on the street. I was delighted by the idea that the unknown driver saw me as someone who wasn't sick. To him, I was just a badass chick who rode motorcycles in empty library parking lots on Christmas Day.

Jeremy stood behind me, promising Dad that he and Brendan would never leave my side. Intoxicating adrenaline flowed through my veins, numbing the always-present pain in my spine.

"Okay," I said, ready to go. "Bye!"

With a flick of the throttle, the motorcycle lurched forward, yanking me with it. Brendan and Jeremy sprinted next to me. I leaned on the throttle and left them in my dust.

Wind blasted against my face, ripping my hair back and whistling through my helmet. Turning 180 degrees, I met back up with the boys, slowing down as they ran beside me.

"I'm doing it!" I yelled to Jeremy over the roar of the engine. He answered with a quick thumbs-up.

Returning to my starting point, I realized that I didn't know how to stop this machine! Brendan and his dad yelled to pull back on something, but I could barely hear them. Engaging the brake too late, I hit the curb, lurching forward and then backward as Jeremy and Brendan worked to steady the bike under me.

Dad ran over with the video camera in hand. "What do you think, Rachel?" he asked, as if interviewing me for the evening news.

"Very cool, man!" I said, punching my fist in the air. "I'm riding a motorcycle!"

I knew I'd have to pay for these past few minutes—probably by spending the next few days stuck in bed due to increased back pain—but right then, I couldn't stop smiling.

CHAPTER 8

Some Rabbits Need Wheelchairs

With heavy eyelids, I leaned back against the fluffy soccer-ball pillow that I always used in my wheelchair. This math tutoring session was putting me right to sleep.

Why was this woman droning on about whether the Greeks did or didn't believe zero was a number? I hadn't even asked about zero. We hadn't even been *talking* about zero. For heaven's sake, the assignment was on "distributive property."

I stifled a yawn and tapped my pencil on the paper in front of me. "How do I do *this* problem?" I asked, trying to move the conversation along.

"Oh," she said, peering down at the packet. "Remember that car we were driving in earlier? In this picture over here?" She pointed to a stick figure drawing she'd made to illustrate the associative property at the beginning of our session. "Well, the car isn't going to get there if the pickle and the squash aren't driving it, and the pickle won't talk to the squash if it doesn't feel like it. So obviously the answer to that question is $2(x-2+4) = 65.23445$." *Well, obviously.*

I didn't know how to respond to that. Why was she talking about pickles and squash? I was too tired to even think about it. Finally, I heard the sweet relief of bells as Mom entered the tutoring center to save me. As soon as we left the building, my fatigue evaporated. I hated this pattern of being so exhausted when forced to do math, but as soon as I was done, I felt fine. Why couldn't I be fine while I was doing math?

Dorothy

Although Rachel's physical pain hadn't diminished, she definitely seemed more clearheaded than she had the previous year. Not wanting her to fall too far behind her grade level at school, I had started looking into the availability of online classes— which, in 2007, weren't common. At first, I couldn't find any program that suited our needs. They all had precise start and stop dates and firm deadlines for completing assignments. None of them made allowances for students who might need extra time to finish the coursework. Then, somebody told me about Brigham Young University's online high school program. Rachel could start a class at any time, move at her own pace, and have up to a year to complete an individual course. This looked like it might work for us.

To try it out, we signed up for the first semester of ninth-grade English, and she had no trouble with it. Then we tried algebra, and that turned out to be a whole other beast. While I'd been able to oversee her English lessons, algebra was out of my league. And though my husband used quite a bit of math in his work, teaching algebra concepts wasn't in his wheelhouse either. We signed Rachel up at a math tutoring center in our town, using the BYU online program as a guide for her course of study.

When the tutoring service didn't work out, we hired a pleasant young woman who was majoring in math at the local university.

She came to our house twice a week to help Rachel prepare for the first semester's final exam in the online algebra class. This tutor was a cheerful person who seemed able to communicate math concepts to Rachel in a relatively painless way. Rachel liked her, and they had fun together. She was also patient and kind with my daughter's occasional memory lapses.

When Rachel got a C on the final exam, we all celebrated it like the great victory it was. Funny how our standards had changed. Pre-Lyme, Rachel would have felt like a failure if she'd gotten anything less than an A. But at this point, we had a new motto at our house: Just do what it takes to get through high school. We treated each class as if it were pass/fail. In terms of qualifying her for graduation, a C worked just as well as an A.

After leaving that less-than-helpful tutoring session with the squash lady, Mom and I felt we could both use some shopping to help reset the day. We entered a department store with a pretty good track record of having clothes I liked and headed for the Juniors department.

"Look!" I pointed at the mannequin on display. "Sparkle jeans!"

They were beautiful! They looked like something straight out of Hannah Montana's personal collection. We gathered a few things to try on and made our way to the dressing rooms.

A sign on the accessible stall read: "SORRY FOR THE INCONVENIENCE. THIS AREA IS BEING USED FOR STORAGE."

"You've got to be kidding me," I muttered. We found a clerk sorting through clothes on the display racks. "I can't fit in the regular stall," I told her. "Is there any way I can use the wheelchair-accessible one?"

She walked to the stall and opened the door. Floor-to-ceiling boxes occupied most of it. Mom and I rolled our eyes at each other but voiced no complaints. Instead, I said, "I think there's room for me to squeeze in there," and I did.

Later, on the drive home, my mind filled with all the epic movies I planned to make while wearing these incredibly awesome sparkle jeans.

Dorothy

As Rachel became more willing to go out and about, we often found ourselves in places that claimed to be wheelchair-accessible but certainly were not. Once, Rachel and I tried on clothes in the accessible dressing room of a well-known national retail chain. When it came time to leave, we couldn't open the door to get out. Somebody had parked a line of shopping carts in the little hallway in front of the dressing room, blocking our exit. When I stood on a chair in the stall and peeked over the doorway, I didn't see anybody around to help. I had to shout until somebody heard me and came to move the carts. If no one had responded, I suppose I could have called the store's switchboard on my cell phone. Luckily, it didn't come to that.

Another time, we went to a movie matinee, figuring the theater was less likely to be crowded on a weekday afternoon. We nabbed a wheelchair space in the back row that was right next to a seat for me. So far, so good.

The issue came in the middle of the movie when Rachel needed to use the bathroom. As we approached the restroom, a young woman walked in right ahead of us. Although there were plenty of available stalls, she bypassed them all and marched directly into the wheelchair-accessible one at the far end. Since we couldn't use any of the other toilets, we waited. And waited. And waited. Finally, she emerged from the stall, and Rachel went in. Since then, I have made it a point of honor not to use the accessible stall when there are other options. You never know who might enter right after you, in desperate need.

It had been a few months since my sparkle jeans had entered my closet, and I was happy to report that, even after multiple washings, they hadn't lost much glitter at all. However, I wasn't wearing my sparkle jeans today; they were saved for school and other special occasions when I wasn't just sitting in my room all day. No. Today, like most days, I was wearing my green Care Bear pajama bottoms.

Alicia sat in the office chair next to my bed as we played Five Crowns for the millionth time this week.

"I win!" she squealed, clapping her hands and thrusting her fist in the air. We played Five Crowns for what felt like hundreds of rounds each day, so winning wasn't what actually excited her at this moment. She only cared because winning meant she got to sign the score sheet in our notebook.

Recently, we'd begun having the winner autograph the score sheet. I'm not gonna lie—it raised the bar big-time, and now everyone in our friend group took winning very seriously.

As Alicia signed her name along the bottom of the page, we suddenly heard rain slamming against the skylights in the adjacent sunroom. Rain! The heavens had broken open.

"Rachie!" she squealed in delight, knowing my love of rain. "Let's go!"

"Where's the tarp?" I called out to my parents, sliding from bed to the office chair and down the hall to my wheelchair. Dad handed us the tarp and Alicia and I bolted through the front door, not wanting to miss even a drop of the precious stuff falling from the sky. The rain was really coming down in buckets. My all-time favorite weather!

Alicia sat on my lap, and we covered ourselves with the tarp, making a fortress against the deluge. It was hard to describe my relationship with rain. Joyful, childlike elation didn't begin to scratch the surface.

When I'd been a little kid, whenever the skies opened up, my mom would say, "Time for a rain walk!" We'd put on raincoats, rain pants, and rain boots, and race outside to witness the world transforming around us. Puddles came together as if by magic, turning leaves into imaginary boats. And the sweet scent of wet earth enveloped us like a comforting hug.

Rain walks were different now—my wheelchair got soaked, and we hadn't found a great way to protect it when it was moving. So, I'd learned to enjoy rain *stays* instead. It wasn't the same, and if truth be told, I yearned for the days of rain walks with my mom. But this was good, too.

Alicia giggled, musing aloud as to what our neighbors were thinking right now, seeing us sitting out under a tarp in front of my house. I was snug and satisfied within our sanctuary, as the glorious essence of rain recharged my batteries and raised my spirits.

Lifting my foot made the tarp crackle loudly. I peered down at my damp socks, put on by yours truly that morning. For more than a year now, I had been at the mercy of my parents or Alicia, or sometimes Shira, when it came to putting on my socks. But recently, after a change in medication, I'd been able to tug them on really quickly, all by myself. It was a victory—small but crucial, and not unnoticed.

Dorothy

Some days, Rachel seemed capable of pushing her pain into the background and focusing on something else. For instance, she would shoot videos with her friends and spend hours editing them, often teaching herself new techniques. One time, she and Alicia painstakingly created a Claymation-style cartoon. First, they fashioned little figurines out of modeling clay and devised a storyline to go with them. Then, they carefully shot the video one frame at a time. After each one, they'd move the figures slightly, and then shoot another frame. The result was an animated video, where the characters appeared to move on their own. I was astonished at their creativity, patience, and skill. Surely, I thought, Rachel's ability for sustained concentration on this meticulous project meant that treatment was helping, that she was getting better. Wasn't she?

Yet her energy and willingness to participate in life ebbed and flowed. On other days, the toll extracted by the continuous pain seemed insurmountable. She'd stay in bed for hours, despondent and fatigued, uninterested in talking, eating, or doing anything at all. I'd try my best to bring her out of this depressed state ("Let's watch *Gilmore Girls*! Let's paint a picture!"), but she didn't want me there. Sometimes, I'd go into my bedroom, shut the door, and quietly cry.

During these times I would try to remember what Sandy often said during our therapy sessions: There will be ups and downs. Don't ride the emotional roller coaster.

Today was the day! Christine, Shira, Alicia, and I were filming our remake of the first episode of *Hannah Montana*. While my friends had been in school or at their various sports practices, I'd carefully gone through the episode and copied down each word so we could work from the exact script. I was playing Hannah Montana and got to wear my sparkle jeans!

Dad had built us a huge blue screen, which I had learned was a tool used to create special effects. It was a ten-by-ten piece of plywood, painted bright blue. Filming in front of it let us edit in a different background later. Dad had constructed it in our carport, placing the blue screen upright against the side of our shed. I slipped out of my wheelchair, lowered myself to the concrete driveway, and crawled in front of the screen. With the help of my shock-absorbing knee pads, I balanced on my knees and Christine angled the camera to make it look like I was standing normally. Later, after editing, I would appear to be standing on a stage full of shining lights, singing at a real concert.

I was at my best when I was engrossed in a project requiring so much attention that my brain couldn't focus on how much my body hurt. Filming offered me a break, both physically and mentally. When Shira turned on the music, I *transformed* into Hannah Montana. The beads on my white, sparkly tank top danced back and forth with my every move.

I batted at the blonde wig as it fell in my face, waved to the imaginary fans in front of me, and then began lip-syncing to the song "Just Like You."

When neighbors walked by as I was performing, I could only imagine what they were thinking. When they saw me out of my chair, balanced upright on my knees and smiling, I bet they thought, *Oh wow, she's so much better!*—as if they knew anything about what was happening with me. It made me so mad! It was the same when we went to our neighborhood potlucks, and I overheard grownups telling my parents how happy they were to see that I was improving. I *wasn't* improving! I found stupid comments like these very upsetting.

Mom assured me these were "well-meaning" remarks, but I didn't see it that way. I'd been in pain every second for two full years now. And statements like that, well-meaning or not, came from ignorant people who didn't know what it was like to live the way I did. If they didn't see me cry or at least scowl, did they think that proved I wasn't sick? They didn't understand that sometimes I could smile or laugh—or lip-sync to Hannah Montana—while the pain pounded up and down my spine as strongly as ever.

For months now, fears of these unwanted judgments had kept me inside the house or behind the safety of my fenced-in backyard. Whenever I heard, "I'm so glad you're feeling better," it infuriated me. How *dare* they tell me how I felt? They didn't see the panic attacks, the hours of screaming, or the hole I'd kicked in my bedroom wall. They didn't see my journal, where I wrote almost daily that I wanted to die and leave behind all the pain and suffering.

They didn't know that when they saw me outside with friends, I was putting on an act for both the world and myself. I was pretending that for just a moment, I was a normal fifteen-year-old girl. Yet, instead of just saying "hello," they undermined my truth and helped only themselves to feel better about the situation.

A week after filming our remake episode of *Hannah Montana*, my body had been herxing in a big way from a change in medication. I'd been out of school the past few days because of it. A heavy, invisible weight pinned down my arms and legs in bed, rendering them useless. I had no energy to do anything. *Gilmore Girls* played softly in the background, but I didn't have the strength to pay attention to it.

Then, the doorbell rang, and I heard Mom open the front door. In walked Jenny and Cassie, two friends from school, who had come for a surprise visit.

As they dropped their heavy backpacks on the floor of my bedroom, I instantly felt what my family had come to refer to as "the

Jenny and Cassie effect" ("J&C effect" for short). It was a magical phenomenon. When I was in the presence of Jenny and Cassie, I could somehow stave off added symptoms and distress. Whenever I herxed now, Mom's first suggestion was always, "Why don't you call Jenny and Cassie?" because it was *that* helpful. The only drawback was that once they left, the herx symptoms came back just as strong as ever. The magic only worked when they were physically present. But we took what we could get.

"We have a proposal," Jenny said, plopping into the chair next to my bed. "Would you help us make a video for our book report?"

Basking in the temporary relief of the J&C effect, I listened as the girls animatedly explained that if they made a video book report, their teacher said they wouldn't have to actually write one.

"Let's do it," I said. Harnessing strength I hadn't felt for days, I pulled the computer table over to take notes.

A few weeks later, Jenny and Cassie returned with their completed script about the book *Lily's Ghosts*.

"All of the ghost parts need to be done upstairs on the green screen," Jenny commented. The novel featured a teenage girl who spent the summer in a haunted house. Although most of the movie would be filmed downstairs, each scene where Jenny played the ghost had to be shot upstairs, on the green screen Dad had set up for us there.

There were different scenarios where a blue or green screen would be the preferred option for special effects. But for our purposes, it came down to what the actors were wearing. You couldn't wear blue in front of a blue screen, or green in front of a green screen, without being rendered invisible. My dad also helped us set up studio lights for the green screen upstairs, which were critical for this project.

It was Saturday, and we'd carved out all morning to film. The hardest parts would be the ones we did upstairs, because I'd have to be out of my wheelchair during that time. I would need to crawl up the stairs and scoot around on my hands and knees from there. Not being able to lean back at a reclined angle would also be a problem for sure.

We started with the scenes we could film downstairs in the kitchen so I could stay in my wheelchair for the time being. Holding the camera in front of me, I sat as still as possible, so my wheels wouldn't creak and ruin the take.

I loved this project. I loved that *I* was needed, for a change. I was usually the one doing the needing.

When Jenny stumbled over her line and stopped to look at the script, I set the camera on my lap and leaned back in my wheelchair. My spine hurt a lot more now than it had before we'd started filming. What I really needed right now was to go back to bed for the rest of the day. But tough. I'd just have to power through it.

I never understood how some people could take a short break and actually feel better after it. The only way my back pain would lessen is if I got into bed and stayed there. But that wasn't an option, so I pressed on.

When it was time for the scenes upstairs, I employed the "backward push-up" technique I'd devised to get up to the second floor. I started by sitting on the bottom step with my back to the stairway. Then, pushing hard with my arms, I hoisted myself up to the next step. Slowly, carefully, I continued the process until I reached the top. I was out of breath and my arms were tired, but I didn't let that stop me. We set up the tripod, so I didn't have to hold the camera, and I leaned forward in a contorted position that released some pressure from my back. The more we filmed, the more eager I was to start editing the footage. This would be my first professional movie! And my name would be in the credits for their whole class to see!

Dorothy

Our Lyme doctor told us about the importance of detoxing. A Lyme patient's body can become clogged with toxins, making it hard to eliminate the bad stuff and blocking the entry of good stuff, like medications and supplements. He recommended some sessions with an alternative healer who specialized in specific detoxification protocols for Lyme patients. The practitioner was located in Nevada, about a three-hour drive from our home.

Today was our first session with the new naturopathic doctor, a woman named Grace, who was going to help my body detoxify. It had been a long, uncomfortable drive to Nevada, but we finally arrived at a two-story building with no elevator. There was a waiting area on the first floor, but the main office was upstairs. Mom went up to tell them we were here, while Dad and I stayed below.

To pass the time, I read *Wise Girl*, a book about an actress named Jamie-Lynn Sigler who'd gotten Lyme disease while working on a series called *The Sopranos*. I'd loved *The Sound of Music*, and thinking her show was about a family of singers, I'd ordered the first installment of Season 1 on Netflix. (Spoiler alert: It turned out to be about the Mafia. Surprise!)

I wasn't very far along in the book when a tall woman with glasses descended the stairs and smiled at us. Introducing herself, Grace took a seat in the waiting room and began going through my health history. Then she asked if there was any possibility that I could make it up the stairs.

I liked her, so I offered to climb the stairs like I did at home. I slipped out of my chair and employed the "backward push-up" maneuver. These were the steepest stairs I'd ever encountered.

Upon reaching the top, I peered down the hall, catching the eye of a woman in the upstairs waiting room. Embarrassed to be seen on the floor, I turned away, watching as Grace and Dad carried my wheelchair to the top.

Grace spoke about the importance of supporting the body while going through Lyme treatment. She handed over a gargantuan list of supplements for me to take daily, in the hopes that they would help us get beyond this plateau we'd encountered with my treatment.

Grace pointed to three columns on the paper, indicating breakfast, lunch, and dinner. Placing a checkmark next to each column, she painstakingly explained the reasoning behind each supplement and the time of day they were needed. I stopped listening after she noted that I needed to take fifty chlorella pills each day. *Fifty!* All before breakfast! Yeah, we were done here.

We left feeling less than uplifted. But we'd be back in a few weeks.

The following weekend, Christine was sitting next to my bed, playing Tetris.

"Oh my gosh! That looks perfect!" I squealed, replaying the video clip on my computer. "Look at that!"

Christine looked up to see my latest edit. Earlier today, after we'd filmed me pushing my wheelchair up to the car door, we had pulled a switch. Off camera, Christine and I had swapped clothes, and then she'd sat in the wheelchair. I'd filmed her standing up and getting into the car. In the edited video, the transition from me to her appeared flawless. From that angle, we could only see her from the back, and it looked like *me*. Like *I* had stood up out of the wheelchair and walked. Mesmerized by what we'd created, I replayed it over and over.

We did lots of these special effects videos now, filming on the blue screen nearly every weekend. Sometimes, the final product showed us flying on broomsticks. Or using superpowers to blow things up. We'd be seen teleporting from one location to another, moving objects with a flick of our wrists, or looking like we both were standing. With the help of the blue screen, I could go anywhere, do anything, be anyone. And I *loved* it.

Dorothy

As Rachel neared the end of her ninth-grade school year, she was doing better in many ways. I knew she was still in constant pain, but I was proud of the times she could rise above it and find ways to enjoy life anyway.

So, I thought nothing of it when a school counselor asked me to come for a meeting to discuss Rachel's plans for the tenth grade. I was thrilled with the headway my daughter was making. Previously, she'd been unable to retain information from even a single paragraph, and now she could hold her own while studying Spanish, English, algebra, and American Sign Language. She was still in pain, still needed a wheelchair, and still struggled with fatigue and other symptoms—but her mind was clearing. Working on her classes in small bites, an hour here and there, with plenty of rest in between, allowed her to make steady progress. Additionally, producing videos with her friends had unleashed an astonishing level of creativity. I now saw her inner spirit waking up after lying dormant for ages. Hope had returned to our house!

Regrettably, that was not how her school saw things at all. I walked into that meeting expecting to see a guidance counselor. Instead, I was met with a committee of people, including a district administrator who seemed very unhappy with me. She said it had recently come to her attention that Rachel was attending only one class at the junior high. She said this violated district policy and was grounds for charges of truancy. With the school year almost over, she'd let it go for now. However, she warned me, high school would be a different story, and we shouldn't expect to "get away with anything."

Is that what we'd been doing for the past two years? *Getting away with something?* I patiently tried to describe Rachel's health problems and offered a letter from our doctor. The administrator didn't want to hear it. When I told the committee about Rachel's progress in English and algebra, one of them sputtered angrily, "You can't honestly believe that an online class is as good as sitting in school with a trained teacher!" I was flabbergasted. Was that what they thought I was saying? I was trying to meet my daughter's medical and educational needs, which sometimes conflicted with each other. I explained to the committee that because Rachel's ability to do schoolwork was improving, she hoped to take two classes at the high school the following year—drama and English. They stared at me as if I were speaking a foreign language. Not possible, they said. In order to take two classes at the high school, she would be required to take an additional four classes through the district's independent study program. I knew these were not online classes. The program involved meeting with a teacher in person once a week and working out of the textbook on her own the rest of the time.

Six classes at once? That was a big leap. Hadn't anything I'd said sunk in? Rachel was in no position to attempt a full schedule. While cheering her progress, Dr. Landers had strongly advised us not to let her take on too much at once. He said he'd seen too many kids with Lyme begin to improve, return to full-time schooling, and then have a serious relapse. Following his guidance, we wanted to gradually ramp up her activity, one baby step at a time.

Two classes at the high school might not have seemed like much to this committee, but it would be a huge undertaking for Rachel. If she could manage that, we might slowly increase her workload. Of course we wanted her back in school. But we didn't want to set her up for academic failure or a medical setback. That's why we'd wanted to start with only those two classes. Not possible, the school committee insisted. I left the meeting disheartened, unsure of what to do next.

Today was the beginning of the last week of ninth grade, and I had a full schedule! This morning I'd see Taylor for therapy, and right after that, I would have my last session with the math tutor before taking my online final later this week. Then, I'd go to school for Spanish, and after that, on to my new acting class where I would take part in an upcoming production of *Peter Rabbit and Friends*. I played Peter's mother. As it turned out, some rabbits need wheelchairs!

Acting breathed life into me. The adrenaline that accompanied the bright lights and excitement of a packed theater somehow suppressed my pain, at least temporarily. As our rehearsal got underway, MJ, our director, called out for me to move backward a bit, next to the hay bale. Today, we were "blocking." That's the process of planning the position of each character on stage and how they would move.

I followed the director's instructions and jotted them down on the script that was sitting on my lap. I looked out into the dark theater, imagining what opening day would be like with every seat filled. My legs dangled down off the chair as I wrote, not propped up on my footrests like usual. This building was more than one hundred years old and barely accessible by wheelchair. The only way I could reach the stage was to go down a dark, winding hallway—and the only way I could fit through that hallway was by removing the leg supports and footrests from my wheelchair. Sometimes I replaced the legs once I was on stage, but it was a hassle. So, during the blocking, I just kept them off, even though it was uncomfortable.

"Let's start from the top," MJ called out, her voice echoing throughout the empty theater.

That meant *me*! As Peter Rabbit's mother, I had the first line in the whole play. It was an important responsibility that I took seriously. Rolling to stage right, I waited for the lights to turn on—my cue to begin!

"Peter . . . Peter . . . time to wake up!" I called across the stage, loud enough to be heard by people in the last row. Anyone who knew me knew if there was one thing I was good at, it was projecting my voice for all to hear! My brother would say that I needed lessons on being quieter, not louder.

As we continued through the scene, I felt pride in my work. I'd gained new confidence here, knowing there was no one to hide behind when I was onstage. Everyone would see me. Everyone would know I was different. And I was learning to be okay with it.

A week later, I found myself alone in the house for the first time in quite a while. Alicia had left to eat dinner, Mom and Dad went for a walk, and so I was on my own. The TV played in the background as I crocheted a blanket for my friend Sheila from ASL class. Then the phone began ringing from its charger by my bed. The caller ID read *private caller*, which meant it definitely wasn't anyone calling for me. I never picked up the phone unless I saw it was a friend of mine. Since Mom wasn't here, I should just have let it go to voicemail.

But I couldn't. I didn't know why, but as I looked at the words *private caller* flashing across the screen, I felt like I should pick up the phone. It rang four times. One more ring, and it would go to voicemail.

Gah! I grabbed it at the last second. "Hello?"

"Hello, I'm calling for Dorothy Leland," a woman said quietly.

"Um . . ." I wasn't supposed to tell strangers that I was home alone. "My mom can't come to the phone right now. Can you call back later?"

She paused. "I don't know when I'll be able to call again. I have Lyme disease, and I'm actually in a psychiatric hospital right now. Someone gave me your mom's number and said she might be able to help me."

"Oh . . . " A sense of purpose urged me to say more. "I have Lyme disease, too. And I was also in a psych hospital." I'd never told anyone that last bit before now.

She said that no one believed her, and she didn't know what to do.

"Doctors didn't believe me either," I replied. "I know how horrible that feels."

We talked together for a little while. I shared my story and heard parts of hers. I told her about my Lyme doctor, and how she should make an appointment to see him because he was the only doctor who ever really paid attention to what I had to say.

"You know," I commented at the end of our talk, "I almost didn't pick up the phone when you called, but I'm glad I did."

"Me, too."

Dorothy

The woman Rachel had talked to called back the next day, and I learned more about her story. During her years of working as a registered nurse, she'd experienced many episodes of strange physical and psychological problems, and at one point she tested positive for Lyme disease. But her doctors refused to accept that diagnosis, she couldn't find anyone willing to treat her for Lyme, and her mental health had spiraled downward from there. Finally, feeling suicidal, she had checked herself into a psychiatric facility. The hospital allowed her to make periodic phone calls, and somehow, she'd connected with someone who knew me from the CaliforniaLyme online support group. That person suggested that she call me. I gave her the contact information for our Lyme doctor and talked a bit about what we'd gone through. In a way, that was the beginning of my work as an advocate for Lyme patients outside of my own family.

Mom and I were in Nevada for treatment with Grace, the naturopathic doctor, and this time we planned to stay for three days. Our hotel was part of a big casino complex, filled with dazzling neon lights and impressive water displays outside. It looked like a palace.

There were slot machines everywhere, brimming with heavy smokers hoping to hit it big, bombarding us with their toxic fumes around the clock. There was no escaping them. To make it to the safety of the elevator and the rooms above, we had to hold our breath all the way from the front doors, past the gift shop, and across the long reception area.

As Mom steered me toward the elevator, I held my sweatshirt up to my face, breathing deeply through its filtering fabric, and stifled a cough.

Mom charged forward. Once we were inside the elevator, the smell of smoke began to dissipate. We got out on the tenth floor, slowing down to gaze out the expansive windows at the beautiful pool and hot tub far below. This place was so extravagant!

Dorothy

If anyone had told me that I would be pushing my teenage daughter in a wheelchair through the smoke-filled lobby of a casino full of slot machines, I would have said they were out of their mind. And yet, here we were. Most of the city's thousands of hotel rooms were found in big casino complexes. During future trips, we switched to a hotel where we could enter and go straight to the elevators without exposing ourselves to the smoke-filled casino. After going to all this trouble for detoxification, we certainly didn't want to poison ourselves anew each time we passed through the lobby!

After I'd rested up from the morning's treatment, Mom and I headed out for the evening's entertainment. She had gotten us tickets for a performance of *Dancing Queen*, a showcase of ABBA songs held at another casino. We had to circle the parking lot three times before we found a spot. It was a busy place.

Once out of the car and in my wheelchair, I felt every jolt from the extra-bumpy roadway beneath me. I sat up straight, hoping it would somehow lessen the impact I felt.

"Would it be better if we slowed down?" Mom inquired.

"No," I said through gritted teeth. "Just keep going so it's done."

My first full breath wasn't until we reached the sidewalk on the other end of the street. What a horrible way to begin the night.

As we entered the casino, I was overwhelmed by the number of people walking around. As a wheelchair user, I had come to dislike crowds. People walked into me constantly, and they tripped over my feet that were sticking out further than anyone expected. I always ended up apologizing to everyone else after *they* ran into *me*.

Mom and I stood in the entryway, waiting to get our bearings, when a hotel employee offered to guide us to the buffet. We followed her through the crowded lobby until we reached a black metal contraption.

"Here we are!" she said triumphantly. "You pick up this phone here," she pointed to an object resting on the wall by the metal box, "and it will call security. Just let them know you need to use the elevator, and they'll come over with their key."

I looked past the woman at the staircase behind her. Just ten steps were all that separated us from our destination. I watched as able-bodied people bounded up those steps like they were nothing. Well, they *were* nothing, for them.

A spark inside me diminished; I didn't want to use this stupid metal box to get up a small flight of stairs. This elevator didn't even have walls—everyone climbing the steps could *see* me, sitting all alone because it was too small to hold more than one person.

I wanted to go *home*.

Dorothy

When I'd purchased the tickets to *Dancing Queen*, I had specifically asked about wheelchair access. No problem, they'd assured me—everything was fully accessible. Yet, right at the outset, we were confronted with a ridiculous apparatus meant to carry the wheelchair up a handful of steps. Hadn't these people ever heard of *ramps*?

The woman left as Mom picked up the telephone, and soon a man arrived to unlock the elevator.

I wheeled myself in, but the gate couldn't close because my wheelchair was too large. I lowered the legs into the most compact position possible, but I still wouldn't fit. We were making a scene now. People were staring. I hated this.

My chair wouldn't fit in at its usual reclined angle, so Mom unlocked the top and brought it upright. I couldn't draw a breath!

With the gate finally closed, the elevator started to move slowly. Mom waited at the top—it took her only seconds to hop up those ten steps. I could have crawled up them faster than this. It would have been just as humiliating, but way quicker.

As soon as I escaped the death trap, Mom lowered the back of my chair, and I could breathe again. We trudged onward to the buffet, hoping to reclaim our evening. French fries improved every situation.

After dinner, it was time to go back down those dreaded ten steps. We wheeled over to the elevator and watched as an older gentleman in a wheelchair tried, without luck, to get it to work. He and his wife had somehow gotten the key from the security team. But, since nothing was moving, Mom offered to help. I peered over my shoulder, seeing another person in line behind me. *Great.*

Finally, with a rumble, the apparatus slowly descended. After another minute, it returned for me. This time, we didn't mess around—Mom removed both legs from the chair and carried them down the steps.

After a less traumatic but equally unpleasant ride down, we reattached the legs and headed toward the theater for *Dancing Queen.* We watched as everyone else walked through the two doors and down the steps like normal people. A woman wearing a hotel uniform offered to lead us to our seats in the wheelchair-accessible section. She guided us around a strange back way, through dark, skinny hallways perhaps meant for prop guys and actors going backstage. After many twists and turns, she led us to seats at the very edge of the theater, right under the speakers. We were so far over we couldn't even see most of the stage. Wheelchair-accessible seating was clearly an afterthought at this establishment.

The lights dimmed, an announcer spoke, and then—*BAM!*— the music of ABBA erupted like a cannon blast from the speaker just feet above us. The vibrations felt like daggers slicing down my spine.

Even with my hands clasped over my ears, the sound pierced my eardrums, and pain ricocheted throughout my head. When the first song ended, I told Mom that we needed to leave *immediately.*

Retracing our path through this rigged fortress was not easy, but somehow we pushed through the dim hallways and got the heck out of there. Once in the car, Mom said, "Hot tub when we get back to the hotel?"

"Yeah. Let's do it."

Dorothy

That summer, between detoxification protocols and trips to Nevada, we contemplated what to do about high school in the fall. The administrators said we had three choices:

1. Attend high school full time, which our doctor said was out of the question, and we agreed.

2. Enroll in the independent study program full time, which wouldn't allow Rachel to take drama or see friends at school and would be too rigorous an academic load.

3. Take two classes at the high school, along with four in the independent study program, which, again, was too heavy a schedule.

Whenever I'd asked why those were our only choices, I heard the same puzzling reply. "It's much better for your daughter this way."

Huh?

That summer, a friend put me in touch with a mother who had several special-needs children attending local schools. Although her family's circumstances differed from ours, she knew a lot about how the system worked. After hearing my story, she said simply, "Funding."

"What?" I asked.

"That's how funding works," she explained. "If your daughter only took one class this past year, the district didn't get any money for her from the state. If they let her attend just two classes at the high school next year, they *still* won't get any money. A student must be enrolled in a certain number of classes in order for the school district to receive funding for that student."

"What if she isn't capable of meeting that minimum?" I asked.

She shrugged. "They just want her enrolled. Play their game. Go through the schedule and pick out as many easy classes as you can—art, cooking, whatever seems most manageable."

Following her advice, Rachel decided to enroll in drama and English at the high school, along with the least academically rigorous classes we could find at the independent study program. I wasn't sure she could pull it off, but Rachel wanted to try, and we honored that.

Shortly after returning home from our recent Nevada experience, I put down my crocheting and paused the *Hannah Montana* episode playing in front of me. From my room, I could hear what sounded like someone stepping quietly upstairs above me. Mom and Dad were out walking the dog, and I was home alone this evening. I really wanted to watch my show on the big TV upstairs, sitting on the comfy recliner, but I was too scared to leave the safety of my bedroom.

For reasons I didn't understand, I found myself constantly afraid these days. I was terrified that a murderer would leap out from the dark shadows of our living room and reach through the gap in the stairs to grab me. When I heard creaks and groans in the wood beams of our house, I instantly feared for my life. When Mom had walked out to the mailbox last night, I wanted to beg her not to go because I just *knew* she would be killed. The mailbox was just a few steps beyond our driveway—but I had *cowered* in bed, holding my breath until I knew she had returned safely.

Then I heard that sound again—the creak of somebody walking upstairs. Or maybe they were walking *down* the stairs, coming for me. I had told Taylor this week about how I was so afraid that Mom or I would be kidnapped, and how it didn't make any sense. I'd never felt like this before.

There it was again, the sound! In a panic, I grabbed the phone and dialed 9-1-... I held the receiver in front of me, equally scared of being murdered as I was of cops showing up at my house again. The last time they'd come, I'd left in handcuffs.

Breathing heavily yet silently, I told myself that this wasn't real. There hadn't ever been anyone in our house who shouldn't be there. I disconnected the call and dialed Mom's cell instead.

"Mom?" Tears filled my eyes at the sound of her voice. She was alive. "Are you coming home soon?"

Dorothy

I did not understand how petrified Rachel would sometimes get when she was left alone in the house. In my view at the time, she was improving both physically and mentally. Leaving her on her own for short periods seemed entirely appropriate. I do remember that she often called us while Bob and I walked the brief loop around our neighborhood. I think I assumed it was impatience on her part—she wanted me to *do* something for her, or she wanted company while she watched TV. I had no idea she was so afraid. In retrospect, realizing how oblivious I was to what was actually going on with her still hurts my heart.

CHAPTER 9

Sixty-Seven Is Too Many Pills

The week before high school was due to start, Mom and I went to campus to check things out. Since one of my classes was on the second floor, we picked up an elevator key at the office. Typically, students were supposed to take the stairs, not the elevator, but obviously that wouldn't work for me.

We soon ran into our first glitch. When I inserted the key and the door slid open, the elevator was entirely filled with buckets, mops, and other cleaning supplies. After a janitor removed them for us, we rode up to the second floor and promptly ran into another problem. The elevator brought us to a concrete platform outside the main structure. The only way into the building was through a heavy door that did not come with one of those big blue buttons to push to open it. No matter how hard I tried, I could not both pull the door open *and* move myself out of the way at the same time. It couldn't be done.

"You'll just need to have a friend ride the elevator with you every day to open the door," Mom proposed, in typical problem-solver mode.

Given our difficulties that first time, we returned for another dry run the day before classes began. This campus was *big*, and getting from drama to English within the six minutes between periods would be a tight squeeze.

When Mom and I reached my first classroom, I set the timer on my wristwatch. "Okay, let's go."

Mom trailed behind as I made my way from drama toward my English class. The elevator was clear across campus, and I was out of breath by the time I got there. I reached into my pocket for that small golden key and realize it was missing. Shoot—I'd left it at home!

"Let me just go up and see if your English teacher happens to be here," Mom said and headed up the stairs.

As I sat by the elevator, irritated at myself for forgetting something so vital, my watch beeped. My six minutes were up. I made a mental note to put the key in my backpack once we got home, so this didn't happen again tomorrow for the real thing.

As I sat there, a woman approached me from behind and introduced herself as Sally, from the front office. "How are you doing today?" she asked.

"I'm fine," I said guardedly. I couldn't put my finger on it, but something about Sally made me uncomfortable. I was grateful to see Mom's legs appear at the top of the steps behind her.

Mom dove right in, saying that I couldn't open the doors on the second floor and explaining that there was an elevator, but no blue button to push, rendering the second-floor classes non-wheelchair-accessible.

Doing her best impression of Professor Umbridge from *Harry Potter*, Sally seemed totally unconcerned. Mom tried again, this time asking about wheelchair-accessible bathrooms around campus, which brought a smile to Sally's face.

"You can choose from *two* different wheelchair-accessible bathrooms!" she announced with pride, as if it was something to put in the school newsletter.

She led us to the first, located deep within the administration building. However, there was no button to open the main door to the building. Mom wasn't shy about pointing this out.

"She can't *get* to your wheelchair-accessible bathroom if she can't *open the door* to the building first."

Sally's body stiffened. "Anybody at this school would be more than happy to open the door for her," she replied.

Mom was getting cranked up for a forceful rebuttal, but I caught her eye and shook my head. There was no point. I wanted to be done with this lady.

We continued our unplanned tour, heading to the second of the two "wheelchair-friendly" bathrooms. This one, thankfully, actually *was* accessible. It had an automatic door and everything.

Dorothy

With the start of high school, Rachel and I began a new routine. Her two classes were both after lunch, so, if she felt up to it, I'd take her there early enough to eat with her friends. She enlisted a classmate to help her navigate the elevator and kept her brand-new cell phone handy in case of emergencies. In 2007, cell phone use by teenagers was growing, and the school had technically banned them from campus. We got permission for Rachel to have one with her as long as she agreed to keep it turned off unless needed.

I turned the key to the elevator, and soon my friend Maya and I heard it crackle to life. After taking its sweet time lowering from the second floor to the first, it groaned open and we stepped inside. It was tiny, dark, and creepy.

Maya pushed me from drama to English every day now. I was grateful for her because this elevator was straight out of a horror film.

For reasons we couldn't fathom, the walls were covered with smelly, yellowed cloths that hung from the ceiling on metal hooks. We often pressed our hands into the fabric where it jutted away from the wall, just to make sure there was no one hiding behind it ready to kill us.

Maya opened the hallway door for me, and I pushed myself through, dodging the students filing in and out of classrooms. As we entered our own, Maya grabbed the very first desk on the left and pulled it into the center of the room—the only place it could go that didn't block the board or other students. I rolled into the recently vacated spot and scooted as far as I could to the side so students behind me didn't trip. I would be deskless if it weren't for Maya, who graciously let me use the side of hers to house my binder and pencil case.

As I looked around my classroom, it was easy to tell that most of these students didn't want to be here. We all knew we weren't in the "smart" class. This was basic tenth-grade English, which may have felt pathetic to some of my peers, but it felt pretty darn exciting for me. I never thought I'd live to see high school, let alone be able to take actual classes here like everyone else. I loved that I'd get to leave home for two hours each day to be around regular people doing normal, boring things. I was pretty sure no one in this room saw themselves as lucky to be here, but they really should have. They had no idea how fortunate they were.

High school was so weird. It was obvious that most of the kids took drama just because they thought it would be easy, not because they had any interest in acting. But I *loved* acting. I wanted to be surrounded by others like me, but instead, half of our class just sat there doing nothing for the entire period. And our teacher allowed it!

Last week, I'd been partnered with my friend Kelly, and we'd come up with a script and performed it. It had been great! But this week, I was assigned to work with Kimberly, a ridiculously superficial girl who looked truly humiliated whenever I dared to be in her presence. She chatted with her friends all the time, over in the corner, and when I tried to get her to practice for even a minute, she just brushed me off and said, "We'll be fine."

Well, I knew we would *not* be fine. Not if we didn't practice. I knew my lines, and I knew *hers,* too, but I would've bet money she didn't even know the name of our scene.

I headed over to where Kelly and her partner were and watched them practice. Drama had so much potential this year. I hadn't been in the right place for it last year, but now I was. I was looking forward to being a real high school student, performing real plays with others who loved acting as much as I did. But it was obvious now that I hadn't understood how little most high school students cared about anything school-related.

Due to stupid rules within the school district, I had been forced to take two classes at the high school and *four* classes at the independent study school, which my whole medical team agreed was way too much for me right now. So, we had picked the easiest, most doable classes, and we were making it work on our own terms.

Every Tuesday, Mom dropped me off downtown at the independent study school for a one-hour session with my teacher, Ms. Trish. I actually really enjoyed our time together. I'd started the year off easy, taking cooking, art, physical education (PE), and ASL. (The school allowed me to get credit for what I was learning in my weekly ASL class at the church.) Obviously, if I wanted to graduate, I'd have to take some tougher classes starting next semester. But we'd see how well I could handle this for now. The art class was in person, but I did the rest on my own at home. Each week, I showed Ms. Trish the new signs I'd learned in my Monday night class, and I reviewed the cooking projects I'd completed and what I had done for PE.

Mom and I teamed up for PE. When I felt good enough, we went on a short walk around the neighborhood, and I pushed myself. On days I wasn't up for it, she pushed me, and I focused on breathing, which was a workout for my lungs. Ask any yoga instructor—breathing is exercise. It totally counted.

Cooking had been fun, too, especially since my next-door neighbor Christopher often came over to cook with me! We'd been buddies since I was three and he was two. So far, we had made pies, rice pudding, and had even attempted to make churros. The churros didn't turn out so well, but they'd tasted okay—they just looked a little funky. Instead of being long, thick, sticklike treats, they'd ended up looking like one-inch flimsy worms. I had still gotten credit though, so that's what mattered.

The best part about independent study was that I got Ms. Trish's undivided attention. In school, I'd always been surrounded by thirty or more students, so each of us would get very limited one-on-one time with our teachers. But here, I was the only student! It was amazing, and I loved telling Ms. Trish all about my life. She was always so happy to see me, and it was now a highlight of my week.

Mom and I traveled to Nevada for treatment about once a month, sometimes twice. I had to miss two days of school each time, which stressed me out because I hated being behind, but we made up for it by having fun on our trip. On our excursion today, Mom held open the door to our favorite pottery painting place. I pushed myself inside, heading for our usual table.

"Have you been in before?" a woman with a purple apron asked. *Have we been in before . . . ha!* "Yes." I smiled. "And we also need to pick up what we painted two weeks ago."

Mom and I had been painting ceramic light switch plates for some time now, with a goal of putting them in every room of the house.

My bathroom now sported a bright green-striped one I had painted a month ago, and Mom had made a lovely blue one for her office. We always came here right after our first appointment with Grace before heading to the hotel for the evening.

Shelves on one side of the studio were lined with unpainted mugs, plates, animal figurines, and other items to choose from. As I wheeled over to examine them, a pretty bowl with a matching lid caught my eye. I picked it up and placed it on my lap.

"No switch plate today?" Mom asked, taking one for herself.

"No," I pushed myself up to the table. "I want to paint this for Taylor."

Alternating between teal, blue, and yellow paint, I carefully colored in the stars and moon that were etched into the lid of the bowl. Then I wrote "Hope Holder" across the back in puff paint. Taylor still told me often that she was holding my hope for me, since long ago I'd lost all hope that I would get better. I figured that if she was going to hold it for me, then she should at least have a special place to store it.

Dorothy

In fall 2007, we started thinking about the approach of an important milestone—Rachel's sixteenth birthday. Birthdays fourteen and fifteen had largely been pain-filled, angst-ridden, and brain-foggy. We hoped to chart a new course with number sixteen. Because our previous trip to Pismo Beach had been so successful, Bob and I took another look at places offering beach wheelchairs. This time, we chose Santa Cruz, a three-hour drive from our home, and Rachel invited several of her neighborhood friends to come along.

For two years, whenever I'd gotten into the van, I'd always had to sit up front in the fully reclining seat. Today I was trying something special for my sixteenth-birthday road trip. I was sitting with my friends in the very back seat, which actually reclined slightly. So far, I was handling it. Was this change because of the Lyme treatment or the supplements I was currently taking? Who knew? Each day I swallowed tons of pills, so any number of them could be the reason I was feeling better. But regardless, I couldn't have been more thrilled to be hanging in the back with my people on this three-hour drive.

We arrived at the house well past dark. We could hear, but not see, waves crashing against the beach nearby. We squinted our eyes, trying to locate the water. Wind danced in my hair as each breath of salty air filled my lungs.

Shira pushed my wheelchair to the front of the house, stopping at the steps leading up to the door. We'd known this place wasn't wheelchair accessible, so we'd come prepared. Dad handed me the knee pads we'd brought for this very reason, and I crawled and scooted my way up the stairs and in through the open door.

The next morning, as we devoured our cereal, Mom returned with the rented beach wheelchair. It was huge, with wheels much bigger than the chair we'd used last year at Pismo Beach. Recalling how hard it had been to roll the chair across the sand last time, I worried because Jeremy wasn't here to help out like before.

Once at the beach, I hoisted myself up onto my massive throne and immediately saw the benefit of the wider wheels. Shira pushed me across the sand to the water's edge with hardly any effort at all. Lowering myself to the ground, I had only moments before the first wave washed over me, taking my breath away with its frigid temperature. Shira splashed in the cold water with me until our bodies had had enough. Then I scooted backward away from the water to where the sand was drier and warmer in search of a place to dig a hole. Using the shovel we'd brought, Shira carved out the perfect resting spot for me, reclined angle included. Only the best for this birthday girl.

I couldn't believe I was sixteen. Ever since I had gotten sick, birthdays had been bittersweet. We tried to make the most of them, with parties and fun outings like this one. But I couldn't escape the feeling that I had lost time I would never be able to get back. Where had it all gone? Three years in, and I still didn't know what it was like to be a real teenager. I couldn't carry a normal course load of classes, and I couldn't learn to drive. Long ago, I'd stopped dreaming of making the high school varsity soccer team. In fact—long ago I'd stopped dreaming of anything.

The sun warmed my face as I reclined against my sandy bed. The sound of waves crashing nearby mixed with Shira and Christine's boisterous comments about their castle, and everything felt right in this moment.

"Rachie!" Alicia motioned for me to look at her masterpiece of suns, happy faces, and hearts written in the sand, surrounded by each of our names. Christine shrieked with laughter when part of their castle collapsed into the moat. I was so grateful to be here today with these remarkable people who had walked alongside me these past three years. I felt that this trip was to celebrate *them* as much as it was to celebrate me.

Back home from my birthday trip, life didn't take long to remind me that I was no longer in paradise. See, there's a bone in your chest called the sternum . . . and out of the blue, mine sometimes felt like it was being stabbed with a screwdriver. It would hurt so much I couldn't breathe. This tended to happen when I was bending forward, like when I was brushing my teeth. Suddenly I'd feel a sharp blow to my chest. It hurt too much to move. My heart would start pounding, and I'd wonder if I could even make it out of the bathroom.

When I did manage to call out, Mom would help me back to bed and put an ice pack on my chest. After a few minutes, the pain calmed down to its normal level. It made no sense how this came and went so suddenly.

My sternum pain was intense, but so far no one could tell me why it happened, or how to prevent it in the future. I had to be so vigilant at school to not bend forward at that angle for fear that I'd be trapped away from home and away from Mom when it happened.

While it was worse when I leaned over, my sternum and ribs *always* hurt if I pushed on them. I assumed it was like that for everybody, until one day Shira told me she could poke her ribs without any discomfort—and had always been able to do so. Well, *that* was certainly a shift in perspective.

Dorothy

Every tenth grader in our school district was supposed to put in at least twenty hours of community service. As defined by the district, this might be volunteering at a nonprofit organization, working at a homeless shelter, or tutoring elementary school children. As an administrator at the independent study school explained to me, the idea was to get the students out in the community so they could make a contribution and have new experiences. She said it was time for Rachel to choose what her service project would be.

I stared at the woman across the desk. She clearly had no understanding of Rachel's situation. I tried explaining how much pain Rachel was in, how fatigued she often was, how it took everything she could muster just to carry the full academic load the school district had demanded of her. But this lady was unmoved. I suggested an alternative community service project. Rachel had recently taught herself to crochet beautiful blankets. What if she made more blankets and donated them to the local women's shelter for holiday gifts? It would be something she could do on her own schedule when her energy levels allowed. It would be creative, and yes, it would be an act of generosity and service.

No, no, no, the administrator responded. That was just sitting at home. Service projects should get students *out* into the community, learning new things.

"Rachel would love to be out in the community learning new things," I replied quietly, stifling my desire to shout at this woman. "Unfortunately, that doesn't work for her right now." I made a counter proposal. "What if, in addition to making the blankets, Rachel interviews somebody who works at the shelter and finds out more about their work there? That would be learning something new. She could write a paper about it." The administrator finally agreed, but she let me know she wasn't happy about it.

With *Gilmore Girls* playing in the background, I carefully pushed my crochet hook into the small hole at the top of my blanket, looped the yarn over it, and brought it back up through the opening. Unlike the other blankets I'd made so far, this one was extra special. It was part of my community service project, and it was going to be a Christmas gift for a woman at a domestic violence shelter near us. I loved using brightly colored yarn. Plus, I loved being able to make a difference in someone's life, even in a small way.

Mom had gone to a Lyme disease conference and would be away for several days. So, it was just me and Dad here, which was sorta weird, since for the last few years it almost never had been just us two—but it was also cool. Earlier today, he'd taken me to an ice-cream parlor that had a sugar-free flavor I could eat, and they'd topped it off with fresh strawberries and nuts. Then he'd driven me to the store to buy yarn for another blanket. We'd gone down multiple aisles packed full of different types of yarn. We'd picked up some that had sparkles and some that were fluffy. I was eager to get started on this project!

Dorothy

In 2007, all students in our state had to pass the California High School Exit Examination (CAHSEE) in order to qualify for a diploma. The idea was to ensure that nobody graduated without meeting minimum standards for reading, writing, and mathematics. The test was first given in tenth grade, with opportunities to retake it the following years. The thought of possibly failing the test filled Rachel with anxiety. I tried to soothe her concerns by pointing out that she'd be able to take it again later if necessary. She wasn't buying it.

The two-day CAHSEE test had been looming in my future for months now, but I'd come to understand that to everyone else, it was a joke. Many of my classmates took multiple Advanced Placement classes, so this test seemed like nothing to them. The week before the test, I had asked some kids in my drama class how they felt about it, and they laughed, saying only an idiot could fail. Well, there you had it. Apparently, I was an idiot. I was also someone pretending to be a tenth grader, but who had really dropped out of school after only two months of eighth grade, then had come back for one ninth-grade Spanish class and two tenth-grade classes.

The first day, I took the English portion and felt like I'd done okay. But math, on the second day, was a different story. Even though I'd been working with a tutor twice a week, my memory was still shot. Sometimes I couldn't even recall what we'd worked on during the previous session, so she needed to review it all again before we could move on.

With my lack of understanding in the math department, I felt there was no way I could possibly pass the CAHSEE. Fidgeting with my pencil, I glanced at the clock for the hundredth time and saw that our next break was in forty-five minutes. That was when I'd finally get to go to the bathroom and call Mom to come pick me up. I couldn't finish this test—there was no point. Why even try when I knew I was going to fail?

As I waited for the break, I looked down at my math problem. Percentages. I'd learned about them at one point—something about a decimal, and you either did or didn't do something to it. Move it? I thought so. Left? Right? I thought left, but maybe not. *Gah!* I couldn't get enough air! It was so hot and stifling in here.

I moved on to the next question, feeling just as unsure about it. Time passed at a snail's pace. The guy in front of me had turned at least five pages while I'd turned just two.

"Pencils down," the moderator called out, noting that we had just ten minutes to use the bathroom and get a snack.

Would they know I was missing when I didn't come back?

Once in the bathroom stall, I took my flip phone out of my bag, trying to muster up the courage to call for my getaway driver. For the past hour I had thought of nothing else except calling Mom and getting the hell out of here. What was stopping me now?

I tapped my fingers gently against the armrest of my wheelchair. The clock was ticking. As more people entered the bathroom, I left and sat outside, staring at the parking lot full of cars. I *could* call

Mom—but then what? I knew I was bad at percentage problems, but if I left now, there was a 100 percent certainty I would fail the test. If I stayed, then even if I *did* fail, I could at least say that I didn't give up.

I decided that mattered to me.

Following a girl who held the door open for me, I wheeled back to my desk. When given the go-ahead, I picked up my pencil and turned back a few pages. After reading the problems again, I decided that when dealing with percentages, you *do* move the decimal point to the left. Twice, in fact.

And with that, I plunged forward.

Dorothy

As the months dragged on, Rachel continued taking oral antibiotic therapy along with a boatload of herbal supplements. She and I still made periodic trips to Nevada to see her naturopathic doctor for detoxification protocols and other therapies. When we weren't at the clinic, we painted pottery, ordered room service, and watched a lot of television at the hotel. It was okay but kind of tedious.

In March 2008, we decided to mix it up a bit. During Jeremy's spring break from college, we turned Rachel's usual Nevada appointment into a family trip. Having her brother in the car certainly made the drive more entertaining for all of us. And having the two kids share a suite meant Rachel and I got a break from almost constantly being together—something we both needed. Furthermore, since Bob and I were able to stay in a room down the hall from our kids, we finally were able to enjoy some much-needed alone time. A win-win situation, if ever there was one.

Jeremy and I were bunking together in what we were told was a handicapped-accessible suite at one of the big casino hotels. It brought back memories of family trips to Europe and Costa Rica before I had gotten sick. I climbed up on the bed, adjusting the pillows under my back and knees to get as comfortable as I could.

"I want the first shot to be me in the fluffy hotel bathrobe, luxuriating in the empty bathtub," I told my brother, channeling my inner cinematographer.

For weeks, I'd been planning an epic music video I wanted Jeremy to film for me. Mom wasn't the best at taking direction when it came to quality filmmaking, so this time I'd brought in reinforcements!

"Do you want the camera at your height in the tub, or above you?"

He was good. This was why we kept him around.

"I—" I began, cut short by the sound of a fire alarm going off in the hallway, immediately followed by seizure-inducing lights flashing urgently throughout the room.

"*Ahhh!*" I shrieked. Pain. Pain everywhere, all at once. "Oh my God!" I exclaimed. "The *bed!*"

Realizing that my mattress itself was somehow shaking, I rolled to the edge and flung myself off, landing with a thump on the carpeted floor.

"What's happening?" I cried out, blocking the blinding strobe lights with my hand.

Jeremy stared at the bed with a puzzled look on his face. "It's vibrating."

It turned out that we didn't get the accessible room for *wheelchair users.* Instead, we'd been given a room outfitted for people who were Deaf and hard-of-hearing. So, when the fire alarm went off, instead of a loud siren, we'd been given a light show and a roller-coaster ride. They wanted to make sure any sleeping occupants were jolted awake in case of emergency.

We now knew the importance of being highly specific about my needs whenever checking into a hotel room.

Dorothy

Despite the rocky start with the vibrating fire alarm, our Nevada "vacation" was wonderful. Between our medical appointments, Jeremy patiently helped Rachel film all the videos she wanted, the four of us painted light switch plates at the pottery studio, and we tried out a variety of good restaurants. And while I can't recall the name of the film, I remember us all piled on the hotel beds, laughing uproariously at a very funny movie. Mostly, I just loved being all together as a family.

Back home from our brief vacation, I was filming a video with Alicia in my bedroom, but we stopped when Mom came in with a bin full of supplements. I let out a loud sigh and took the pills and the cup of juice Mom handed me.

I was taking sixty-seven of these dang things every day now, and I was sick of it. I used to gobble down multiple pills with no problem, but no more. Now, as soon as even one small pill went into my mouth, my throat seemed to close up in protest.

Mom left, and I picked up the least foul-smelling capsule and placed it on my tongue. But my throat wouldn't cooperate. I took a swig of the juice, but no matter how much I willed my throat to open, it just wouldn't do it.

"What if you film yourself taking pills backward?" Alicia suggested. We'd entertained ourselves for hours this morning by filming normal tasks, such as crumpling a piece of paper, and then editing it to play backward.

"Worth a try," I said.

As the pill got soggy and disgusting, soaking in the juice that was now warm and icky in my mouth, I handed Alicia the camera. As soon as the recording light turned on, my throat worked perfectly. I easily downed each pill, and then we headed outside to film Alicia jumping off playground equipment.

Dorothy

The filming-pills-to-play-backward trick worked a few times, but even that soon lost its effectiveness. I could tell Rachel wasn't being contrary. Instead, it was as if her throat was rebelling. Afraid that she'd soon be unable to take any pills at all, I suggested we take a hiatus. For a few weeks, she took only her prescription medicines and probiotics—none of the many supplements. This certainly simplified our routine, but it came at a cost. Rachel's energy ebbed considerably, and she felt fatigued most of the time. We started slowly adding some of the supplements back into the mix, which helped.

Every Thursday afternoon, I had my stupid two-hour art class at the independent study school. While I enjoyed seeing Ms. Trish on Tuesdays for my one-on-one review of homework assignments, art class wasn't like that, and Ms. Trish was not there. When I signed up for the class, I'd thought it would be fun to draw and paint with a small group of students and an art teacher. But it turned out that I hated this course with a passion—and I couldn't quit because I needed it to graduate.

Today, we were stuck learning two-point perspective drawing, which seemed to be the absolute worst type of drawing out there.

No matter how much the teacher explained it, I couldn't do it right. Whatever happened to the saying "There's no wrong way to do art"? Because, as my teacher thoroughly explained, there was *indeed* a wrong way to draw two-point perspective.

Kyla, one of the other four victims in this artless art room, took out a little bottle and emptied two pills into her hand. I knew she had sickle-cell anemia because we'd chatted as a class about how she slept nearly all day because of it. That's why she came to this independent study school instead of regular high school.

I watched her swallow the capsules and replace the container in her backpack.

"Do you have to take a lot of pills?" asked another one of our classmates, a girl who always left early for volleyball practice.

"Yeah," Kyla said with a sigh. "I take a lot of pills every day. But you get used to it."

I perked up at not being alone in the too-many-pills department, and asked, "How many do you take?"

"Let's see . . ." she mumbled quietly as she counted on her fingers. "I take seven each day."

My heart sank.

"Wow!" the volleyball girl exclaimed as if seven was a lot of pills.

I thought back to a recent phone conversation I'd had with an online Lyme friend. She'd told me I shouldn't complain about taking a measly sixty-seven pills, because she took more than one hundred. Like it was a contest, and she was winning. Like the fact that I'd been gagging on only sixty-seven pills was insignificant in light of her triumphant feat. I felt abandoned and ashamed. I had vowed during that conversation to never make anyone else feel the way I'd felt that time—invalidated. Even if seven didn't seem like a lot to me, it was a lot to Kyla. And that's all that mattered.

"Oh, man," I sympathized. "That stinks."

The following Tuesday, I had my scheduled hour with Ms. Trish to go over my assignments. On this occasion, she was still with the student before me, so I waited for him to leave before wheeling myself toward her cubicle.

"Hello! Come in, come in!"

She waved me toward my usual spot by the desk. She had an extra energy about her today. She smiled broadly at me and said, "I just *love* it when all my students pass the exit exam!"

Why was she telling me this? She wasn't the type of person to rub failure in my face.

"What do you mean, *all* your students passed?" I asked guardedly.

Still grinning, she repeated, "*All* my students passed!"

"Am I one of your students?" I asked. What was she implying? For the past six weeks, I'd been certain I had failed the CAHSEE. I'd put it behind me and moved on.

"*Of course* you're one of my students!" She swatted her hand in the air at my silly question.

"Wait." My eyes widened. "You're saying *I* passed the test?" I spoke the words cautiously, preparing myself for her to laugh, telling me no, I did indeed fail—she'd meant all of her *other* students passed.

"Yes! *You* passed! You passed the high school exit exam!"

My mouth dropped open. "Even the math part?" This couldn't be true. I needed to get her answer on record before someone popped up out of nowhere to say she was just kidding.

"You passed both the math and the English tests!" She smiled from ear to ear.

I exhaled all the breath I'd been holding in. "Oh my God! Oh my God!" I was going to graduate from high school!

Later that same week, I was shoving fries in my mouth as I stared at the group of people across the courtyard at the Deaf social event. These were held monthly at this shopping center, so Deaf people could interact with one another, as well as others who knew ASL. Anyone learning sign language was welcome to attend. I'd asked my parents to bring me because I wanted to join in, but now I couldn't fathom how I was going to make my entrance. Mom and Dad had cajoled me to "just go over and say hi." As if it were that simple.

I recognized one person at the event from my ASL class, but she hadn't attended for a long time. She might not remember me. Everyone was signing so fast. I would look so stupid if I went over there and then didn't know what anyone was saying. Or what if no one even looked up from their conversation to notice I was there?

After my fries were gone, I forced myself to push back from the table, leaving Mom and Dad to finish their meal without me as I headed toward the group of signers. I rolled past, pretending to be casual as I looked around me.

Right away, the woman from my sign class locked eyes with me, smiled, and waved me over. Thank God.

"Hello!" she signed.

Instantly, many of the people in the circle looked toward me. I waved and signed, "My name R-a-c-h-e-l." Then I showed my unique name sign that had been given to me by my first Deaf friend, whom I'd met at Girl Scout camp when I was nine.

And just like that, I was part of the group! I watched as a young woman continued her previous conversation about being a camp counselor.

This was what I'd always wanted—to communicate in this amazing secret language that no one else in this plaza could understand but us! I looked back to see Mom and Dad watching our group. They didn't know what we were saying either.

We were soon joined by my friend Owen from ASL class.

"What's up?" he signed, stepping over the knee-high wall to join our conversation.

He and I had met through ASL but soon found out that we attended the same high school. We'd recently been hanging out together at lunch sometimes.

"I thought you working tonight?" I signed.

"Schedule change," he signed back.

I closed my fist except for the thumb and pinkie, as I moved it forward and back to show the "oh-I-see" sign.

A hand flapped off to my right side, the signal in ASL that someone was trying to get our attention. I turned to see a man I didn't know, looking straight at me with a concerned expression on his face.

"You wheelchair why?" he signed at me.

Who was this guy? And why was *that* the first question he asked me? To my frustration, this interruption prompted Owen to leave our conversation and join another. Now it was just me and this creepy old dude.

"L-y-m-e d-i-s-e-a-s-e," I spelled out, feeling forced by social obligation to answer his intrusive question.

Before he had time to ask anything else, I turned my head in the opposite direction, trying to make eye contact with *anyone* so I could have an excuse to get away from this man. No such luck. His hand waved in my direction once more. To ignore it felt rude. I didn't know what to do. If I pretended not to see it, I was afraid he would move on to the next most appropriate way to get someone's attention in the Deaf world, which was to lightly tap their shoulder. I sure didn't want that! I turned back to him.

"Treatment?" he signed, as he pulled up a chair next to me.

What in the world? Why was he asking me these questions? We were at a social event, for goodness sake, not a medical appointment! I felt so uncomfortable. I also knew that Mom and Dad, watching me from across the courtyard, had no clue that there was a problem. I peered around and spotted Owen deep in conversation with other people. I'd get no help from him. I was on my own. Even if I had wanted to, how could I explain in a foreign language what types of treatments I was doing? I didn't even understand in *English* what treatments I was doing! "Take pills. Many," I responded, hoping to shut him up.

His shoulders slouched, and he shook his head, as if he knew for a fact my treatment was all wrong. To my surprise, he said aloud, "What alternative treatments are you doing?"

This guy was not even Deaf! Why was this much older, hearing man asking me personal health questions that were in no way his business? Besides, it's considered rude to speak without also signing at a Deaf event. He should have *known* that.

"I don't know. Many," I signed, not speaking. I felt trapped by this insistent line of questioning and didn't know how to get away from him.

"R-e-i-k-i, you try?" he signed.

I had never tried Reiki, but I actually knew what it was because Mom had been learning about it recently. I wanted to leave. I looked back toward Owen once more. If he hadn't left the instant this guy showed up, I wouldn't be in this predicament. I didn't get many opportunities to use my signing skills, and this stupid man was ruining everything. I looked frantically for an escape route. My wheelchair was backed up against the wall, and my only way out required this man to move out of the way. Mom and Dad weren't far, but for all they knew, I was having a good time. "Yes," I lied, figuring maybe that answer would make him happy. If he was happy, maybe he'd leave.

"Where?" he demanded in ASL.

Where? Why did he care where I went for my fictional Reiki sessions? "Sacramento," I signed, since that was where Mom went.

He shook his head and signed, "Too far."

I didn't know what to say anymore, but I had to get out of here.

"I need to go now," I signed, indicating that he had to move out of my way.

"Here's my card," he said aloud once more, without signing. "I do Emotional Freedom Technique, which will really help you."

Not gonna happen, buddy! Indicating that I needed to go, I pushed past him and fled.

Moments earlier, I had felt so happy and proud of myself. I had been wanting to come to this Deaf event for months, and I'd finally gotten up the courage to do so. Now, once again, a stupid grown-up had ruined everything. Why couldn't people just leave me alone? Why did that guy think it was okay to grill me about my health? In what world would that be deemed acceptable? Instead of leaving the event with new friends, with promises to meet up soon, I left feeling violated, never wanting to attend another in case this guy showed up. But why was I surprised? Of course, this was how it would go down. I shouldn't even have come.

Back at school a few days later, I typed my student ID and password into the keyboard in front of me. My English class was being held in the computer lab today so we could explore our education options for after high school. I was actually excited to see what was out there!

A woman with shoulder-length brown hair introduced herself as one of the counselors. Listening as she explained how to use this computer program, I clicked on some buttons that brought me to a different page. At the top it showed a drop-down menu with "university" and "community college" options.

Mom, Dad, and I hadn't talked a lot about what was to come. However, we'd discussed it enough to know that the plan would be for me to graduate from high school and then go to a local community college. That way I could live at home and continue to take things slowly.

When I clicked on "community college," it brought up a list of schools in the area, and the programs they offered. Up near the top was "American Sign Language," so I clicked on that, too. A list of ASL programs popped up, such as interpreting, theatrical signing, and other courses I could take about Deaf culture.

"Oh no, no, no," the counselor said behind me as she reached over and took the mouse from my hand. "Don't click on community college." She wrinkled her nose. "You don't want that. You're going to a four-year university, so click here." She backed out of the page on American Sign Language and handed me the mouse.

But I *wasn't* going to a four-year university. At least not right away. Mom and Dad had made community college sound like a perfectly fine idea, but this lady acted like it was garbage. I felt like if I told her I *wanted* to go community college, she would think I was garbage, too.

Fighting back tears, I wasted the rest of my computer lab time by looking up Cal Poly, which was where Jeremy was right now. Why was I here if I couldn't even look at what I wanted to look at? School was such a waste of time. This was bullshit.

Dorothy

Though Rachel was clearly upset when I picked her up from school that day, she remained tight-lipped on the trip home. I had learned it was better not to push at such times, so I made idle conversation until we pulled into the driveway. At that point, unleashing a flood of tears, Rachel told me what the counselor had said and how it had made her feel. I was furious that a school counselor would make such an ignorant statement—not just to my daughter, but to *any* high school student. The counselor didn't know the personal circumstances of the teenagers in that class.

Why voice such a damaging, stigmatizing opinion? She ought to have had her credentials revoked!

Then I firmly said to Rachel, "That woman is clueless. She knows nothing about you or what *you* need. And her opinion about community college is just plain dumb. Ignore her. What she said is rude and *wrong*."

Throughout her illness, I'd had to step carefully around any discussion of the future with Rachel. A big part of her believed she'd never be free of pain or out of the wheelchair—and she resented it bitterly whenever she thought people didn't take her situation seriously. Talking about anything that was further down the road than her next medical appointment was a dicey proposition, often prompting her to lash out at us. Thus, Bob and I had tended to avoid such touchy subjects and focus solely on the present as much as possible.

But on that day, looking at my unhappy daughter, who had again been failed by an adult who was supposed to help her, I took a chance. "Rachel," I said with determination. "I think we need to declare some priorities." I told her these were the three things on my list:

1. Get you walking again.

2. Get you a driver's license.

3. Get you a lime-green VW Bug so you can drive yourself to community college.

"And after that, sweetheart," I said, "you can do anything you want to do."

I didn't know how Rachel would react to what I said. Was it too much "future talk" for her? Would she get angry at me, as she had many times before? Was I making things worse instead of better?

She sat quietly for a few moments with a neutral expression on her face. Then, she smiled slyly and said, "Does it have to be a VW Bug?"

Kelly walked beside me as we headed to drama class. Today we were making the plaster of Paris masks for our final performance before school let out for the summer.

"If we can just mold them today, then I can bring them home and get them painted," Kelly said.

The corridor was packed. I hated crowds because they made me feel suffocated and in the way. I apologized as someone bumped into me from behind. Kelly continued discussing masks, but something else caught my attention. Looking to my right, I noticed a tall boy standing at his locker, facing away from me, but right in the path of my wheelchair.

There were people all around—I couldn't move out of the way. *Don't step back*, I silently implored. *Don't step back.*

But he didn't pick up on my mental telepathy. Clenching my armrests with both hands, I watched as he slammed his locker door shut and stepped backward. To my horror, the back of his legs rammed into my chair, his knees buckled, and this six-foot-tall senior landed squarely in my lap.

Time stood still, and just like in slow-motion videos, I heard only deep, elongated sounds all around me. Kelly seemed miles away.

Mystery man froze momentarily, surely as shocked as I was by this turn of events. Then time sped back up and sound returned to normal as he whipped his head around, now just inches from my own. His eyes widened with alarm. Lashing violently from left to right, he tried to get off this carnival ride he'd never meant to get on in the first place.

I was speechless. My arms rested helplessly atop my wheels as I watched this show from my front-row seat. I wanted to move, but my muscles no longer received signals from my brain.

He thrashed back and forth, which repeatedly sent my right wheelchair leg slamming into the locker. He was *so* heavy. Pushing his hand on my armrest, he managed to put one leg back on solid ground. Then he pulled his other leg off me without making eye contact.

"Sorry," he mumbled to the pavement before booking it down the hall.

Later, I told Mom how humiliating it had been to have some random guy fall into my lap with everyone watching.

"Well . . ." she said with a smile, "imagine it from his point of view."

CHAPTER 10

No One Cries Forever

After Taylor and I had finished our therapy session in my bedroom, I switched to my office chair and pushed myself out into the hallway. Where was Mom? The door to her office was closed, and I could hear her talking on the phone.

Pushing the door open, I whispered, "Mom. We're done. You need to pay Taylor."

She held her hand over the phone receiver. "It's Casey," she said. "Calling for you."

Casey! Casey and I had been emailing back and forth for the past two weeks. Dr. Landers had connected us because Casey had Lyme and had been at the same pediatric hospital I'd stayed at before I knew I had Lyme disease. Casey also used a wheelchair and was just as sick as I had been a year ago. And she was *my* age!

"My mom and I are in the car on the way to a doctor's appointment," Casey explained once I got on the line. "Your mom said you were busy, so we chatted with her for a bit!"

Until now, Casey and I had only communicated via email, and although I wanted to explode from excitement, I forced my voice to remain calm. Hearing her describe the day-to-day struggles of performing simple tasks, such as taking a bath or eating at the table, deeply validated my own experience these past three years.

"Rachel!" her mom shouted into the car's speakerphone. "It's so nice to have someone who gets what Casey is going through!"

"I know!" I said, smiling at the phone as if they could see me. "I know."

Later that week, I watched as Alicia, perched up high on a branch above me, collected cherries for the two of us.

"Here, Rachie!" She lowered a handful to me.

Popping one in my mouth, I was instantly aware of the distinct flavor of a cherry picked by someone else. It was like the way peanut butter-and-jelly sandwiches don't taste as good if they are cut straight across instead of diagonally. No one knows why, but it's a fact. Same with cherries. They taste best when you pick them yourself. This marked the third cherry season I'd been stuck on the ground. How many years would go by until I could be the one up in the tree again?

My whole life, we'd lived next to this orchard, and climbing these trees each summer was a huge part of living here. Back in the day, my friends and I would sit in them for hours, picking cherries and carelessly spitting out the pits at friends unfortunate enough to be on the lower branches. That was how cherries were supposed to be eaten— not while sitting useless under the tree. Not picked by someone else.

Our friend Christopher arrived from down the street, and he joined Alicia as they gathered cherries for our pie. I turned away, watching neighbors throwing Frisbees for dogs at the nearby greenbelt. When the bag was full enough, we headed back inside. Together, we pitted the cherries, rolled out the crust, and created our beautiful pie. After Christopher placed it in the oven, the three of us played Age of Empires on the computer while we waited for it to bake.

The scent of fresh pie wafted throughout the house, pulling Dad in from another room. Wandering over to say hello, he expressed a desire for a piece of our hard work.

"Don't worry, Bob, I've got you," Christopher said.

The pie was delicious. It was warm and flaky and better than anything you could ever buy in a store. Alicia smothered her slice in whipped cream, making an evil laugh as she did. But even in the midst of this happy moment, a weight pressed hard against me. It had been a good day—I shouldn't be sad. I should be grateful and enjoy this moment. I was *lucky*. I had so much going for me, so many wonderful people in my life. But as I ate my pie, I felt tears fighting to break free. I had wanted so much to be up in that tree today.

Dorothy

Two pivotal events in the world of Lyme disease occurred that spring. One was the release of the Lyme documentary *Under Our Skin*, the project I'd helped out on two years earlier. After its world premiere at New York's Tribeca Film Festival, the documentary became available for purchase on DVD. I ordered a copy immediately, and Rachel and I waited with excitement for it to arrive by mail.

About the same time, the book *Cure Unknown: Inside the Lyme Epidemic* was published. It had been written by science journalist Pamela Weintraub, whose whole family had contracted Lyme disease. I obtained an advance copy and wrote an article about it for a local newspaper. It was another step into the world of Lyme disease advocacy for me.

Mom sat next to me in the office chair as we watched the new *Under Our Skin* DVD on my computer. With my extra weakness and pain, possibly from a herx, it was a stay-in-bed day. Since I couldn't crawl upstairs to watch the film on the big TV, we made do with the computer in my bedroom. The movie showed a lot of different people with Lyme disease, but I was most interested in Marlena—a teenage girl in a wheelchair, just like me.

My eyes widened as the girl's mother talked about how doctors hadn't believed her. How they had accused Marlena of making up the pain. We were alike in so many ways. She'd grown up doing ballet. I'd grown up playing soccer. She'd scooted around the house to get to her wheelchair, just as I scooted around the house to get to mine. She was in pain and had debilitating fatigue. Me too. This girl was telling my story.

Dorothy

Under Our Skin spelled out in mesmerizing detail everything we'd spent the previous three years learning. There were untold numbers of suffering people systematically denied care by the US medical establishment. This was due in large part to the authors of the Infectious Diseases Society of America's Lyme disease guidelines. This was a powerful group of researchers with demonstrated financial conflicts of interest concerning Lyme disease. There was an endless rabbit hole of political and economic machinations involving insurance companies, government officials, and the targeting of Lyme-treating physicians by state medical boards. But Rachel and I were most fiercely captivated by Marlena and her family, whose story so closely reflected our own. When, by the end of the movie, that girl got out of her wheelchair and walked, Rachel and I held each other and wept.

"I want that to be me," she sobbed in my arms.

"Me too, baby, me too."

For years now, I had been such a burden to my family. Before Lyme, I had done chores, helped out with things around the house, and had been a normal kid doing normal kid things. I used to play soccer and took tap dancing lessons, which I assumed must have cost *something*, but nothing like what my parents were shelling out for my treatment these days. We were in Nevada again, and yesterday's bill had been one thousand dollars to cover both the office visit and the new supplements we'd ordered. One *thousand* dollars. Today we turned around and paid another six hundred just for the treatment. Mom hadn't been trying to show me the bill, but I'd seen it on the counter before she had picked it up.

And that didn't even count our two-night stay at the hotel, the food we ate in restaurants, and the cost of the pottery place we went to every time we were in Nevada. All because we were doing treatment for *me*, and it wasn't even working. If I wasn't in my family anymore, Mom, Dad, and Jeremy could spend this money on fun things for *themselves*. They could have so much freedom if I wasn't such an oppressive weight holding them back.

I tried not to think about money. I tried not to think about how much worse I made everyone's life just by existing. Because when I did, it became all-consuming, and I realized what a horrible person I was. My parents threw away tons of money and got nothing in return. I didn't contribute to this family. I didn't contribute to anything. I didn't think anyone could argue that I was worth even one thousand dollars—let alone the many times that amount Mom and Dad had already spent.

Dorothy

Rachel had been using the wheelchair for three years at this point. While antibiotic therapy and herbal detox protocols seemed to clear her brain and help in other ways, nothing took away her pain. I spent hours online every day, desperately seeking new possibilities.

Whenever I heard that somebody's pain had been helped by Reiki, medical massage, Bowen therapy, craniosacral bodywork, cold lasers, far-infrared saunas, or microcurrent devices—I wanted Rachel to try whatever it was right away. However, my daughter did not share my enthusiasm. She immediately shot down every new idea I proposed. I had to take comfort in the fact that she was still willing to continue with our Lyme doctor and the alternative therapy practitioner in Nevada. But while I stopped telling her about what my research turned up, I never stopped looking.

And then, one fateful day, Casey—the other teenage girl with Lyme—called again. Although the two girls still had never met in person, they had become good friends through email and talking on the phone. It warmed my heart to know that Rachel had someone to talk to who understood what she was going through. I'd spoken with Casey's mother a few times and felt that we had a lot in common, too.

I could hear the excitement in Casey's voice crackling through the receiver.

"Twelve steps!" she sang out. "I walked twelve steps!" Her parents had taken her to a new, specialized chiropractor, she told me. His treatment had reduced her pain enough that she could take twelve steps with a walker after just *one* session with him. "It was like a miracle," she told me. "You've got to see him too, Rachel!"

My mom had been wanting me to explore different kinds of healing stuff for months now, and I'd always said no. Doctors were never the answer—they just made everything worse, and they never believed me. But Casey was a lot like me, and this guy had actually helped her. What if I could take twelve steps too? After I hung up the phone, I got on my office chair and propelled myself down the hall, yelling "Mom!" at the top of my voice.

Dorothy

After months of resisting any suggestions I'd offered for new treatments to try, Rachel was now begging to see Casey's chiropractor. I said I'd call him and see what I could find out. Dr. Becket and I spoke for an hour. After listening to my summary of Rachel's situation, he described his methods. He specialized in upper cervical care, which focused on correcting misalignments of the neck—especially the top two vertebrae, called C1 and C2. He said that having those two vertebrae out of alignment could impair the central nervous system, causing all kinds of problems, including symptoms like Rachel's. First, he would take high-resolution X-rays, which would give clearer information than standard ones. Then, he'd perform a variety of other diagnostic measures to determine what was going on with Rachel. If her situation warranted it, he'd make chiropractic adjustments to realign her neck. Yes, he'd seen many patients with Lyme disease. He didn't treat Lyme disease per se—he treated misalignment of the neck vertebrae. But often this treatment helped to clear up many symptoms Lyme patients experienced, he said. No guarantees, of course. He had an opening for us in two weeks if we were interested. We were.

A few days before we were due to see Dr. Becket, I woke up early from a vivid dream. In it, I had been driving my white van up a steep hill, looking through the windshield at Rachel walking by. In the dream, I had thought, *Oh, good, she's walking again.* As I lay in bed in the dim morning light, pondering that mental image, I wondered, *Can dreams foretell the future? Or is this just an expression of my deepest wish for my daughter?* When my husband woke up a bit later and I started to tell him about it, he looked at me in amazement and said, "I dreamed Rachel was walking too."

Mom, Dad, and I drove two hours through heavy traffic to see Dr. Becket, the upper cervical chiropractor that Casey had told me about. While Mom filled out forms on my behalf, I spoke with the nice lady behind the counter. Her genuine smile lit up the room as she stopped everything to talk with me.

A big man with longish blond hair and wearing scrubs came out. He reached down to give me a firm handshake. I thought he looked nice, like a big teddy bear.

Dr. Becket led the three of us back to his office. There, we saw a flat stool in the corner and an exam table. He also had a computer with strange instruments attached to it.

"Well, let's get right to it. Can you rate your pain on a scale of 1 to 10, with 8 meaning you're in tears?"

His question threw me off. I disliked the pain scale anyway, but to change the rules and say I must be in tears to call something an 8 or higher? That didn't seem right.

"I . . . *uh* . . ." What could I say? I didn't want to categorize my pain as a 7, making it seem less than what it truly was. *It's unbearable. It ruins my life and makes me want to kill myself.* Why couldn't I just say *that*? Instead of a stupid number, why didn't doctors ask for adjectives to describe pain? *Excruciating. Agonizing. Pounding.*

Why did I have to pick an arbitrary number that meant nothing to me?

And what idiot came up with "8 means you're in tears?" Did he expect me to cry for three years *straight*? No one cries forever! And crying was an expression of an emotional state more than anything. I could experience just as much pain, but if I was surrounded by friends, I might be laughing. If I was with doctors who upset me, I might be sobbing. It didn't change the pain; it changed my response to it.

There wasn't enough air with the four of us crammed into this tiny room. Clearly, we'd made a mistake. Why had we even come here? What had we been thinking?

The doctor was waiting for me to respond.

"I guess it's a 7," I replied quietly, even though labeling my pain as a 7 offended me to the core. Like I was belittling it. As tears stung my eyes, I thought, *Can I change my answer? I'm crying now.* But I said nothing aloud.

The doctor then told me that he needed to feel around my back, shoulders, and neck. My tears fell harder as I looked at Mom, shaking my head "no."

"Her shoulders are hypersensitive. She doesn't want anyone to touch them," Mom said in a hushed voice.

Just two short weeks ago, she'd spoken with him at length via phone, judging whether it would be worth it to drive all the way down here in person to meet him. Had he not learned anything from that phone call?

He reached for some kind of device, which he called a paraspinal thermal scan, and asked me to sit up straight and hold my hair to the side. Pushing the gadget firmly against the top of my neck, he slowly slid it downward. As he did so, an image popped up on the computer screen in front of us. Pointing to various parts of the diagram, he said there was definitely something wrong. The X-rays would show more, he told us, but this clearly indicated that the top bones of my neck were out of place. He said this made it difficult for my brain to communicate effectively with my body. Then he placed a stethoscope on my chest and planted his hand firmly on my shoulder. *No!* It felt like a fireball had detonated where his hand was touching.

I can't breathe! 100 out of 10! The pain is 100 out of 10!

I wanted to die. I wanted his stethoscope to show that my heart was no longer beating, that the pain was all gone because I was gone too. Shutting my eyes tightly, I saw deep red lines behind my eyelids, with lights flickering all around. Coughing as I choked on air, I tasted the salt from my tears.

After an eternity, he removed his hand. Shaking, I stared down at the speckled gray carpet, feeling the burn of his handprint tattooed on my right shoulder blade.

Dr. Becket's voice sliced through the suffocating silence.

"Your nervous system is entirely haywire," he said. "It's going nuts, and it needs to calm down."

He explained that my nervous system wasn't holding up its end of the bargain. My intense bone, joint, and muscle pain, as well as my shoulder hypersensitivity, were all being dictated by a struggling nervous system.

In shock, I didn't know what to feel. Part of me believed there was a special place in hell for people who touched my shoulders after I'd told them not to, but another part recognized that this doctor *believed* I was in pain and wanted to help. He just had a twisted way of showing it.

Leaving Mom and Dad behind, he led me to an adjacent room, where I transferred to a thin X-ray chair. Dr. Becket moved as fast as humanly possible through this small room, knowing that it was hard for me to breathe when forced to sit straight up. He may also have realized that we'd gotten off to a rocky start, and this was his one chance at redemption.

When we rejoined my parents in the treatment room, Dr. Becket exhaled deeply.

"I never promise anyone that they will get better. If anyone ever promises that they can fix you—run. But I do believe I can help you." He wanted us to come for treatment every Monday, Wednesday, and Friday for the foreseeable future. A two-hour drive each way!

Leaving through the back door, Mom pushed my wheelchair over the uneven concrete parking lot toward our van. I hoisted myself into the front passenger seat and leaned back, resting my eyes, as Mom and Dad fumbled to get my chair in the trunk.

As Dad backed the car up and drove toward home, I realized that I felt slightly hopeful. As if somewhere deep in the black abyss, a faint candle had been lit.

At my next appointment with Dr. Becket, I had to lower myself to the floor in order to position myself against his flat blue stool so we could begin treatment. Unlike a normal stool, designed for sitting, this one was meant only to hold your head in a contorted, uncomfortable position. Following his instructions, I squished my face against the stool as my legs flailed out to the sides. His hands gently felt around my neck for the right spot before pressure engulfed me, feeling as if all of his weight was crashing down on a single vertebra in my neck. When it was over, I took inventory—feeling as though something had to have snapped in the process.

"Okay! That's it!" he said cheerily, stepping away from me. "You can get back in your wheelchair."

We'd just driven for two hours to be seen for *two minutes*?!

Dazed and dizzy, I hoisted myself up into my wheelchair as he explained that my body-wide pain might stem from my C1 vertebra being out of alignment, as shown in the X-rays taken the previous week.

He pointed to the image, where we could clearly see that the two sides of the spine weren't symmetrical. One jutted far out at an angle, while the other was in line with the rest.

No wonder Lyme treatment wasn't helping my sternum and rib pain! Everything from my neck down had most likely been out of alignment for ages!

As we waited in the lobby for fifteen minutes as instructed, everything felt off. So much so that it was hard to identify what exactly I was feeling.

I turned to Mom. "My neck doesn't hurt," I said quietly, more confused than excited. "But my back and ribs hurt much more than they did before." I wanted to be happy. This was the first time in years that I could point to a moment and say that my neck was not painful—but at what cost?

With each passing minute, my rib pain intensified, and with each shallow breath, my lungs felt as though they were being stabbed by dull knives.

When our fifteen minutes were up, we headed to the car, and Mom chirped about how great it was that we were already seeing progress.

Yeah, I thought. *Progress of the "one step forward, two steps back" variety.*

We got in the car and headed down the street to Whole Foods. As we drove, my ribs screamed for my attention, but I focused on my neck. I had *no* neck pain. *How is this possible?* The bones in my neck had hurt for so long, and until now I couldn't even imagine what it would feel like to not have that constant, sickening, deep bone pain.

I wanted to enjoy this incredible change, but my ribs made that impossible. I couldn't even take a normal breath in anymore.

On the drive home, things got worse. *Way* worse. My iPod couldn't even begin to distract me from the excruciating pain radiating down my spine. My heart was beating fast, and it was hard to breathe. I tried not to panic. *If only I could get out of this car,* I thought. But I was stuck here for another hour. This was a *terrible* plan.

Twisting my neck back and forth, I tried to find any position that was even remotely tolerable. Suddenly I felt a *pop* somewhere deep in my neck. Then, instantly, the shooting pain in my spine died down, right as my neck pain came roaring back into focus.

What in the world had we signed up for?

I took a deep breath—the first I'd had in hours—and thank God, I was now able to do so without my lungs feeling punctured. But the pounding in my neck had returned with hurricane force. I could feel each individual vertebra, and they were all hopping mad.

I reached up to gently cradle my neck in my hands. But the second my fingers made contact, a jolt of fire burned at their touch and catapulted down the skin of my shoulders and back.

I couldn't believe this.

I lightly touched my neck again.

"Oh my God," I blurted out. "The hypersensitivity has spread to my neck."

Dorothy

When we arrived home after more than four hours of driving that day, Rachel was in worse pain than ever. Couldn't my girl ever get a break? But the doctor had warned us about this and urged us to stay strong. I clung to that advice and did my best to keep Rachel calm. I was watching a TV show with her the following afternoon when Dr. Becket phoned. I went into another room to take the call and shut the door behind me.

> "How's it going?" he asked.
>
> "Simply dreadful," I replied. "When we first left your office, her neck had stopped hurting. But by the time we reached home, all her pain had skyrocketed."
>
> "I know this is difficult, but she's got to hang tough. It's so important not to give up now." He told me that people often quit too soon. "Promise me you'll keep coming. Tell her things will get better."

I woke up Sunday morning and lay in bed, staring at the ceiling. What undesirable surprise awaited me today? Taking inventory, I scrutinized every sensation in my body. *Hmm.* The pounding in my neck was gone once more, just like it had been right after the adjustment two days ago.

I sat up.

Still no pain in my neck.

Not wanting to screw anything up but still eager to figure out what was going on, I gently placed my hand on my neck, right below my ear. I breathed a sigh of relief. No more hypersensitivity in my neck.

My back pain had returned to baseline as well.

Thank God. What a roller coaster.

Dorothy

Thus began our new summer routine. Every Monday, Wednesday, and Friday, we loaded up the van and took the two-hour trek to Dr. Becket's office. After each short visit, we'd eat lunch at Whole Foods and then head home. Rachel had an iPod full of music, along with books and magazines to help pass the time, but the drive was tedious. Finally we hit upon an elegant solution. Bringing her friend Alicia along for the ride solved two problems at once: The girls could entertain each other, and having a third person in the van let us use the carpool lane. This simplified the trip considerably.

"Find a train track," Alicia read aloud from Rubberneckers. The card game allowed me to spend my mental energy looking for things like a gas station, a green truck, or a license plate from a different state, instead of on the constant pain I felt from vibrations in the road.

"I don't think we will see a train track for a while, Alicia," Mom commented, as she made her way over to the HOV lane on the left.

"Put that one aside and pick another," I said, adjusting my position slightly to see Alicia sitting in the seat behind Mom.

"Okay, find a semitruck," she read.

Turning to my right, I watched as we passed by a large tractor trailer. "Done."

Before we knew it, we were sitting in the waiting room of Dr. Becket's office. Mom and I headed back to the treatment area while Alicia stayed and chatted with his receptionist.

"How are you feeling today?" Dr. Becket asked as I positioned myself for the paraspinal thermal scan hooked up to the computer.

"The usual," I replied.

The cool plastic of his scanner slid gently down my neck.

"This looks good!" he exclaimed. "This looks very good!"

I smiled. Good was good. He pointed to the monitor, showing us that my body was adjusting itself and doing what it needed to do.

"We're going to leave it alone for now. Your body is doing exactly what we want. Let's let it sit for the time being, and we will check again on Wednesday."

Say what?

I looked at Mom. Was he not going to do another adjustment? Had we just driven two hours for no reason?

I rolled out of the exam room feeling like I had been punched in the gut. I found Alicia sitting in the corner, talking to strangers. Her superpower was an ability to connect with just about anyone, no matter their age or background. Seeing us, she said goodbye to her new friends and scampered over.

I wanted to break down. My back hurt extra because I'd just spent two hours in a vibrating vehicle, and now I had to turn around and do it all again—all for a pointless appointment. But I couldn't cry with Alicia here, so I tried out a weak smile instead.

"Wow, Rachie, that was really quick!"

"I know."

Mom paid for our nothing of an appointment, and we climbed back into our van and went to Whole Foods. As Alicia and I settled in at a table up front, Mom brought us forks, spoons, and knives made out of potatoes. (They might have looked like plastic, but the utensils really were made out of potatoes. It was a sustainability thing.)

My oatmeal looked delicious. It was topped with walnuts, cranberries, raisins, seeds, and a heap of shredded coconut. As I raised the spoon to my mouth, an employee walked over, introduced himself as Marty, and placed beautiful red flowers in a Whole Foods cup at the center of our table.

"Thank you!" the three of us said, practically in unison.

Marty stayed for a bit to chat, saying he'd seen us here before. I put down my spoon and explained how we drove all this way for medical treatment.

"You all just looked like you could use some flowers!" he said gently before wishing us a great rest of our day and waving a friendly goodbye.

Peering around, I saw that no other table had flowers. Just ours! I bit into my warm, gooey, perfectly textured oatmeal while admiring our special gift. Marty was right—we could use some flowers today.

Back in the carpool lane, we sped past cars that had all but stopped in the right three lanes of the highway. Another accident. We saw a lot of accidents these days.

"Ground, green, gravel, g- . . . g- . . . gliding! That plane is gliding!" I was so proud of that last one.

We were playing a game where you pick a letter and name everything outside the car window beginning with that letter. For instance, depending on the letter, you might refer to the road as *ground, tar, asphalt, freeway, highway,* or *street.* It really worked your brain muscles.

"Ooh, gliding is a good one," Mom commented.

"Grass, you said green but not grass," Alicia stared intensely out her window. "Grandma! Look! There's an old lady—I bet she's a grandma!"

We were comfortable with our new routine. Three days a week, we picked Alicia up early in the morning and brought her along with us to my appointment. School was out, and she didn't really have anything else to do. So, although she was clearly helping us more than we were helping her, I liked to think it was mutually beneficial. Like a weird version of summer camp.

Each treatment day basically went like this: We made the long car ride to Dr. Becket, spent two minutes getting adjusted, waited fifteen minutes in the lobby after the adjustment, went to Whole Foods where Marty was waiting to give us flowers, ate, got back in the car, drove two hours home, and dropped Alicia off. I then spent the rest of the day in more pain, followed by the next day when I was usually in less pain. And repeat.

"Gentleman," Mom added. "There's a gentleman in that car. And there are gray clouds. And a golden sun."

She's good.

CHAPTER 11

Two-and-a-Half-Inches Taller

After a couple weeks of treatment with Dr. Becket, he told us about a research study he was doing with a special type of grounding machine. It used energy from the earth to somehow help fix people. I didn't really understand what he explained—it sounded like magic to me—but the gist was that he thought my shoulders could benefit from this treatment. I was on the fence until he noted that a top athlete was using this machine over in China as we spoke, preparing for the 2008 Summer Olympics in Beijing.

It was settled then. If it was good enough for an Olympian, it was good enough for me.

After he adjusted my neck, we moved to another small room where a machine with a bunch of wires attached to it sat next to an office chair. My gaze landed on the sticky square pieces at the end of each wire. I didn't like where this was going.

"Where do you put those?" I asked cautiously.

"Two will go up here," he said, pointing to the top of my shoulders without touching. "And two will go right below the shoulder blades."

Danger. Danger.

"I can't have anything on my shoulders," I said, feeling let down. This was not new information for him, so why were we even discussing it? "Can we put them lower on my back?"

"No, we need to put them right on the shoulders themselves to get the most benefit."

I *hated* this. So far, no one had ever recommended a treatment specifically to help my hypersensitive shoulders. Now, Dr. Becket's experimental machine offered that possibility, but it sounded like it might also cause me a lot of pain. I felt conflicted. Though I strongly doubted this new gadget would actually help my shoulders, what if it did?

"All right," I said grudgingly, sucking in my breath as he placed the electrodes.

Both hands formed fists as I held myself as still as possible. The sticky electrodes felt cold against my skin. Dr. Becket set a timer for thirty minutes and left the room.

My body didn't know what to do with the sensation of stickiness. My shoulders writhed back and forth as my right arm jutted out to the side. My left shoulder elevated, forcing my neck down in a painful thrust. Tightening my face and squeezing my eyes shut, I used all my power to will my body to settle down.

Fighting the urge to pull off the wires and call it quits, I leaned back in my wheelchair, pressing my head against my puffy soccer ball pillow. My feet flattened on the footrests as I ran my fingers across the little picture Alicia had taped to the side of my wheelchair. She hadn't been able to come with us today, so I was all on my own.

I am okay. I am okay.

I inserted my earbuds in the hope that Katy Perry could take my mind off the sticky little devils plastered to my shoulders. When the timer beeped, Dr. Becket returned, explaining that from now on, our new routine would be adjustment first, followed by thirty minutes with the grounding machine.

At least now we wouldn't be driving four hours round trip for a two-minute appointment.

Dorothy

That summer, we also started regularly going to our neighborhood swimming pool. If we took her wheelchair right up to the edge of the shallow end, Rachel could lower herself out of the chair and slip into the water. Then, with the help of a pool noodle, she could keep herself afloat while her legs simply trailed behind her. Being in the water let her move about and play with her friends in a way she couldn't on dry land. It became her happy place.

As she splashed around with Alicia and Shira, Rachel seemed to be moving her legs more with each passing day. Apparently, playing in the pool was a useful adjunct to Dr. Becket's treatment. When he told us he was taking his family on vacation for two weeks and would be unavailable for treatment, he encouraged us to keep up with the swimming. As disappointed as I was that he was leaving us, I appreciated the break from all the driving.

As I approached the pool, I remembered what Dr. Becket had said about the importance of swimming. Staying stationary was the worst thing a person could do, apparently. Movement was the key to keeping your body in proper alignment.

Lowering myself into the water, I took a deep breath, fell forward, and let my body go limp. With my face under the surface, I brought my legs into a fetal position underneath me. This eased my back pain for as long as I could hold my breath. When my lungs couldn't last any longer, I lifted my head out of the water and inhaled deeply before doing it again.

I finally understood why lying motionless in the water helped my back and neck pain so much. It had to do with alignment and taking pressure off my spine. If I'd had a snorkel with a long enough breathing tube, I would have happily stayed in the fetal position all day, but Alicia was waiting for me. Wiping the water out of my eyes, I held on to the wall as deep pressure stormed back into my neck and spine.

Alicia threw an orange diving ring across the pool. "Let's go!"

Releasing my noodle, I dove below the surface in pursuit of the sinking ring. I didn't wear goggles since they always fogged up. But even with the water blurring my eyesight, I clearly spotted the orange toy making its slow descent. My fingers grasped the plastic ring just before it reached the bottom.

Resurfacing, I breathed heavily as I tossed the ring clear across the pool for Alicia and slowly made my way over to her. During the past few summers, I hadn't been able to swim with my legs. They'd just dangled behind me while my arms did all the work. But lately, things had been different. I found I could kick them gently in the water, growing muscle and confidence as I did.

Dorothy

Rachel's mental and physical status seemed better than it had been in ages, and I desperately needed a break from our routine. Jeremy had a summer job near Seattle, and Bob and I decided to visit him for the weekend. We arranged for Julia, a college girl who had grown up next door to us, to spend the weekend with Rachel. Julia was always like an older sister to Rachel. As Bob and I drove to the airport, I felt a weight fall from my shoulders.

Unlike other teens who got to go over to friends' houses or go away to camp, I didn't have such luxuries. I couldn't even be driven around by a friend's parent, because they weren't set up to haul my wheelchair. So, no matter where I went, or what I did, Mom was *always* there. Especially after all our driving to and from Dr. Becket's office, both of us really needed a change of pace.

Julia was upstairs watching *Deadliest Catch* and working on her needlepoint. Alicia and I were downstairs in my bedroom, playing *Marble Blast Gold* on my computer.

Alicia looked at me conspiratorially and said, "Do you think we could sneak upstairs without Julia hearing us?"

"*Um*, yeah, I do!" I said with conviction.

I clicked a blue-and-yellow icon at the bottom of the computer screen, which opened up my audio recording software. "What if we record ourselves down here for a few minutes, and then play it really loudly so she'll think we're still down here?" Sometimes I was blown away by my own genius.

Alicia grabbed the microphone from my desk and squealed into it. "Hi, Rachie!"

We talked back and forth, eventually just describing all the objects in my room to keep the conversation going.

"Okay," I put the mic down. "I think we have enough."

I turned the volume up and pressed play.

"Hi, Rachie!"

I smiled at Alicia, confident our plan would work. I got in my office chair, and we slowly made our way out of the room and down the hallway toward the stairs. I winced at the noise made by the plastic wheels against the floor, but the loud conversation from my bedroom drowned out the sound.

Lowering onto the bottom step, I quietly hoisted myself backward up the stairs. Alicia followed, crawling on all fours up the steps below me. We stopped when we reached the top, watching Julia across the way, calmly sitting on the couch.

Though we made no noise, she absentmindedly looked over in our direction. "Oh my God!" she gasped, bringing her hand to her chest.

Laughter erupted as we high-fived.

This weekend was going to be amazing.

Dorothy

Our trip to Washington state was wonderful. We spent time with Jeremy, played tourist around Seattle, and took a ferry to visit my aunt on Whidbey Island. She asked about Rachel's situation, and I explained as best I could. "She's started a new treatment," I said. "I think it might be helping."

On August 1, Dr. Becket returned from his vacation, and Mom and I resumed our regular drives to his office. On the way back home that day, I inadvertently discovered that I could sit up straight in the van and still breathe easily. *What?* For three years now, whenever I had sat up straight, my spine would feel like it had been stabbed with a dagger, and I couldn't get enough air. This new situation didn't compute. I reclined in the seat once more, afraid to keep sitting up straight until I figured out what was going on.

I opened up Solitaire on my iPod and tried to focus on it. Yet the thought kept nagging at me. If I sat up straight, I'd be able to see out the window better. I never got a good view from down here. Should I give it another go?

No. I scolded myself for even thinking about trying to sit up in the car again. That was *not* an option. I didn't do that. I couldn't. I wanted to; I'd *always* wanted to—but I couldn't breathe when I sat up. It was clearly a fluke. It wouldn't last. If I got all excited about it now, it would only hurt more when life went back to normal.

Once we were home, Mom pulled my wheelchair out of the car and brought it over to me. I lowered down into it and headed straight for my room. I crawled into my bed, like always, but this time I sat up straight.

Taking a deep breath in, I felt my rib cage expand and then compress. No sharp pains deep in my lungs. No lack of oxygen in the room.

"Oh my God," I whispered aloud. The pounding I'd felt in my spine for the past three years was gone! I'd been so focused on my breathing that I hadn't even thought about my lack of back pain!

I could breathe while sitting up! And my back didn't hurt. This wasn't just in my mind. This wasn't a dream. This was *real*. I looked up to see my reflection in the full-length mirror on the wall across from my bed. I was *sitting up*.

I reached for the computer and opened up my journal.

"I AM WRITING THIS SITTING UP STRAIGHT!!!!" I wrote in all caps, with plenty of exclamation marks. "I'M SITTING UP RIGHT NOW!!! OH MY GOD!!!!!!!!!!!"

I leaned back against my pillow and then sat up once more. I took another deep breath, feeling both elated and terrified now that everything was changing.

I turned the computer's camera on and watched myself onscreen. I was nearly seventeen years old, and the last time I'd been able to breathe normally while sitting in this position was when I was thirteen. This morning, the first thing I'd felt when I woke up was the constant pounding in my back. Then, after a seemingly typical Dr. Becket appointment, it now had gone quiet.

What did this mean for my future?

"Mom!" I yelled out.

Dorothy

I came running at Rachel's call. "It doesn't hurt to sit up straight!" she shouted. "It doesn't hurt, and I can breathe!" As I looked at her in astonishment, a world of possibilities flew through my mind. Even if she never got out of the wheelchair, just being able to sit up straight would improve her quality of life tremendously. Car rides would be easier. Attending school would be easier. Eating meals at a table would be easier. Was this really all from Dr. Becket's neck adjustments?

She moved to her office chair, and we went out to the living room to retrieve her wheelchair. It no longer needed to be reclined! I adjusted it to an upright position, and we took this "new" chair on a spin around the neighborhood. The world around us seemed brighter and more beautiful that day.

The next day, I sat in my wheelchair in the center of the garage, looking out as Dad cleaned the van in the carport. While I watched, Mom was on an important Lyme call. She did a lot of Lyme advocacy these days. Whenever Dad turned off the vacuum cleaner, I heard the rise and fall of her voice coming from inside the house.

In the corner of the garage, I spotted a box filled with sports supplies from when I was younger. Dusty softball equipment poked out, along with several deflated soccer balls. I wasn't brave enough to reach in and reclaim any of my old possessions. The box was probably full of spiders.

To my left, I saw three bikes, dusty from lack of use. What if I could ride one? It couldn't be that hard—I'd been swimming a lot, and my legs were getting stronger from the exercise.

Dad was bent over, vacuuming under the seats as I wheeled closer to Mom's bike.

I parked alongside it. Using the chair and armrests for leverage, I hoisted myself up and over onto the bike seat.

I was so high up! Pushing my wheelchair away with my leg, I swiveled my neck around to see if Dad saw me.

As if he sensed something, he crawled backward out of the van and looked in my direction. Eyes wide open, he dropped the vacuum with a crash and ran over.

"Whoa!" He came close enough to grab the bike if necessary, but he didn't tell me to get off.

I sat up as straight as I could, feeling my core muscles come to life after years of hibernation.

"Look!" I squealed. "I'm on a bike!"

"I see that! How does it feel?"

"Good! It feels good!"

I moved my bare feet around until I located the metal kickstand. Lifting it up, I steadied myself with both legs out to the sides, with my feet touching the dusty garage floor.

I felt so badass at that moment.

"Watch, Dad!"

I pushed on the pedals, but they didn't move an inch. I tried again. Nope.

Dad lowered the gears, but still nothing happened.

"Here," he said, bringing over his own bike. "Switch over to this." He held it steady while I got on.

Round two.

As I pushed as hard as I could, the bike slowly rolled forward. Gripping the rubber handles for dear life, I kept my balance as the bike lurched back and forth at my quarter-mile-per-hour speed.

Nearing the edge of the garage, I rolled to a stop, backing myself up with my feet. Then I did it again.

And again.

"Mom needs to see this," I told Dad.

"She's still on her call," Dad replied. "Let's film it for her!"

I moaned. "But she needs to see the real thing . . ."

What I couldn't articulate was that this might be *it*. Tomorrow I might wake up in my normal, excruciating pain, and she would have missed the one chance she had to see me ride a bike. Mom *needed* to come out here.

"Can you just tell her to come and look?" I pleaded. "She doesn't have to get off her call, just have her *look* out here."

"Okay," he conceded.

He ducked into the house for the camera and in a moment, Mom peeked out the door, holding the phone to her ear.

Her eyes grew big, and she said a hasty goodbye to the person on the phone.

"Film her, Dad!!" I insisted. "Mom! What did you think when you came out and saw me on the bike?" I demanded with a grin.

"Um, um," she stammered, grasping for words. "I'm amazed. I'm amazed and astounded." She looked at the camera in Dad's hands and continued, "I was in the middle of a phone call, and I hung up, because this is more important." She reached over and hooked pinkies with me, forming our special handshake.

I launched into the saga of how I had climbed up all on my own, and how I'd ridden back and forth in the garage. I mimicked Dad's expression when he first saw me on the bike, and both my parents laughed out loud.

Dorothy

Things were definitely shifting. Rachel seemed willing to try moving her body in ways she hadn't even attempted for ages. Bob and I let her lead the way. We didn't want to screw things up by pushing her to do something and have her rebel against us. Instead, we resolved to stay quietly supportive and see what happened next.

Five days later, I stared at my bedroom ceiling in the early morning light. My crutches—which I hadn't used in three years—kept calling to me from my closet. Alicia had put them there this weekend after finding them in a dusty corner of our garage. She thought I could shoot a video of her messing around with them, but we'd run out of time. But what I hadn't even told her was—I wanted to mess around with them myself.

The house was quiet. With Mom and Dad still asleep, it was the perfect time to try. No pressure if it didn't work—no one even had to know.

I kicked off my sheets, moved to my office chair, and rolled over to the closet. I removed the crutches and placed them across my lap. Bringing the video camera, I slowly pushed myself down the hall to Jeremy's vacant bedroom. Mom and Dad would wake up if a pin dropped, so precautions were essential.

I set up the camera on the tripod in a corner of the room and crawled to the edge of the bed. Standing up on my knees, I placed the crutches under my arms and leaned forward, letting my legs slide off of the bed behind me. My feet pressed against the floor, but before I could get them in place beneath me, I toppled over, landing on the carpet.

Try again.

Back up on the bed, with the crutches positioned in front of me, I pushed my body forward. But again, too much momentum sent me flying, this time head-on into our leather chair in the corner.

Ouch.

My legs were so weak and uncomfortable—I could barely put any pressure on them. My fingers slid across a bump on my left knee, which I bet would turn into a bruise later. I could see the camera's red light was still on. *Good!* It was capturing all of this.

Try again.

Once more, I crawled back up onto the bed. I put the crutches in front of me and carefully slid my legs off the edge. The carpet tickled my bare feet. My atrophied legs felt like spaghetti noodles, but somehow, I kept my balance. *I'm doing it!* Taking a deep breath, I tried to straighten up to a full standing position, but I just couldn't put enough pressure on my feet to manage it.

Leaning backward, I let myself fall onto the bed and paused to catch my breath. My watch said it was 5:12 a.m. I really wanted to share this new development with Mom and Dad. Was it too early? *Nah!* Hoisting myself back up on the crutches, I hobbled down the hallway to my parents' bedroom and tapped quietly on their door.

No answer.

I knocked again.

Dorothy

A knock on the bedroom door roused me from a deep sleep. I stumbled groggily toward it, never thinking it might be Rachel, although she was of course the only other person in the house. Did I somehow think it was an intruder, politely knocking before invading our personal space? I actually didn't think anything—I was still half-asleep. The bedroom was dark, but when I opened the door, light from the hallway temporarily blinded me. I squinted through the doorway, trying to make sense of what I saw. Rachel was standing up tall, directly in front of me.

Mom opened the door, standing eye-to-eye with me and staring for a moment. Then she called out, "Oh my God!"

Dad bolted upright in bed. "What's wrong?"

He looked over at me standing in the hallway and echoed Mom's initial reaction.

Suddenly, I felt like all my previous energy had evaporated. Afraid that I'd collapse on the floor, I pushed past them, saying "I need to lie down . . ." Then I fell forward onto their mattress.

I was exhausted. Mom and Dad returned to bed, and I lay between them as we all worked to slow down our collective heart rates.

"Wow," Mom whispered.

Breathing out a long, slow breath, I nodded. "I know."

"You're full of surprises these days," Dad added.

"I know."

The next day, we were back in the car, returning from another trip to Dr. Becket. "When will we be home?" I tapped my fingers anxiously against the car door as acres of farmland passed by my window. Never had a trip back from Dr. Becket's dragged on *this* long.

"About twenty minutes," Mom said absentmindedly.

I couldn't tell Mom and Dad yet, but I knew with every fiber of my being that when I got home today, I would *walk*. My body had been screaming it at me ever since my adjustment with Dr. Becket this afternoon.

"Can we fix the pads on the crutches so they don't hurt my armpits so much?" I hoped this came off sounding casual.

"We'll look and see what we can do."

"Good."

I leaned back in my seat, pressing my feet on the floor, discreetly seeing how much weight they could hold. From this angle I couldn't get leverage—I'd need to wait until I wasn't tethered to the seat.

What had it been, two minutes now? That meant eighteen minutes until we were home. My heart was beating like a bongo drum. Ever since today's adjustment, I'd had no throbbing pain in my back, knees, or neck. It was like somebody had flipped a switch and turned off the pain. Now only the hypersensitivity in my shoulders remained.

As much as I wanted to sing out this news at the top of my lungs, I forced myself to keep quiet. What if I still couldn't walk, even with the pain gone? What if when I started walking, the pain came back? No one could know that this adjustment had been different from the rest—not until I could try standing up on my own.

After an eternity, we parked in the driveway, and Dad brought my wheelchair around for me. I lowered into it, paying close attention to the sensation of settling into my gel-padded seat, the slick metal bars beneath my hands. I pushed myself forward toward the house, bracing for impact as I passed over the bump of the threshold. I took note of it all—because somewhere deep inside, I knew this would be the last time I used my wheelchair.

I escaped to my room and closed the door behind me. I grabbed the crutches from my closet and sat on the bed. Steadying myself with the crutches, I stood up. Today was different from yesterday; standing felt easier, sturdier. The girl staring back at me in my bedroom mirror was so tall that I ducked my head so as not to be whacked by the ceiling fan.

I could do this. *I'm ready.* Forging my way across the room, I pulled the door open just a crack.

"Dad!" I yelled. "Get the camera and tell me when it's on!"

"One moment! I'm coming!"

I heard him scrambling around the living room as he located our Panasonic video camera sitting on the counter.

"Okay, we're rolling!" he yelled.

As I stepped forward, my bare feet pressed gently on the floor, the floor we got specifically so I could get around on my office chair three years ago—back when we'd hoped this would be just a short-lived adventure.

Turning down the hall, I limped the rest of the way to the living room, feeling immense pressure on my arms from the crutches. Mom and Dad whooped and hollered as I made my entrance and plopped down on the couch with a bow.

"Look at you go!" Dad said, as Mom disappeared into the garage. She came back pushing a big black walker I'd never seen before. "Why don't you try this?"

"I'm not using that," I protested. It was cumbersome—and meant for old, frail grandparents. Not for *me*.

"Okay," Mom didn't argue. "I just thought it might be easier on your arms to use this." She started to take it back to the garage.

"Wait . . ." Stuck between wanting to look cool and wanting to be rid of the crutches, I motioned for her to come back.

Pulling myself up into a standing position with the walker, I realized just how valuable a device this was. It let me stand up straight, instead of slumped over on the crutches. It also allowed for a more natural gait, and my armpits were thrilled with the change.

I started forward, hearing the screech of plastic grinding against the vinyl flooring. Pausing for a moment, I looked at Mom, but she shrugged and gestured for me to keep going. My right leg was doing most of the work, while the left remained bent and largely useless. The floor felt incredibly hard against my tender feet, and my right foot felt like I was stepping on a hard rock.

With each lap around the living room, I stood taller and more sure-footed. Hannah, our beagle, ran around excitedly, caught up in the energy of the moment.

"I want to try standing without the walker!" I said, glancing at the camera in Dad's hands to make sure he was catching everything.

Taking a deep breath in, I prepared for my very first solo stand in three years. Releasing my grip on the walker, I made it to the count of two before falling down to the floor, squealing with delight.

"Two seconds! That's the score to beat!" I announced, thrilled at this new game I'd just discovered.

Pulling myself back up, I tried again.

"One ... two ..." My legs sank further. "Three ... four ..." Down I went.

Soon, I could stand unaided for thirty seconds. Mom came over to pose for a picture, wrapping her arms around me, careful not to touch my shoulders. With her face so close to mine, I realized I needed to look *down* to see her eyes.

"Who's taller, Dad?"

"Well," he examined us for a moment, letting out a little laugh. "You are, Rachel."

"I'm *taller* than she is?" I was astonished.

The evening continued in a whirlwind. Within fifteen minutes, I'd gone from crutches to walker to holding on to Mom's arm.

As we crossed the living room, my left leg struggled to hold any weight, forcing my right foot to repeatedly slam into the ground sooner than expected to prevent me from falling. My feet hurt, but with all the excitement, the concept of shoes had never crossed my mind.

"I want to try walking on my own," I said. "Just to see."

I released Mom's arm and felt only air surrounding me. As I lifted my right leg, my left one collapsed, and I tumbled forward, catching myself with my hands. I squealed with each fall. It was thrilling, intoxicating. I wanted *more*.

When I tried again, my left leg buckled under my weight, but I managed to keep my balance. My arms flailed, going every which way to keep me upright. With sheer determination I made the treacherous voyage across the living room. After stopping for a photo op, I went to my room, unaided, in search of long pants to try walking in. Out of habit, I sat down on my bed as I changed into my favorite pair of corduroys. Mom was crying in the kitchen, but I could tell they were happy tears.

Soon, we invited our next-door neighbors over, and I demonstrated how I could open the microwave, grab a glass from the top shelf, and how I needed to bend *down* to wash my hands in the sink. My audience cheered as I walked across the kitchen and placed my hand on top of the fridge just because I could. They clapped as I made my way to Mom, giving her a hug.

Each time I passed through a doorway, I ducked my head so I wouldn't hit the frame. Dad said I didn't need to do that, but I felt so tall now that I was quite certain I did. Following him out to the garage, I stood against our measuring wall and Dad marked my new height. Over the past three years, I'd grown two-and-a-half inches without even noticing!

The neighbors left and our house was quiet. Exhilarated and exhausted, I realized once more just how much my feet hurt.

Mom brought a bucket of ice water for me to soak my aching feet in, and we all sat down to watch the opening ceremony of the 2008 Summer Olympics taking place in Beijing, China.

Mom smiled at me and whispered, "We had our own Olympic event today."

She said that the Olympic committee specifically chose to open the Games that day, August 8, 2008, because 08-08-08 was an auspicious date in China. I had known nothing of this until then, but I concurred that 08-08-08 was indeed a lucky day.

Dorothy

The next twenty-four hours brought a whirlwind of activity to our house. Neighbors dropped by because they'd heard our good news through word of mouth and wanted to cheer Rachel on. Others came by special invitation. Rachel called her pal Jenny and casually said, "Any chance you can drop by today? I have something I want to show you." When the totally unsuspecting Jenny showed up at our front porch, Rachel opened the door and stood there beaming at her friend. Jenny was so overwhelmed by what she saw that she dropped to the ground and started to cry.

The following day, Dad handed me two black ankle braces. "Try these."

We were sitting on the living room couch, which felt foreign to me. I was used to supplying my own seating arrangement. I pulled the ankle braces on and laced up the green running shoes we'd bought three years before. They'd been in the back of my closet all this time.

Both of my ankles hurt so bad. The bones in my feet felt like they were being crushed into tiny pieces each time I put weight on them. Mom had me periodically soak my feet in cold water, but that didn't offer much relief. The only thing that kept me mobile was the pair of supportive running shoes. When I wore the shoes, I could push through the pain more easily. It was strange. I'd lived with pain for three years, but this felt totally different. For so long, my ankles hadn't had any work to do and then all of a sudden, I was using them nonstop.

Shira was here hanging out with me, and once my new ankle braces were on, I followed her to my bedroom. Last night we'd lowered my bed to a flat position, so now it looked just like anyone else's. No one would even know it could function like a hospital bed.

I was lying on my newly lowered bed to rest my legs when the doorbell rang. I heard Mom's footsteps scurrying toward the door.

"Are the rumors true?" Our neighbor Jill's muffled voice carried through the wall. "Can Rachel walk?"

I didn't catch Mom's response, but I heard Jill say, "Can I see?"

Mom called for me and I hobbled to the living room. Jill was appropriately impressed.

"Wow!" she whispered, tears in her eyes. "Wow."

I smiled through the pain. As much as I wanted to sit down, I also wanted to show Jill what she'd come to see. Jill had been such a support to our family these past few years. She'd even gone to the pharmacy to pick up my medication when Mom and Dad hadn't been able to.

"Rachel needs to rest her legs now," Mom said, giving me my exit.

I waved goodbye and headed back to my room, crawling into bed. I told Shira I was tired, and she headed home.

It had been fun showing off my new walking skills. People's reactions varied from being shocked into silence to screaming and everything in between. But the whole experience was confusing and draining. Ever since last night, things had been constant high energy. I felt like I didn't even know what was happening or who I was anymore. I hadn't had a moment to wrap my head around all this.

I found my black hoodie in the closet and put it on. Then I pulled my hair back and put on the blonde wig I used to wear for music videos. For years now, this wig had been how I'd transformed into my alter ego, April. April was blonde, smart, and had her life all figured out. I was done being Rachel for right now. I needed to be April.

I flipped the camera's screen around to face me and pushed the record button.

"Hi," I said to the camera in a higher-pitched voice than usual. "I'm April. Guess what I can do?" I set the camera down and walked across the room. "I can walk! That's how you know I'm not Rachel. Rachel can't walk."

I went into the bathroom and watched April in the mirror. She looked tall and strong and confident. I stared at her for several moments, longing to feel as sure of myself as she did.

Stepping carefully, I headed back to my room. My gait was awkward and unnatural. How did I use to do this? I couldn't get into a rhythm, and I seemed to be leaning too far forward. I climbed back into bed, still in my April attire. I thought I'd be her for a while longer.

The next morning I sat up in bed and took inventory of what was going on with my body. My neck was stiff as I stretched it left and right. And my calves were tight and uncomfortable. They didn't feel like this yesterday. I swung my legs over the side of the bed and glanced around for my office chair. Then I realized, hey—I didn't need that anymore! I could get out of bed without it. Extending my legs toward the ground, I started to stand up.

Bam!

I collapsed on the floor before I could catch myself. My legs—there was something seriously wrong with my legs! When I touched my calves, they felt tender and swollen. I couldn't get back up in bed; it was too high up from down here.

"Mom!"

Frantically, I tried stretching out my legs, but my calf muscles were too tight and painful. What was happening?

Mom brought my office chair, and I went to the living room the old-fashioned way, feeling defeated.

I *knew* this had been too good to be true.

Mom called a neighbor who was a physical therapist and asked for advice. The woman said that lactic acid had probably built up in my legs. Apparently, this happened to normal people after they did a hard workout. She suggested doing what she called "wall leans" to slowly stretch out my calf muscles.

But I couldn't even attempt wall leans until I could stand up. While I stayed on the couch, we used heat packs to loosen my calves enough to straighten my legs. From there, I tried standing, breathing through the pain as I slowly rose up to my full height. Hobbling to the nearest wall, I leaned forward ever so slightly, fearing that something would snap and make things ten times worse than before.

Luckily, that didn't happen. After a few wall leans, things improved enough that I could limp around the house. This was quite a comedown after my triumphant display of walking over the past two days. But any benefit of wall leaning was short-lived. Each time I sat down—even for a minute—the calf clock reset, and I'd have to start the process all over again. Would it always be like this? What would happen if I went somewhere with no walls to lean on?

"Let's go to the pool," Mom suggested. "Maybe that will loosen up those leg muscles." Alicia joined us. Somehow, we made it from the car to the water's edge. Lowering myself down the pool steps, I gripped the railing tightly in case my legs gave out. Once submerged, however, things were better. The buoyancy of the water allowed me to move freely once more. Everything was easier in the pool; I could kick, stand up in the shallow end, and dive for rings in the deep end. As Alicia and I splashed and played in the water, the anxiety I'd felt earlier started to ebb away.

After a while, Mom said, "It's time to get going. The potluck starts in an hour." Our neighborhood had a potluck every Sunday in the summertime, which we attended as often as possible. I had a feeling today's would be different from most.

As I walked up the steps out of the pool, I instantly felt the difference. My legs were back!

"Mom, look! I can walk again! It's a magic pool!"

After getting home and changing into dry clothes, I placed each foot awkwardly in front of the other, following Mom and Dad down the path to the greenbelt. There would be questions—lots of them. Voices drifted from beyond the bushes as I rounded the corner. *This is it.*

With a deep breath, I made it two steps before hearing "Rachel!" followed by gasping. All conversations halted as I stepped into view. Smiling, I timidly waved hello and continued forward to set up my lawn chair.

Everyone wanted to hug me, so Mom and I took turns reminding the crowd that my shoulders were still hypersensitive and couldn't be touched—which was code for: Don't hug me, let *me* hug *you.*

Relishing the ability to fill my own potluck plate for the first time in three years, I picked every fruit and dessert dish available. All this time, I'd had to rely on my parents or friends to choose my food for me at potlucks, since the picnic table's built-in benches made it impossible to reach from my wheelchair. But no more. While playing Tetris with slices of watermelon on my plate, I heard a buzz of conversation behind me.

Once I sat down in the circle of chairs, neighbors peppered me with questions. *When did this happen? How did this happen? What type of doctor got you walking? Do you still need to see him or are you done with treatment?* I fielded some of them, and let Mom handle the rest.

Shira, Christine, Alicia, and I sat together at one edge of the circle. Then we saw our friend Stephanie walking toward us.

"She doesn't know!" someone whispered. "Rachel, she doesn't know!"

"Hey, guys!" Stephanie called out.

All conversation stopped. Every person in the circle watched, waiting for me to show Stephanie my new superpower.

I obliged. After using my arms to push myself up and out of my folding lawn chair, I took two steps toward Stephanie. But my ankle got caught on the handle of a bag on the ground, and I came crashing down in front of her.

"Wh-what?" Stephanie looked bewildered. "What's happening?"

I'd just fallen flat on my face in front of thirty neighbors, that's what was happening. This wasn't the cinematic entrance I'd been going for.

Scrambling to my feet, I sheepishly told her, "Guess what? I can walk now."

Since everyone's reaction so far had been to try to hug me, I beat her to it and hugged her first. This kept her arms out of reach, so she wouldn't accidentally touch my shoulders.

Things settled down, and Stephanie joined us in the circle of potluck chairs on the grass. But it seemed like everyone else was staring at me like I was an animal at the zoo. "Hey, let's go kick a soccer ball," I suggested. Let the adults do their gawking from afar.

Grass felt funny to walk on. It was lumpy everywhere, and I had to remember to pick up my feet higher than I did on concrete. I carried the ball as we made our way to the other end of the field. I hadn't held a soccer ball in so long. It felt good.

We all spread out, and I dropped the ball on the ground in front of me, preparing to kick it. Boy, my legs were unsteady. This moment was nothing like what I'd envisioned my first day back at soccer being like. I figured I'd effortlessly run up to the ball and lob it downfield, right to my teammate. But instead, I wobbled up to it, stopped to catch my balance, and then slammed my foot amateurly against it. I was trying to kick the ball to Shira, but it launched off in a completely different direction. Christine ran to fetch it.

Pain sliced through my ankle the moment my foot collided with the ball. But it was overshadowed by the excitement and joy of this moment. Memories from years ago came flooding back. Early mornings on the soccer field, feeling the cool, crisp air against my skin. Munching on orange slices during halftime. Leaping sideways as the goalie to block the ball. Hearing Dad's voice cheering louder than all the rest. The feeling of power and strength that wearing cleats and shin guards had always given me.

Christine's voice interrupted my thoughts.

"Rachel . . . *um*," she said, pointing at the circle of parents. "Literally *everyone* is staring."

I turned to see all eyes on us from across the grass. I tried to ignore them. I'd waited three-and-a-half years to play soccer with my friends, and I didn't want anything to stand in my way now. But after a few minutes, I had to stop. My ankles couldn't take any more.

"Want to go to my house and watch a movie? Get away from all this?" Stephanie asked, gesturing at the onlookers.

Good idea.

"We're going to watch a movie at Stephanie's house," I told Mom as our group walked by. Such strange words coming out of my mouth. I never went to other people's houses. Any hangouts always took place at our house, in my bedroom. But right now, the words felt right.

I kicked off my shoes and took a spot on the sofa as Stephanie inserted *The Sisterhood of the Traveling Pants* into the DVD player.

For the past three years, I'd been in so much pain I couldn't walk, or sit up straight, or take part in so many ordinary activities. Now, here I was, relaxing on a couch like a normal person, in someone else's house, after just having played soccer with my friends. I could breathe no matter what position I was in. And although it was true that my ankles were throbbing at the moment, the pounding in my back and knees was gone. I had never believed even for a moment that this could happen. When my Lyme doctor once asked me to envision a life where I was healthy and mobile, I'd refused. I couldn't let myself hold even a glimmer of hope—because I knew that having that hope dashed by reality would be more than I could bear.

Yet, as thrilled as I was to be walking again, I was also filled with anxiety. What did this mean for my future? For the longest time, I'd never wanted to make long-term plans or even think about what my life could be like down the line. I had never believed there would even *be* a down the line.

But for the first time in forever, I realized something. If I could make it through everything I had survived over these past three years, I felt confident I could handle whatever happened next.

CHAPTER 12

The Next Ten Years... and Beyond

I stopped writing daily entries in my journal shortly after I began walking. My life suddenly became filled with new possibilities, and I wanted to get busy doing them. First off, I was determined to get my driver's license as soon as possible. The freedom of taking myself anywhere I wanted to go was so appealing after all those years stuck at home. I also wanted to rearrange my bedroom—no more hospital bed, tray table, or other trappings of a sickroom. And, to my parents' surprise, I had no desire to return to regular high school. In my eyes, high school classes wasted too much time. Now that I could finally visualize a future for myself, I wanted to get on with it—no messing around. I chose to return to the independent study program and do whatever was needed to graduate. I took a full academic schedule, and I even enrolled in community college ASL classes, which gave me dual credits for high school and college.

Dorothy

As excited as we all were with Rachel's progress, there remained a lot of work to do on her health. We still saw Dr. Becket regularly

> for continued sessions with the grounding machine and other treatments to help normalize her nervous system. And it paid off. About six weeks after she started walking, the hypersensitivity in her shoulders and upper back simply went away. After three years, I could finally hug my daughter again!

I still struggled with various Lyme-related symptoms, including problems with concentration and memory. For instance, I found it virtually impossible to memorize facts for tests. No matter how much I studied, I couldn't retain the information. In an interesting twist, ASL came to my rescue. I discovered that I could recall things more easily if I converted them into sign language and memorized that. However, at one point, this almost worked against me. During my senior year, a test I'd aced fell under suspicion because my answers matched the textbook word for word. Some people at the school felt I must have cheated. To defend myself, I stood in front of my teacher and signed and spoke the exact words from the textbook that had been etched into my memory via hand gestures. Vindication! I continued to hone my ASL skills by volunteering each week in a classroom for Deaf children at a local elementary school.

Although my educational path differed from the norm, I caught up with the rest of my class and graduated from high school on time. Despite butterflies in my stomach, I spoke at my graduation about my health challenges and continuing to push through them. That summer, I was hired to work at the same Deaf program where I had previously volunteered.

Dorothy

After high school, Rachel lived at home and attended community college. Although she had been out of the wheelchair for two years by this point, it was still difficult for her to walk long distances or remain standing for any length of time. She also still took a lot of medications and other treatments. Upper-cervical chiropractic had gotten her back on her feet, but she still had to deal with persistent symptoms of Lyme disease and its co-infections. Beginning college on her own turf, with her home support system in place, bought her time to figure out a game plan for the future. When she'd been younger and sicker, I had managed the details of her life—meals, medicines, and doctor appointments. Now, she needed to assume responsibility for all those things herself. Thus, we approached the community college years as a dress rehearsal for when she'd go out in the world on her own, something she yearned to do. As had become our style, she ramped up slowly, taking on new tasks one by one.

While in community college, I continued working at the local Deaf program. Intrigued by how the speech therapist worked with the students, I was inspired to pursue that occupation myself. When it came time to transfer to a four-year school, I chose the Speech and Hearing Sciences program at Portland State University. I was, of course, still a big fan of rainy weather—another benefit of moving to Oregon.

I transferred to Portland State as a junior in 2012. I loved living in the dorms, soaking up knowledge in my classes, and making new friends (including a boyfriend, Bryan, whom I eventually married).

Unfortunately, even though other parts of my life were going so well, my health went sideways again—though differently this time than before.

New symptoms came and went, such as nausea, muscle weakness, heart palpitations, and tremors. Was it Lyme rearing its head in a different way? I sought out various doctors, but no one could figure out what was going on. I had phone consultations with my Lyme doctor back in California, and sometimes he changed up my medications. It didn't help. But I kept pushing forward.

One morning near the end of my first year in Portland, I woke up unable to see out of my left eye. It was like a big, gray Frisbee was blocking my vision. It turned out to be something called central retinal vein occlusion (CRVO)—essentially a blood clot behind the retina.

Dorothy

I was attending a Lyme disease medical conference in Minnesota when Rachel called to tell me about the CRVO. She explained it calmly, but I heard the underlying fear in her voice. Would the sight in her eye be gone forever? What if it happened to the other eye too? I flew straight to Portland, and my husband came in from California. We accompanied Rachel to various specialists, who examined and scanned her eyes comprehensively. The final recommendation: She should receive shots of the drug Avastin® (normally a cancer drug but useful for CRVO as well) injected directly into the affected eyeball. And it wouldn't just be one time, the doctor cautioned. She'd need them periodically for a year or more. I was aghast at that prospect, but Rachel said, "Do it."

With just a couple weeks left in the term, we scheduled my first Avastin® shot for the day after my last final. As scary as this was, however, I couldn't even give my eye my full attention. I had four big finals to study for and a GPA to keep up in order to have a chance of getting into graduate school the following year.

My brain was struggling with knowing what to do as well. If I kept both eyes open, my brain would begin to transpose the images it got from each eye, and soon the gray Frisbee would cover both eyes. This would happen slowly, over a minute or so, with my world getting darker and darker until I couldn't see anything. As frightening as this was, I did manage to find a workaround of sorts. If I kept my left eye closed, and only used my right one, the vision in my good eye wasn't affected. So, in the privacy of my dorm room, I would cover my left eye with a makeshift eye patch. But I was too embarrassed to wear the patch anywhere outside of my room. Unfortunately, my self-consciousness came with a price—headaches, eye fatigue, and occasionally, temporary blindness. Getting through finals was rough. I distinctly remember looking at my biology exam with both eyes open and watching everything slowly fade to black.

With sheer determination, I somehow finished up the school year and then went for that first treatment. Getting a shot directly into my eyeball was less horrible than I had feared, but it was followed by days of agony. Any amount of sunlight inflicted excruciating pain. Furthermore, my left eye felt like it was full of sand, constantly scraping and scratching inside my eyelids. For a few days, I couldn't even open up my good right eye, which now was also highly sensitive to light. I spent my time trapped in my darkened dorm room, with blankets blocking out all light from my window. I dreaded the thought of getting another shot in a few weeks, followed by even more in the coming months.

Dorothy

Even after Rachel started the shots to her eye, I continued searching for information about CRVO. I also asked for help from people
in my Lyme advocacy network. Soon, I received an email from
JoAnne, who had worked at the hyperbaric clinic that Rachel had
gone to some years before. She told me their clinic had partici-
pated in a research study for CRVO and that hyperbaric treatment
was shown to be beneficial. She emailed me a list of medical journal articles that supported that view. She connected me with the
former owner of the center, who strongly encouraged us to get
Rachel into hyperbaric treatment as soon as possible.

I called every HBOT facility in the Portland area. Most were
hospital-based and therefore would not accept a walk-in patient,
but I finally located an independent clinic. Accompanied by her
supportive boyfriend, Bryan, Rachel met with the medical director and began treatment immediately. By this time, she'd had two
shots of Avastin®.

After five hyperbaric sessions, I noticed pinholes of light poking
through the dark circle blocking the vision in my left eye. After a
few more dives, the Frisbee of doom disappeared! I required a much
stronger eyeglasses prescription than before, but other than that, I
had my vision back. When I returned to the retinal specialist, he
was pleased that my sight had been restored. But he gave all credit
to the two shots of Avastin® I'd had, and said he doubted that hyperbaric treatments had had anything to do with it. He said it must
have been my young age—the only conceivable reason why I had
healed faster than anyone else he'd seen to date.

Dorothy

I found it strange that the retinal specialist so readily discounted the possible role of hyperbaric treatment in restoring Rachel's eyesight. I thought it clearly had played an important part. Maybe flooding her system with extra oxygen helped the Avastin® work more quickly? More important to me was the question of what had caused the occlusion in the first place, and how we might prevent such a thing from happening again.

The retinal specialist acknowledged that with Rachel's history of Lyme disease and Bartonella, either of those infections might have been the source of the problem. However, he ran tests to rule out other possible causes, including an ultrasound of the eyeball and a lot of blood work. All results were normal. Ultimately, we received no definitive answer as to why this had happened.

That September, with my vision stabilized, I eagerly embarked on my senior year of college. I scored well on my GRE test and began the time-consuming process of applying to graduate programs for the following year. My goal was to become a speech-language pathologist. Unfortunately, as the school year progressed, my legs and arms became noticeably weaker. I had never fully gained back the strength I'd had in my pre-Lyme life, but this was worse than ever. I also became easily winded and felt like I was living in the body of an eighty-year-old. But I pushed through anyway, not wanting my health problems to waylay my future plans. In June, I graduated with high honors in Speech and Hearing Sciences and was accepted into graduate school, also at Portland State.

But when I started graduate classes in the fall, the weakness in my legs worsened, coupled with fatigue, labored breathing, and heart palpitations. It became increasingly difficult to walk across campus to attend my lectures. Once in class, I found it hard to concentrate, and the complex concepts taught by my professors seemed utterly beyond my grasp. Four weeks into my program, I simply could not continue. I had no choice but to drop out.

Dorothy

A woman I knew through my Lyme work suggested that we look into mold toxicity. She told me there was a lot of overlap between Lyme disease and mold-related problems. And with Portland's notoriously rainy weather, there was a good chance that Rachel was being exposed to mold where she lived and went to school.

First, we had to ascertain what precisely was going on and then figure out what to do about it. We found a mold specialist and had Rachel fly home for his first available opening. He started by asking very detailed questions. We learned that mold illness—often called chronic inflammatory response syndrome (CIRS), can manifest in a wide range of debilitating symptoms. Everything Rachel was experiencing, including shortness of breath, muscle weakness, and a variety of neurological issues, could possibly be explained by CIRS. Subsequent lab tests showed that her body had high levels of mycotoxins—the poisons given off by many kinds of mold. It was time to take action.

I followed the mold doctor's recommendations to the letter, determined to be a model patient and beat this thing once and for all. But it was different from any other protocol I'd done. For one thing, my doctor said I must eliminate any possible exposure to mold for the duration of treatment. "Detoxing from mold while living in a moldy environment," he told me, "is like trying to dry off with a towel when you're still taking a shower—a waste of time." Luckily, I had just moved to a new apartment, which was tested and found clear of mold. For more than a year, I avoided going into stores, restaurants, and theaters. If I had to enter any building to use a restroom or see a doctor, I wore a face mask with a charcoal filter. It was a lonely and isolating time.

Detoxing from mold was both physically exhausting and mentally taxing. My days revolved around medications, which were meticulously planned out down to fifteen-minute intervals. I set phone alerts to tell me every time I should eat food or drink water or take pills. Following this protocol was a full-time job that never allowed for time off. But as the months wore on, strength slowly returned to my body. Eventually, I could handle short walks around my apartment complex, something I hadn't been able to do for ages.

About the time most of my mold symptoms subsided, my soon-to-be husband Bryan got a job offer in Arizona. Hoping for the benefits of a drier climate and eager to see my health problems in the rearview mirror, we enthusiastically packed up and moved to Chandler, a suburb of Phoenix.

At first, all seemed well in Arizona. I began making friends and doing fun new forms of exercise, such as hiking and goat yoga. I started working at an elementary school as a speech therapy assistant, which didn't require a master's degree. I liked my job, but soon, bizarre new health issues materialized, making me wonder if I would have to quit. The problem centered on my left arm. Sometimes, if I exerted it at all—carrying a sack of groceries or taking a pot of soup off the stove—my arm would stop working. It would turn blue and dangle lifeless at my side, feeling ice cold and painful to the touch. After a few hours, things would revert to normal—until the next time it happened. At first, these episodes were sporadic. Sometimes I could carry a package or hold a frying pan with no trouble at all. But then, my arm started "turning off" more often, and I didn't know what to do.

I was always reluctant to discuss strange symptoms with doctors, assuming they'd dismiss me as faking it. But things were reaching a crisis point. I took the plunge and brought up the subject with my new primary care doctor.

Unlike many of my previous medial experiences, this physician believed me. When my arm changed colors and temperature right in front of her, she couldn't very well deny it. But she didn't know how to help me either. She ordered some tests, which showed nothing, and referred me to a specialist, with the same result—zilch.

Dorothy

Once again, someone in my Lyme network offered useful advice. My friend Karen said her daughter's Lyme-related neuro issues had been greatly helped by a chiropractic neurologist. These specialists diagnose and treat a range of disorders affecting the nervous system—and they do it without drugs or surgical intervention. Luckily, Rachel found a chiropractic neurologist not far from where she lived in Arizona and began regular treatments. Unlike other doctors, who seemed stumped by her symptoms, Dr. Russell Teames believed he knew what was causing them and how he could help her.

At our first appointment, Dr. Teames took a detailed medical history and then gave me various tests that involved eye movements.

He said these would give him important information about how my brain was working. For instance, he had me put on special goggles with built-in cameras, and then asked me to track a series of dots moving in different directions. At the end of that session, Dr. Teames said he had a pretty good idea of what was going on. With my history of Lyme-related infections and mold, he believed that my prefrontal lobe had gone "offline," as he put it, prompting other areas of my brain to act strangely in its absence. He said that by getting my prefrontal lobe to "turn back on," the rest of my brain would then begin to self-regulate.

I saw him weekly and grew to really enjoy our work together. Every session looked different. Sometimes I balanced on an uneven surface while tapping dots on a touch-screen TV. Other days, I sat still while he used various instruments on my arms or legs, such as a tuning fork or TENS unit. We used mirrors to trick my brain into thinking it was looking at one arm, when really it was looking at the other, and I wore colored glasses to try to calm down my nervous system. As we regularly worked with my brain like this, I began experiencing fewer days where my arm stopped working—until, finally, it just stayed "on" permanently.

Fixing my arm problem improved my life dramatically. I could lift boxes of school supplies at work, operate my vacuum cleaner at home, and turn the steering wheel of my car with no trouble at all. But soon new health issues raised their ugly heads.

Ever since I had first started mold treatment while living in Portland, I had struggled with food and chemical sensitivities. In time, I'd been diagnosed with mast cell activation syndrome—a condition where the immune system triggers severe allergic reactions to certain substances. I generally handled this problem by avoiding the offending foods and using allergen-free cleaning products. But, about the time my arm stopped being a problem, my food reactions kicked into overdrive. It seemed like practically anything I ate would make my skin break out in a painful, burning rash or cause shooting pains in my stomach. I had to eliminate more and more previously "safe" foods every few weeks. Eventually I could only eat zucchini, meat, lettuce, bell peppers, and coconut oil. If I became intolerant to those foods as well, there would be nothing I could eat at all.

I also began reacting strongly to the cleaning chemicals used at the school where I worked. If I so much as walked past the janitor's cart, my lungs would burn and my skin would turn red-hot and stay that way for hours. When I got home from work, I'd put ice packs on my hands and arms—anything to ease the burning sensation.

Just a whiff of a Clorox wipe, used often in elementary classrooms, would trigger a searing headache and set my skin on fire. Passing by one of the restrooms—with fumes of sanitizing chemicals spilling out into the hallway—would provoke such fatigue and weakness that I had to hold on to the wall for support. If I was going to keep doing the job I loved, something would have to change, and quick.

My answer came in the form of a program called Dynamic Neural Retraining System (DNRS). It was based on the concept of *neuroplasticity*—the ability of the brain to adapt to changing circumstances. Those adaptations can be either negative or positive. When a person is sick for a long time, the brain adapts to that, sometimes continuing to send out certain kinds of signals, even long after the body doesn't need them anymore. Through DNRS, I learned that the years I'd spent dealing with chronic illness had left my brain struggling to function properly, as witnessed by my left arm "turning off" due to mixed signals in my brain. But neuroplasticity means that our brains can also change for the better. I learned that I could create new, healthy neural pathways to stop unwanted symptoms from occurring. I was determined to try.

The DNRS program required more dedication than any treatment I had experienced before. Among other things, it called for me to perform specific visualization techniques, in a precise pattern, for a full hour each day. Finding the time was a struggle. My job kept me busy all day, and at night I was too tired to put in the effort. But I felt that DNRS was my last hope. If I couldn't get a handle on my chemical sensitivities, I would have to quit my job. I began setting my alarm for 4:00 a.m. every morning and did the entire hour before starting the rest of my day. It was exhausting, and I never looked forward to it, but I did it anyway. It turned out to be the missing piece I needed. Not only did my food and chemical sensitivities resolve within a few months, but my strength also returned. I discovered stamina I hadn't experienced since before needing to use the wheelchair in 2005. I could walk far, go on hikes, and participate in exercise classes. I could depend on my body in ways I never thought possible. For the first time since I was a kid, I finally found a place of consistent good health.

Dorothy

If I hadn't personally witnessed Rachel's DNRS experience, I wouldn't have believed it. In the year prior to doing the program, she couldn't get in a chlorinated swimming pool without immediately developing hives all over her body. Eating an ice-cream cone would bring on horrible stomach pains. And accidental exposure to a plug-in air freshener would leave her gasping for breath.

Now, after DNRS, Rachel could do those things and more with no physical reaction whatsoever. It was astonishing. While I did not do the program myself, I watched the introductory videos and read as much as I could about brain retraining. I learned how chronic illness and trauma can make the brain's limbic system go haywire, giving rise to the kind of overreactions to chemicals and food that had plagued Rachel. And I learned how neuroplasticity, the brain's ability to rewire itself, could normalize things.

That's what happened with Rachel. She could now eat anything she wanted to without debilitating consequences. She could walk into a public restroom without reacting to its chemical cleaning products. Now she had the energy, endurance, and vitality to participate in life in ways that had been unavailable to her for years. Months after her DNRS training, Bob and I accompanied Rachel and Bryan to India to attend the three-day wedding of a family friend. We traveled for hours on a plane, visited different locales, and ate exotic foods. The whole exhilarating experience would have been out of the question for Rachel at any time during the previous decade. To me, that trip signified that Rachel finally had her life back.

When I started a blog in my mid-twenties, I came up with the name *Resiliently Rachel*. I loved the alliteration and the way it rolled off the tongue. But mostly, I felt that the concept of resilience embodied who I aspired to be. This contrasted dramatically with my former identity as a depressed, chronically ill teenager, fearing that real life would pass her by. Back then, I would have described myself as crushed, defeated, and weak—anything but resilient. But in looking back, I realize that, although I failed to see it at the time, the quality of resilience was with me all along. It was there when I chose to edit videos during my darkest days, recognizing that the activity could help keep me out of the abyss. It was there when I made music playlists for long, painful car rides to out-of-state medical appointments. And it was there when I wrote nearly five hundred pages in my journal, holding on to the idea that one day my struggles would have a purpose.

Dorothy

Although I accompanied Rachel through the darkest days of her illness, there were aspects of her experience that I didn't comprehend at all. For instance, I never grasped the depths of her ongoing despair during the time she was on IV antibiotics. And I only learned that she'd injected air into the PICC line when she shared details from her journal with me fifteen years later. Reading those words even years after they were written delivered a sharp blow to this mother's heart. Working on this book together forced us to revisit those and other painful times. But the process also clarified for me the strong bond my daughter and I developed through that trial by fire—a connection that endures to this day. I'm proud of the capable and courageous woman Rachel has become, as she negotiates whatever challenges life throws her way. She has indeed discovered her own resilience.

Long ago, as a young, impressionable teen, I had been told by one of my medical practitioners that I would always be sick. That living with Lyme disease meant learning to accept the fact that I would be on many pills each day for the rest of my life. That I would need to find peace with activities that could be done with less energy. I could still have a good life, that person told me, but a different one than I might have chosen for myself. It would be many years before I recognized just how profoundly that one conversation had damaged me. I had somehow internalized that message, and it had negatively affected how I'd viewed my entire future.

It wasn't until DNRS, when I learned about a well-known experiment with fleas, that I realized the limitations I had put on myself. In the experiment, scientists put fleas in an open jar. Since the jar had no lid, the fleas jumped out easily. But then, the researchers put the fleas back in the jar and placed a glass lid on top. The fleas repeatedly crashed into the lid, until they finally learned to avoid hitting the barrier by lowering the height of their jump. However, even after the lid was then removed, the fleas never jumped higher than where the lid *would have been.*

Without a doubt, that misguided advice from a practitioner who thought she was being helpful had conditioned me to lower the height of my jump. I wish that instead, all those years ago, she had told me that in my future I would climb mountains. That I would be free from pain, and that I would rappel down two-hundred-foot waterfalls. That I would eat foods from different cultures while traveling around the world, and I'd ride a zipline high above the treetops. Because that's what was really waiting for me, and what I should have been working toward all along.

Acknowledgments

Rachel

To our early readers: Jenny, Christine, Liz, Becky, Lynn, Jill, Sandy, and Bryan—Your insights helped shape this memoir into what it is today. We cannot thank you enough for your time and support.

Valerie—This book would not be complete without your invaluable input, filling in the gaps along the way.

Dad—You have been our biggest support from day one. Thank you for helping us get this book where we wanted it to be.

Jeremy—Thank you for letting me talk about you in my memoir. Don't worry—I made you look good.

And to every medical provider who believed me and helped get me to where I am today, along with my wonderful friends, I am forever grateful.

Dorothy

Sandy Berenbaum—Thank you for guiding me through the thicket of parenting a troubled teen with Lyme disease and later being my co-author of *When Your Child Has Lyme Disease: A Parent's Survival Guide*.

The brave doctors willing to step out of the medical mainstream to save my daughter's life—Words are inadequate to express my deep gratitude.

Alicia, Christine, Shira, Jenny, Cassie, Tenaya, Julianne, Stephanie, Kate, Julia, and Christopher—You were the neighborhood posse who kept Rachel going through three long years. We couldn't have done it without you.

Jill, Lynn, Mary B, and other friends and neighbors who stepped in and helped whenever they could—Much appreciation!

Jeremy—Teaching Rachel to edit videos was a masterstroke! Thanks for hanging in with us through the tough times.

Bob—When we vowed to stick together "through all of life's changes," we had no idea what was barreling towards us. Thanks for being my wonderful and supportive husband through better and worse.

About the Authors

RACHEL LELAND is a speech-language pathology assistant who loves working with children. Born and raised in Northern California, she currently resides in the Pacific Northwest. These days, she is often found hiking, doing flying trapeze, and filming and editing videos documenting her life, which she features on her Instagram, @resilientlyrachel. Through her words and videos, Rachel seeks to inspire, educate, and offer a beacon of hope to others dealing with chronic illness.

DOROTHY KUPCHA LELAND is president of LymeDisease.org, a national research and advocacy organization. She writes the blog *Touched by Lyme* and spearheads public education efforts for LymeDisease.org. Co-author of the book *When Your Child Has Lyme Disease: A Parent's Survival Guide*, she frequently speaks to groups and the press about Lyme-related issues. Before she became involved in Lyme disease advocacy, she worked as a journalist and a political aide and wrote four books related to California history. She and her husband live in Northern California.

To learn more about Rachel's experience,
visit **resilientlyrachel.com/book**.

To learn more about Lyme disease and to read
Dorothy's blog *Touched by Lyme*, visit **lymedisease.org**.